BEADS
of BORNEO

We gratefully accept the generous support of the
following organisations for this publication:

Ministry of Urban Development & Tourism, Sarawak

Yayasan Sarawak

Ministry of Social Development & Urbanisation, Sarawak
Sarawak Craft Council
Sarawak Shell Berhad
Sarawak Tourism Board

EDITORIAL DIRECTOR
Timothy Auger

EDITORS
Martin Cross
Christopher Khoo

DESIGNER
Felicia Wong

PRODUCTION MANAGER
Annie Teo

First edition published in 2005 by **Editions Didier Millet Pte Ltd**
Reprinted 2010
78 Jalan Hitam Manis,
Singapore 278488
www.edmbooks.com

This compact edition published in 2019

Colour separation by Singapore Sang Choy
Printed in Malaysia by TWP Sdn Bhd

ISBN: 978-981-4610-81-0

Cover photographs, from left: Headling and protective beads; string of blue, turquoise and millefiori beads; Bidayuh beads with hawk bells; Bidayuh Jagoi priestess' necklace; Orang Ulu value beads; and Bidayuh warrior neckpiece.
Back cover: Different kinds of millefiori beads.
This page: Beaded Orang Ulu baby carrier.
Opposite page: Bead string containing colourful late 19th-century millefiori beads.
Page 4: Maloh skirt panel with beadwork.

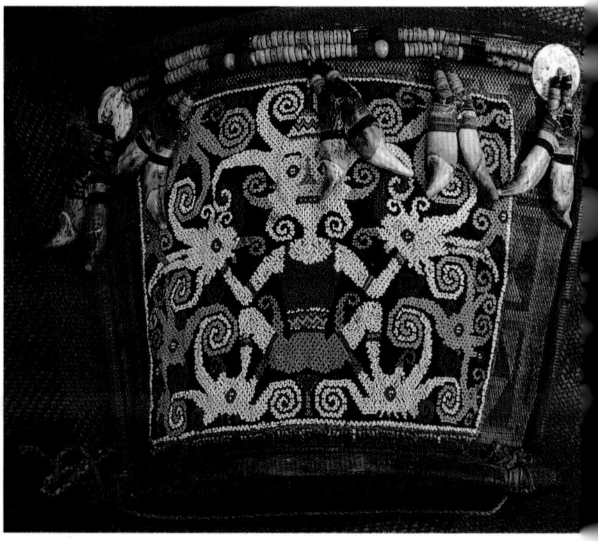

BEADS
of BORNEO

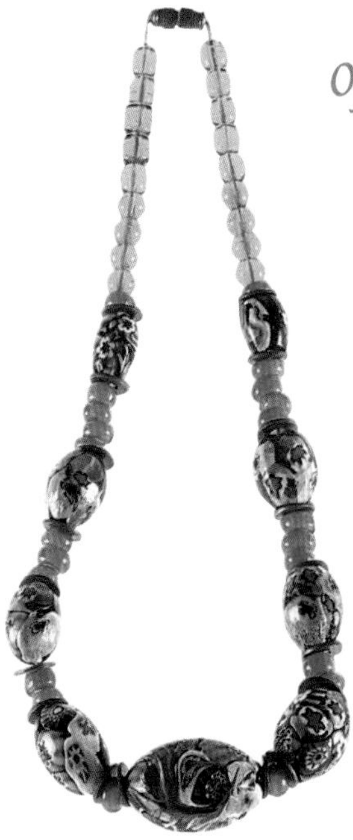

Heidi Munan

edm EDITIONS DIDIER MILLET

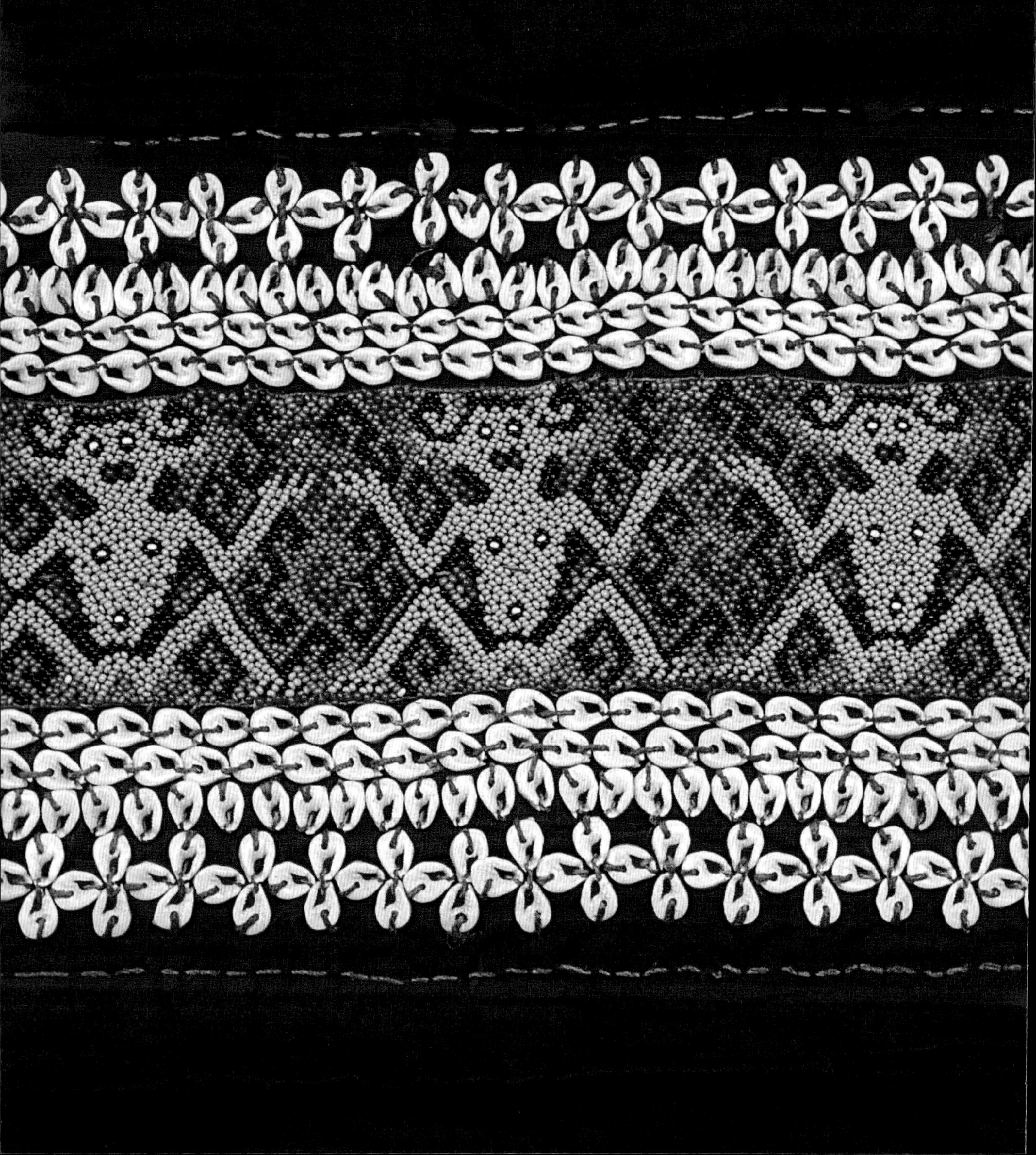

Contents

Acknowledgements

I wish to thank the Sarawak Dayak Cultural Foundation for a research grant. Much help and encouragement came particularly from Datuk Leonard and Datin Margaret Linggi, as well as Janet Rata, Dr Vinson Sutlive and Dr Clifford Sather. Supplementary grants from the Bead Study Trust of UK, the Northwest Bead Society and the Bead Society of LA (USA) funded further travel and professional photography; for these I am very grateful.

Researchers in all parts of the world patiently answered queries and helped out with material (see Picture Credits). There are so many ... but I would like to single out the late Peter Francis Jr of the Centre for Bead Research (USA), and Karlis Karklins of the Society of Bead Researchers (Canada), the late Dr D. Freeman, Dr S. Morris, Dr W. Geddes and Rev H. Southwell.

In Sarawak, collectors and experts in town, village and longhouse have been sharing their knowledge and experience with me:

Datuk Dr Laila Taib, Dr Thomas Chung, Ramsay and Edric Ong, Nelson Tan, Datin Brigitte Wan Ullok, YB Jacob Sagan and Winnie Jolly, Datuk Jacob and Datin Garnet Ridu, Lucy Bulan and David Labang, Albert and Mary Kedit, Dato Balan Seling and Datin Mariam, Lah Jau Uyoh and Roselynn Lah, Datuk Nyipa Batok and Datin Hau, Cecilia Toyad, Datuk Lucas Chin, the Director of Sarawak Museum and members of his staff, Ipoi Datan, Jayl Langub, Robert Sulis and Hamdan bin Buyong of the Native Customary Laws Council.

Alfred Dawat and his extended family in Lawas and Long Tuma gave me an insight into Lun Bawang culture, as did Tagal Paran and Madam Yamu Pengiran in Ba Kelalan. Petrus and Maggie Rajah and Aria Turan in Marudi helped with my trips up the Baram, as did Kijan Toynbee, Vincent Ajeng, Juan ak Entebar, Sheryl and Roland Mattu, and Lesley and Julius Linggod of Miri.

Lucy Bulan of Bario Secondary School put up with endless streams of visitors, who came to discuss the issue of beads when I stayed at the school; Pemancha Henry Jala and family introduced me to many Kelabit bead experts. In the Long Lama-Long Laput area, I drew on the deep knowledge of the late T. R. Lah Wan and Madam Tijan Anyie, and the singers of the unforgettable "bead song" led by Unyang Wan.

Visits to the late Harriette Brodie introduced me to Melanau bead culture; Edmund Salman of the Mukah Museum collected experts K. K. Peteran bin Libai, Pemancha Henry Ely, Mary Sebie binte Usup and many others for a lively bead discussion. Diana Rose took me on a "bead trip" to the Matu-Daro area, which included the last Melanau longhouse.

The late T. G. Oto first introduced me to Bidayuh beads. Others shared their lore: the late Raseh ak Lutong of Mentu Tapu, D. B. Lunti ak Saee of Paya Achau, Jongen ak Abun of Opar, Katib ak Nub of Tibia Kiding, Raymond Daling Jihok and Councillor Ena Kalong.

There isn't space to list the names of everybody who has contributed to this book, but let me assure them all of my gratitude. It may be the place, however, to thank my patient, and occasionally bewildered, editor, Christopher Khoo of Editions Didier Millet.

The exhibition Bead Links, hosted by the Petronas Gallery in Kuala Lumpur City Centre in 2001, first put Borneo beads before a larger audience. Publication of *Beads of Borneo* is another milestone, but not the end of the road. As I travel around Borneo I meet old friends again, and find new ones — and the bead goes on!

October 2004

Introduction

The indigenous people of Borneo have used beads since time immemorial, when teeth, bones, shells and stones were perforated and worn as ornaments. The influx of trade beads, from the early historical period right up to the present, affected bead preferences. Colourful artifacts of semi-precious stone and glass were added to each community's bead treasury, reflecting sometimes specific tastes or needs, and sometimes availability.

My interest in beads developed from meeting "upcountry" people who wore these fascinating ornaments. I soon discovered that the true repositories of bead lore are the old ladies, many of whom moved to towns as the rural-urban drift carried them. Now living in their son's terrace house, they miss their customary farm work and are certainly happy to talk about their people's history and traditions to an eager questioner.

Family travel, field trips, interviews and a study of the relevant literature led to one basic conclusion: The political boundaries which divided Borneo into "Dutch" or "English" segments are simply lines on a map. The people and cultures of this island have their own divisions and meeting points which transcend colonial and national partitions.

Beads of Borneo surveys the island's bead culture as it stood at the turn of the 20th/21st centuries. People — and beads! — are more mobile than they used to be. Large-scale population movements are restricted by international boundaries on the one hand, but promoted by considerations of economic development on the other. Nothing stands still in Borneo; as people move they share and adopt aspects of each other's cultures.

Bead tastes and concepts have changed immensely within the last 100 years. Few people seriously believe in the supernatural properties of beads today. Beads are kept as heirlooms, and as I started taking a serious interest in this fascinating segment of Borneo's material culture, the current owners were quite prepared to share their knowledge. Such information is often prefaced with "in the old days, our people believed that ..."; one generation distancing itself from the pagan beliefs of its forebears.

I do not address large issues in *Beads of Borneo* — after all, beads are small things. The book is my contribution to keeping bead history and bead lore alive. Many of the elders who generously shared their knowledge ended ruefully with: "My grandchildren aren't interested in all this — they're educated!"

By now, many highly-educated Borneans appreciate and study their ancient culture. In time to come, the young ones will be able to read about one aspect of it in this book, to tell them what the status of the bead culture was in the late 20th century. It altered within the time I personally observed it, and it will continue to do so. Only dead things are static.

Commercial beadmaking in Borneo is a change that occurred within the 20th century. So is the influx of new glass replicas of the venerable old beads, products of industrial technology. They are a fitting metaphor for Borneo's indigenous cultures, based in the dim past and stepping confidently into the future.

Heidi Munan
Hon. Curator of Beads, Sarawak Museum, Kuching
October 2004

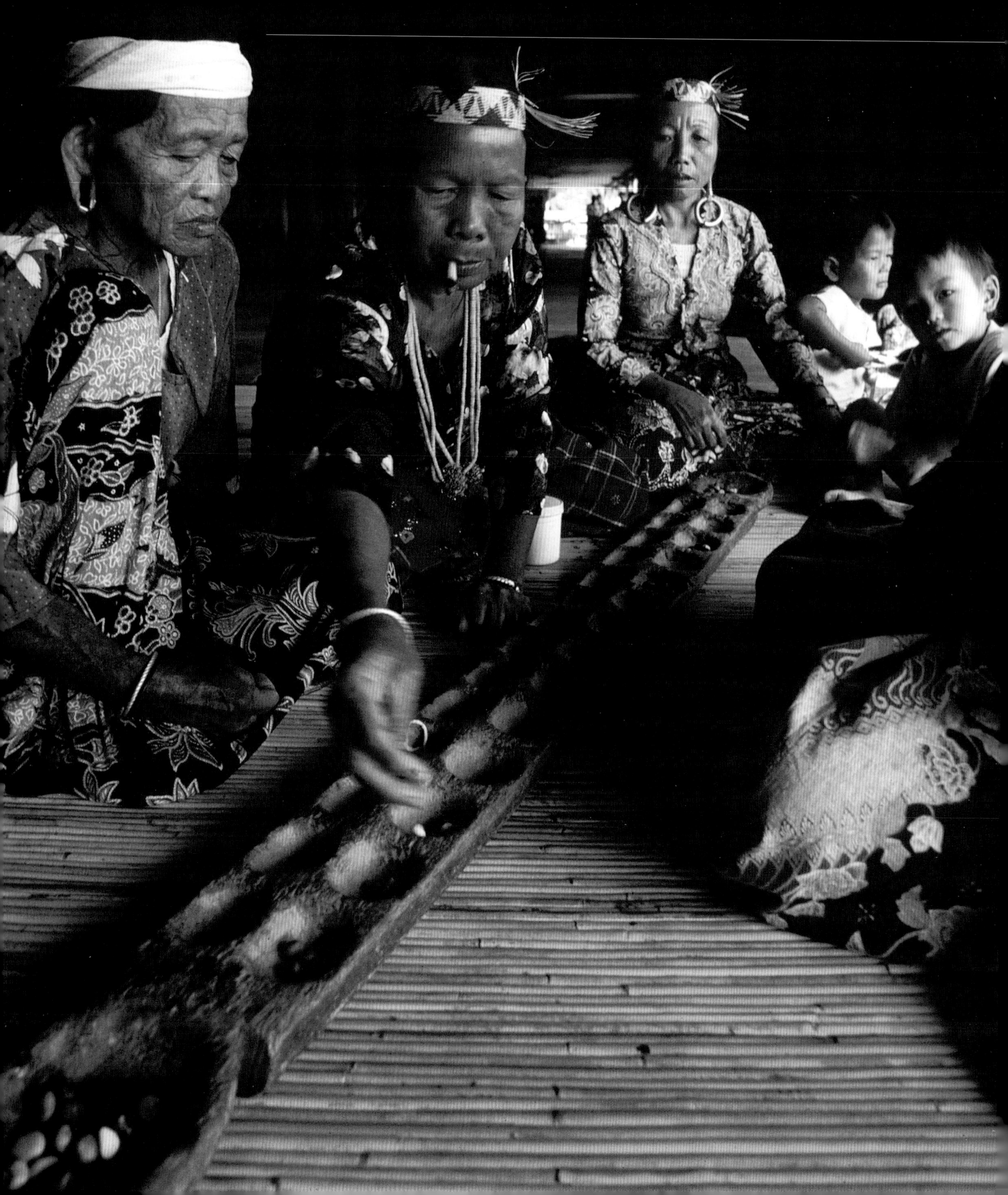

[CHAPTER 1]

BORNEO: THE LAND AND ITS PEOPLE

A historical and geographical introduction to the island of Borneo, and a description of its ethnic groups who still possess a significant bead culture.

FACING PREVIOUS PAGE: Orang Ulu ladies from Kalimantan playing the Malay game of *congkak*. The Orang Ulu are one category of ethnic people who live at the headwaters of the major rivers in Central Borneo.

RIGHT: Borneo, with its diverse mix of peoples, is located right in the centre of the South-east Asian archipelago. It has a land surface area of about 750,000 sq km and lies north of Java, east of Sumatra, south-west of the Philippines and west of Sulawesi.

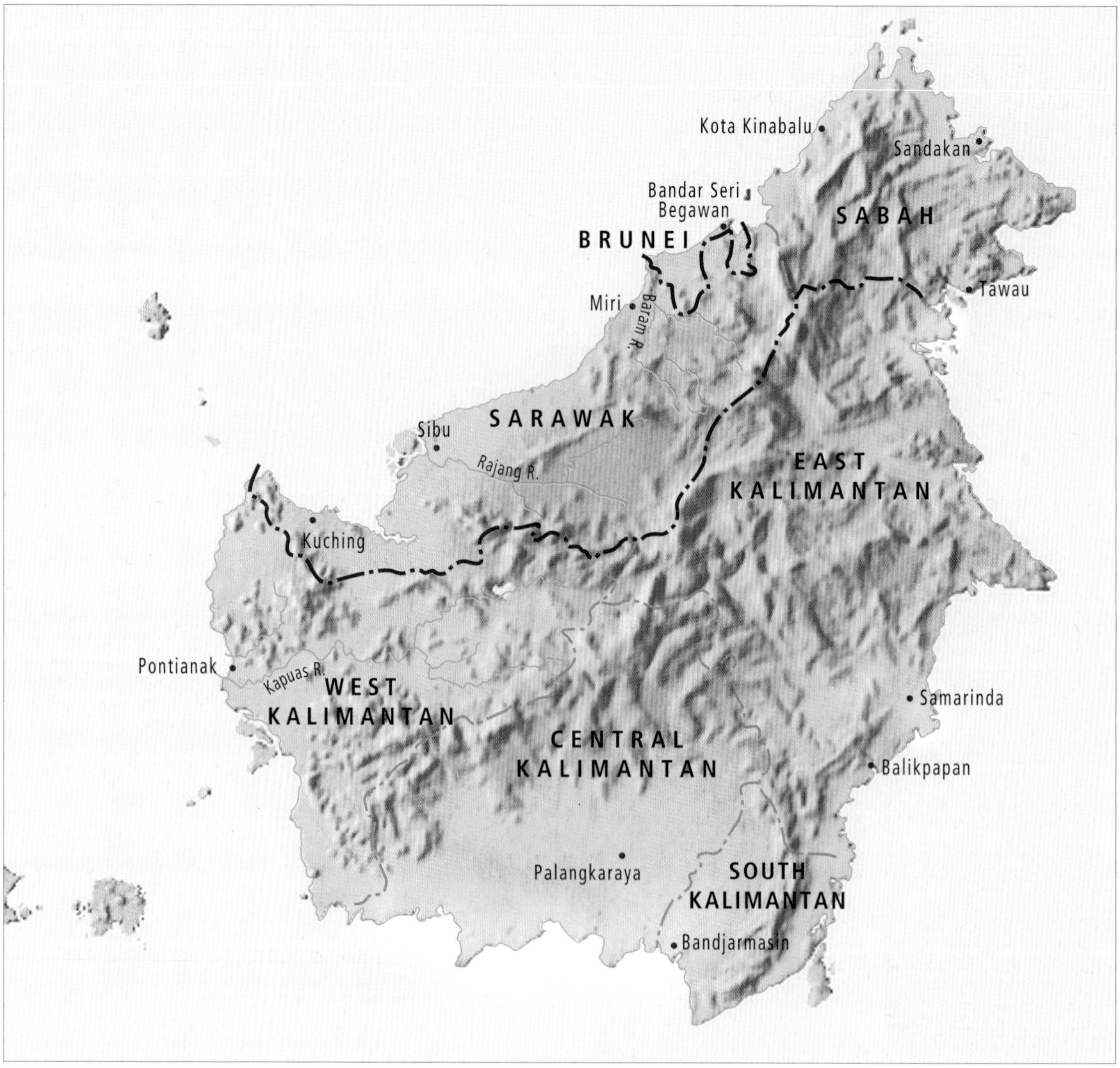

THE ISLAND OF BORNEO

Borneo lies in the centre of the South-east Asian archipelago, north of Java, east of Sumatra, south-west of the Philippines and west of Sulawesi. With a land surface area of about 750,000 sq km, Borneo is larger than any of these more densely-populated and historically more prominent islands.

Chinese seafarers of the Sung period (AD 960-1279) knew Borneo and its produce, but the maritime trade, en route to the bigger markets of Sulawesi and Java, mainly bypassed the looming land mass. The island's coast during this period was sparsely dotted with small townships and rivermouth states, ruled over by indigenous chieftains. The people of the interior governed themselves in small, mostly riverine units. Migrations in search of fresh farmland led to forays into virgin lands or enemy territory. Traditional epics testify to endless rounds of inter-tribal warfare. Sometimes a bigger group annihilated or absorbed a smaller one.

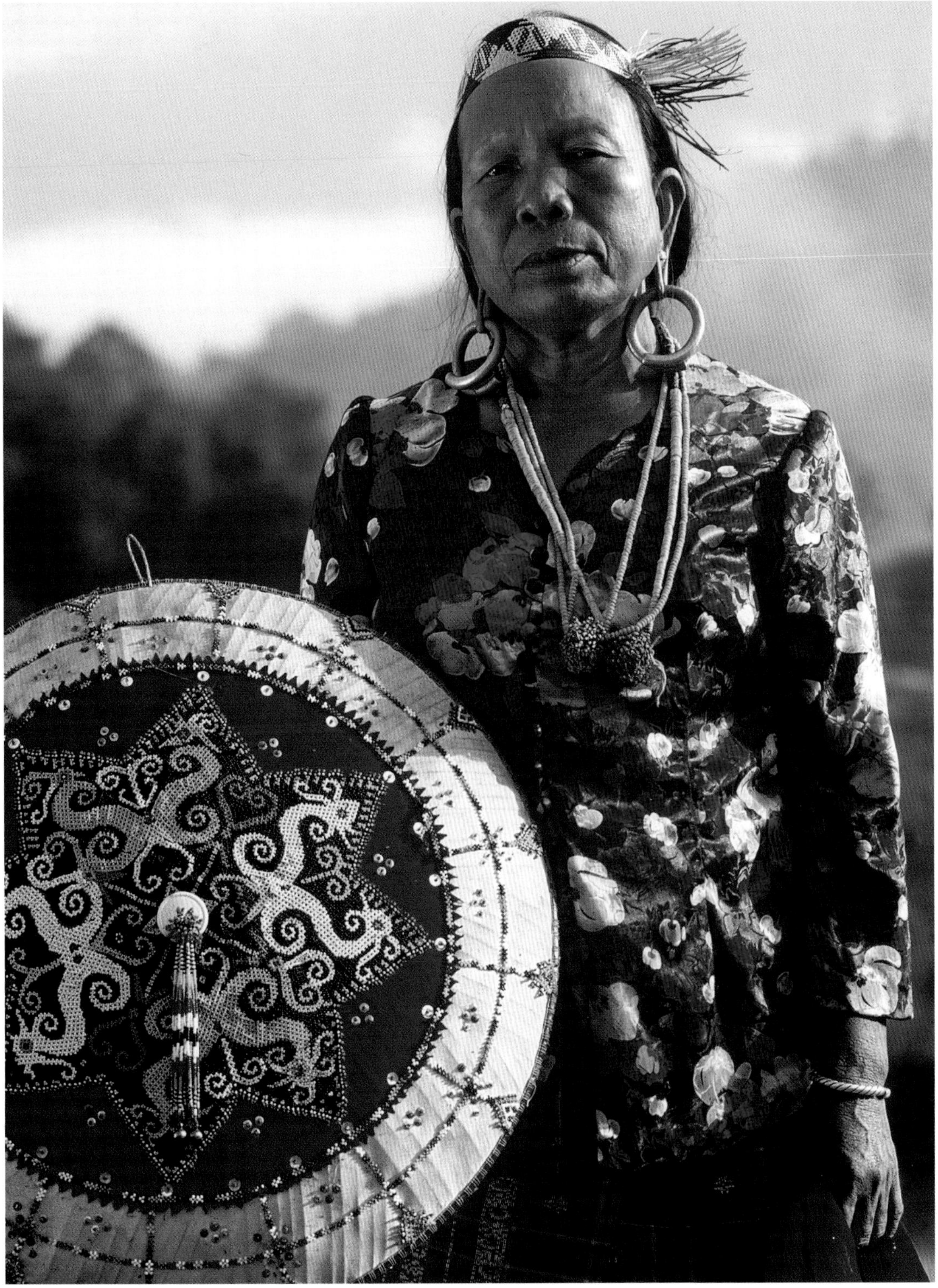

A Kenyah matron from Kalimantan carrying a beaded sun hat. The Kenyah are one of several ethnic groups in Borneo who decorate their hats with bead-work and wear neck-laces of antique beads.

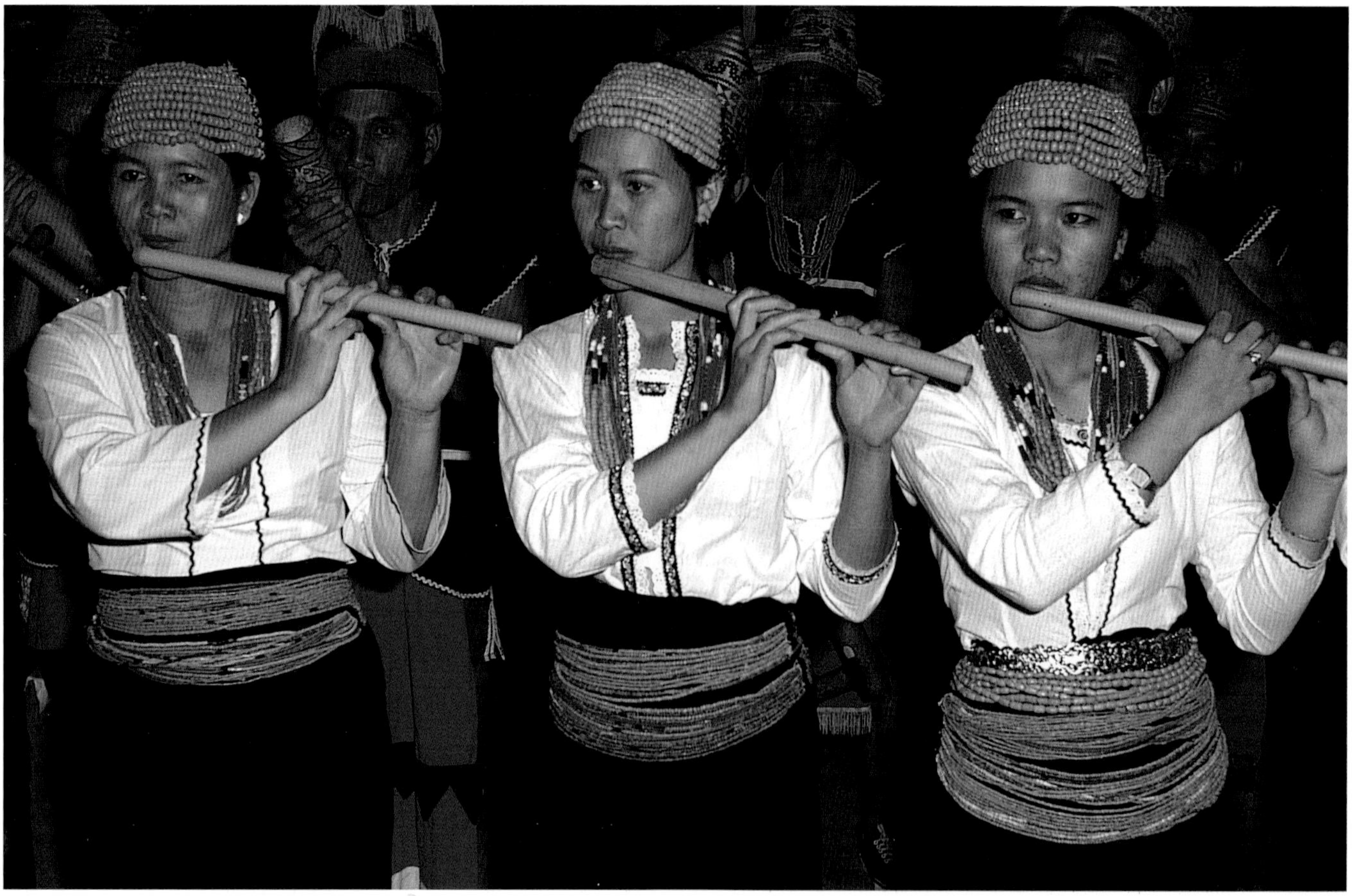

Lun Dayeh girls wearing bead caps, necklaces and belts, and playing on bamboo flutes.

Borneo's indigenous name, "Kalimantan", is said to be derived from the sago which grows abundantly in the coastal wetlands, and which once formed the staple diet of most indigenous peoples here. The name "Borneo", introduced to Western literature by Portuguese explorers in the 16th century, is derived from "Brunei". This sultanate was one of the major trading ports in the 13th–16th centuries. In its heyday, it claimed suzerainty over the northern third or half of the island, and some adjoining territory now part of the Philippines.

In the 19th century, the Dutch extended their rule from the riverine capitals of the south, west and lower east coast. Sarawak in the north-west was occupied by an English gentleman-adventurer who was eventually given the title of Rajah by the Sultan of Brunei. The British North Borneo Company established itself on the northern segment of the island.

To the people of Borneo, especially the Dayak, a collective term referring to a number of very different peoples on the island, these political divisions meant very little, merely lines drawn on a map by black-coated officials in London or Amsterdam. Some of these lines cut right across tribal and cultural affiliations. Today, the term "Bidayuh of West Borneo" includes both Malaysians and Indonesians.

Since 1963, the East Malaysian states of Sabah and Sarawak have covered the northern part of Borneo, with the Sultanate of Brunei situated in between. The remaining four-fifths of the island are divided into four Indonesian provinces: East Kalimantan, South Kalimantan, Central Kalimantan and West Kalimantan.

CLOCKWISE FROM TOP LEFT: Orang Ulu headman wearing value beads and leopard-tooth ear ornaments; Murut man in traditional dress with blowpipe and parang; Orang Ulu traditional longhouse; and Kenyah woman in everyday dress, wearing some old beads.

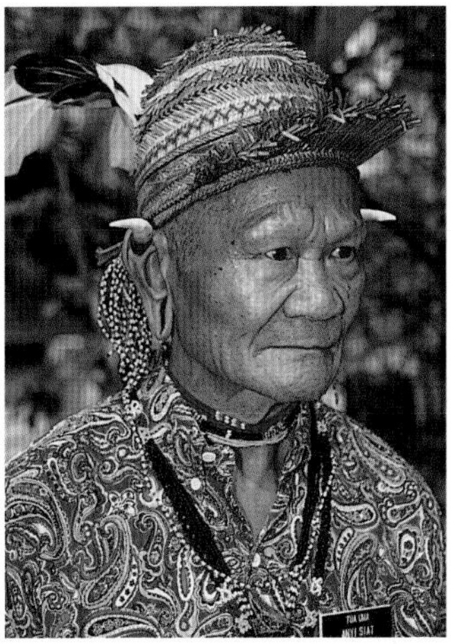

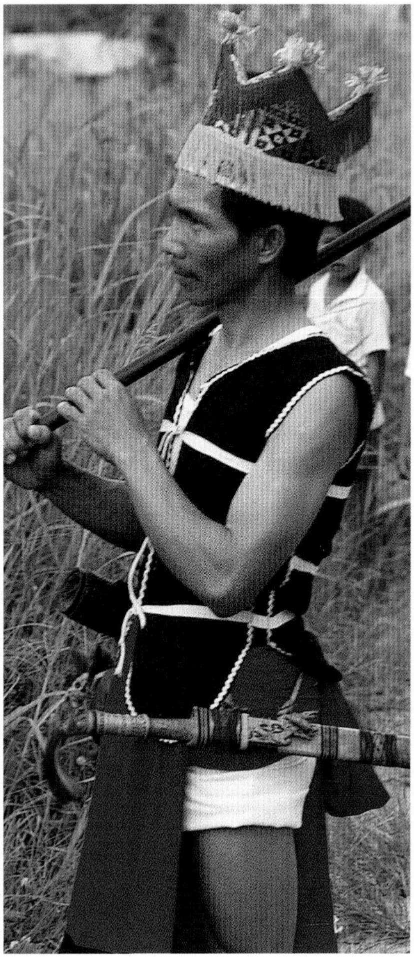

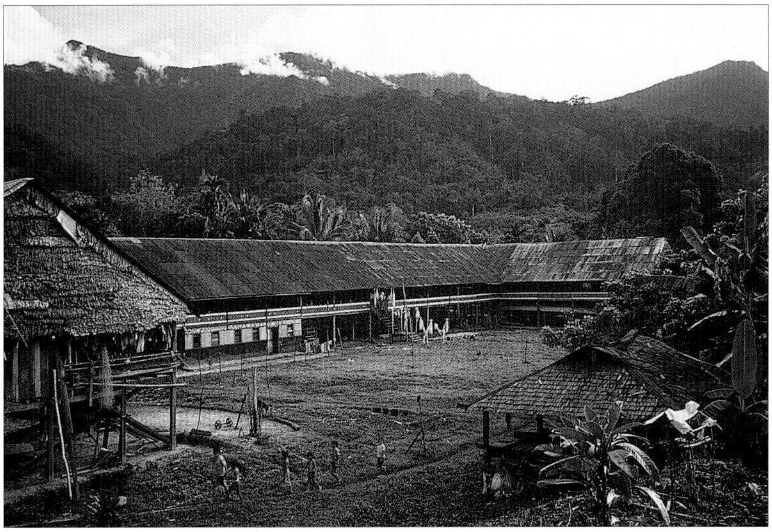

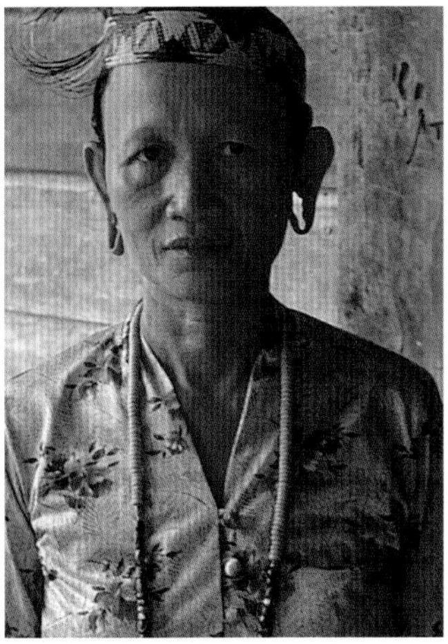

Within the last 30 to 40 years, the rural population of Borneo has been flocking to the towns in search of the educational, medical and social facilities which are not available in remote locations.

This movement has affected traditional cultures. Many young people have lived in centralised school boarding houses from the age of six because of the dearth of village schools. These people, who later moved downriver in search of work, know little of their own material or spiritual heritage.

The main towns of Borneo, listed clockwise from the north-western corner, are Kuching, Sibu and Miri in Sarawak; Bandar Seri Begawan in Brunei; Kota Kinabalu, Sandakan and Tawau in Sabah; Samarinda and Balikpapan in East Kalimantan, Bandjarmasin in South Kalimantan, Palangkaraya in Central Kalimantan, and Pontianak in West Kalimantan. All these and smaller townships harbour considerable numbers of Dayak, visually indistinguishable from the heterogeneous populace of an urban centre of the South-east Asian archipelago.

THE PEOPLE OF BORNEO

The people living along the coast and lower reaches of Borneo's rivers are popularly called "Malay" by virtue of their religion. However, many are in fact indigenous converts to Islam, not ethnic Malays. "To become Malay" is a popular term for "to embrace Islam" in Borneo – the new convert adopts the

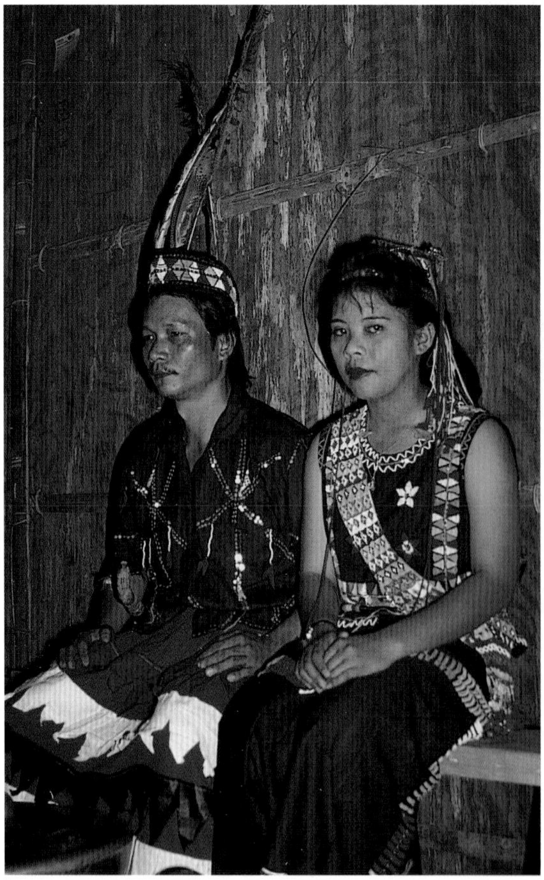

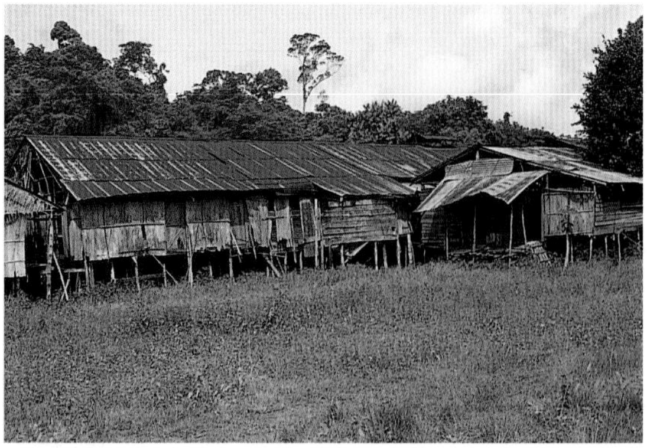

RIGHT: A Murut couple dressed up in traditional finery at their wedding ceremony.

EXTREME RIGHT: A traditional Murut longhouse.

lifestyle, dress and dietary habits of his new mentors. Muslim migrants from the neighbouring islands of Java, Sulawesi and Sumatra are more likely to retain their ethnic identity.

Borneo also has a sizeable Chinese population, who are mostly descendants of 19th-century immigrants, though earlier arrivals had settled in the gold-mining districts of west Borneo.

Of Borneo's roughly 20 million inhabitants, between a fifth and a quarter may be classified as Dayak. This general term was adopted by the Dutch explorers who heard it from their Malay guides. It means "inland", where most non-Muslim natives were to be found.

"Dayak" is a term similar to "Western", a rough, collective definition to cover a number of very different peoples. The Dayak of Borneo share some common characteristics – until quite recently, all of them lived in longhouses, situated mostly near navigable rivers which served as the main traffic routes. They were rice farmers, self-sufficient in the necessities of life. Longhouse communities tended to lead frugal lives, punctuated every now and then by impressive religious festivals which involved large-scale feasts.

The rainforest surrounding the settlements yields building materials, supplementary food, and fibre for clothing and mat-making. The Dayak collected jungle produce, which they took to the coastal markets to be bartered for useful articles like iron and plain textiles, or luxuries imported from far-away lands such as fine textiles, ceramics and beads.

Young Dayak men, intent on proving their worth, undertook the hardest task in swidden agriculture – the felling and burning of virgin jungle.

In the slack periods of the agricultural season they went on trading and raiding forays, returning richly laden with trade goods or the spoils of war, which included enemy heads. Headhunting was an integral part of inter-tribal warfare in Borneo until the early 20th century, and there were localised flare-ups during the Japanese Occupation of 1941–1945.

BORNEO SOCIETIES

Some Dayak societies are egalitarian while others were strongly stratified until recently. The higher

CLOCKWISE FROM EXTREME RIGHT: Kelabit lady wearing bead cap and ear weights; elderly Kayan couple in festive dress; and elderly Kenyah man in traditional costume, doing a war dance.

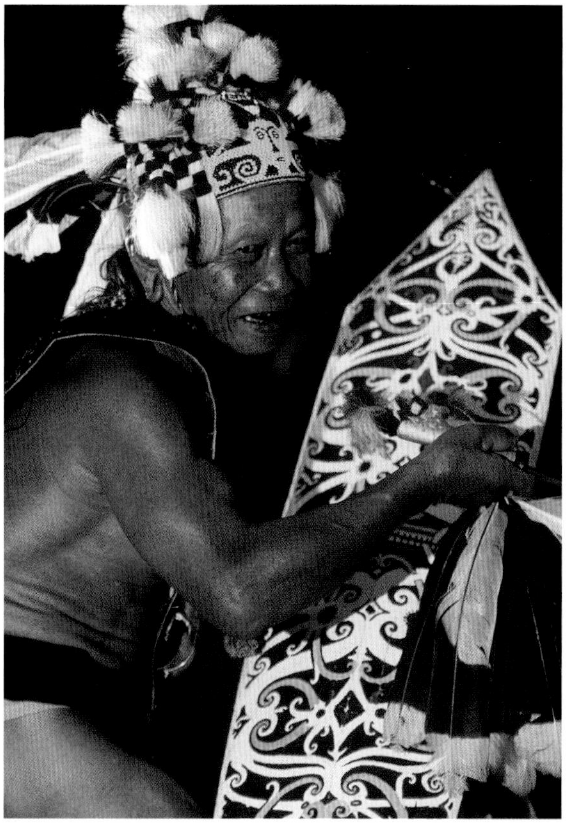

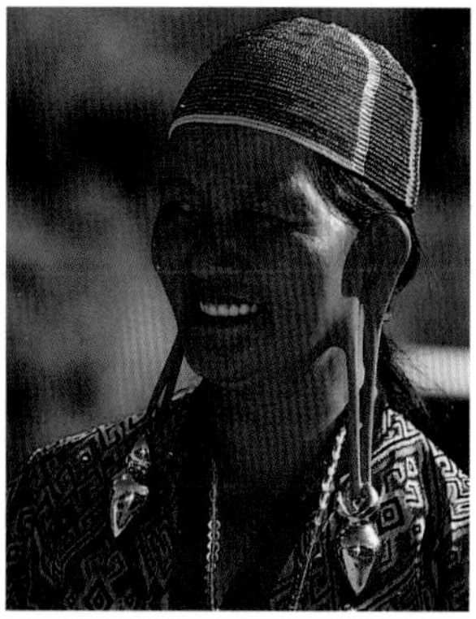

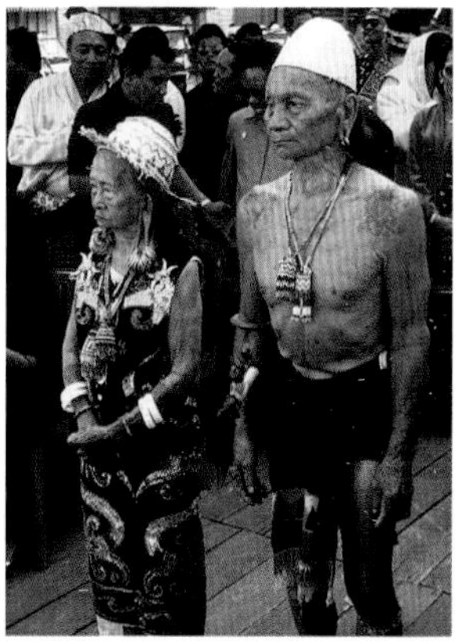

classes reserved many privileges for themselves, including the use of certain ornamental motifs on their houses, clothes and personal belongings. The aristocratic families of the Orang Ulu, a people who live at the headwaters of Borneo's major rivers in Central Borneo, constructed elaborate repositories in the form of carved burial posts or elevated ossuaries for their dead. The term *ulu* means "upriver". Other societies practised earth burial. Some Bidayuh people in West Borneo, possibly due to early Hindu influences, cremated their dead. Today, earth burial is the norm.

Borneo straddles the equator. Very little clothing is needed for creature comfort. The traditional everyday costume for most Dayak groups consisted of a loincloth for men, a short skirt or a set of two apron-skirts for women. A headband or headcloth for indoor use and a shady hat for outdoor wear completed the outfit. Both sexes wore jackets for semi-formal occasions. Children went mostly naked, though little girls might wear pubic shields suspended from a string, or a hip-lace of beads. In contrast to these very plain garments, ceremonial and festival costumes were lavishly ornamented with animal claws, teeth and feathers, silver, and beads.

It is almost impossible to enumerate all the ethnic groups of Borneo. In addition to the main divisions, there are many sub-groups. The movement of farming communities in search of land exposed them to new neighbours who might influence their culture or language, be influenced by them, or produce yet another hybrid sub-group. Many communities named themselves not by ethnicity but by the river where they settled. Some names commonly used in ethnographic literature pertaining

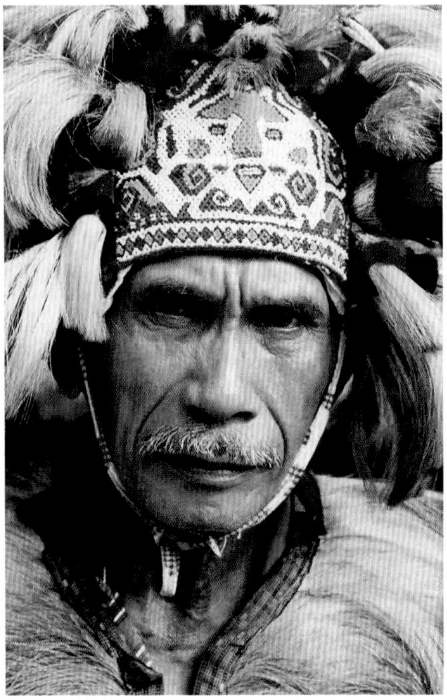

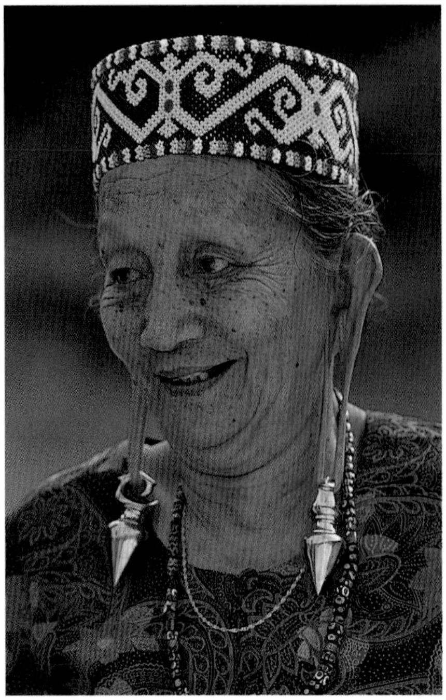

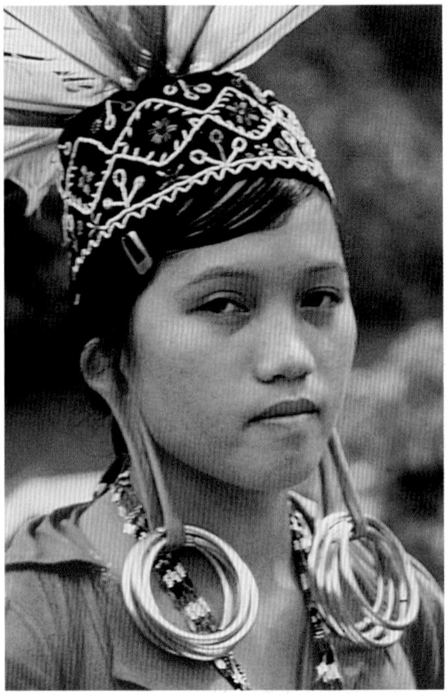

FROM LEFT: Iban elder wearing beaded headdress; Orang Ulu woman wearing bead headband and antique bead necklace; and Kenyah girl wearing beaded cap with feather trim.

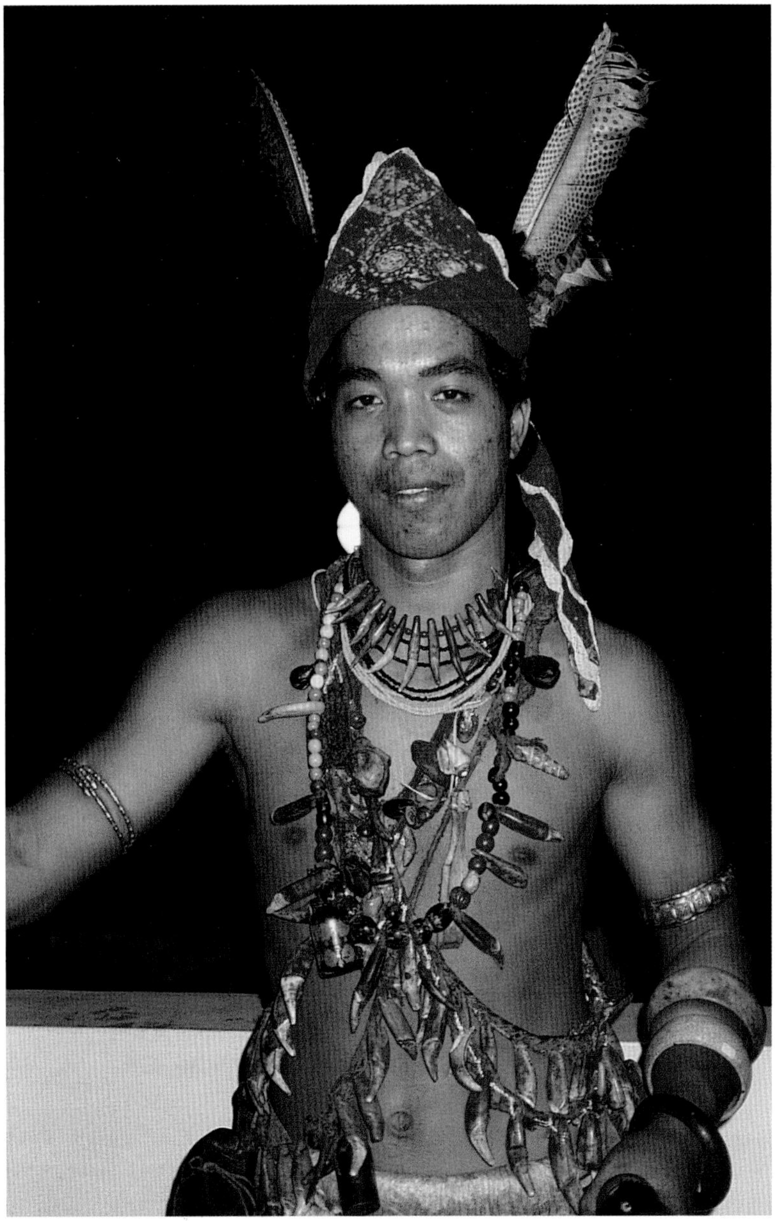

Young Bidayuh man dressed up in traditional warrior's gear during a Gawai festival.

to Sarawak are obsolete today: The Sea Dayak are now known as Iban, the Land Dayak as Bidayuh, and the Murut as Lun Bawang, Lun Dayeh or Lun Lod. A major grouping of indigenous Sabah people call themselves collectively Kadazandusun.

Below is a simplified summary of ethnic groups who still have significant bead cultures, with some indication of where their "homeland" is located.

Although many of these people have moved to the coastal towns of Borneo or even further afield in search of a living, they often return to home villages and longhouses at festival time to maintain family bonds and renew their cultural ties. To the reader who is not familiar with Borneo, this information is relevant when cultural connections, exchanges and trade patterns are discussed in the following chapters.

ORANG ULU

"Orang Ulu" is a useful if not very accurate collective term meaning literally "upriver people", as most of them live at the headwaters of Borneo's major rivers in Central Borneo – the Apo Kayan highland in East Kalimantan, and the headwaters of the Rajang and Baram rivers in Sarawak. Orang Ulu groups include the Kayan, the Kenyah and related groups, and the Kajang on the upper Rajang in Sarawak. The Modang are ethnically an Orang Ulu group that has migrated to the lower Mahakam basin in East Kalimantan. Much of the distinctive

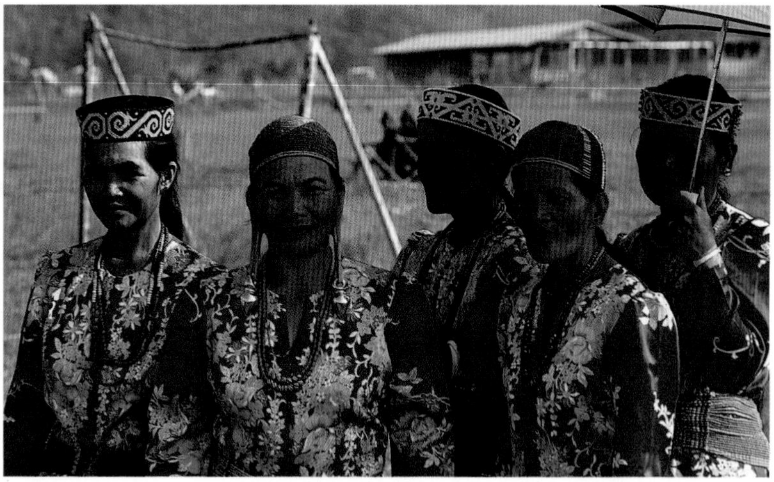

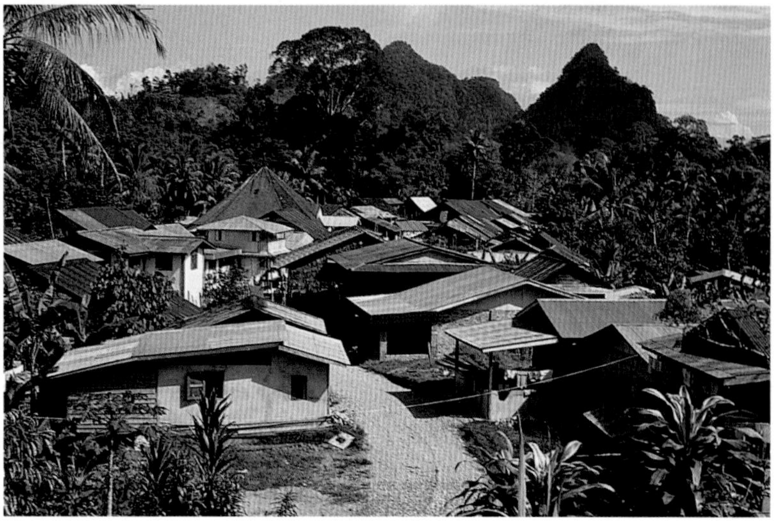

TOP: Kelabit ladies celebrating National Day at the Bario. They are wearing either beaded headbands, or the traditional Kelabit bead cap or *pata*.

ABOVE: A modern Bidayuh village situated in the hills near Kuching.

indigenous art of Borneo is the handiwork of the Orang Ulu.

In the past, Orang Ulu society was strongly stratified. Even artistic output was regulated by status in the old days – only the aristocrats were entitled to have large murals in front of their family rooms, wear gorgeously-beaded caps and waistcoats, and be entombed in tall, striking repositories that proclaimed the rank of the deceased to all comers, human or spirit. A gifted artist of the lower classes could produce these artifacts for his chief, but he had to be compensated with special beads to "protect his eyes" when he executed designs above his social level.

KELABIT AND LUN BAWANG

The Kelabit and Lun Bawang are sometimes classified with the Orang Ulu, mainly because they too live in the Sarawak highlands, centred around Bario and Ba Kelalan respectively, and their societies are stratified. These two groups are skilled rice farmers – their irrigated wet paddies with intricate networks of channels and sluices are a major achievement of pre-industrial technology.

Another distinctive feature of these cultures is the use of buffaloes for tilling the soil, as beasts of burden and as status symbols. The owner of many buffaloes is still considered a rich man, and a high-ranking bride was, in days gone by, worth many buffaloes. In the past, the Orang Ulu, Kelabit and Lun Bawang made extensive use of bark cloth, pattern-darned for greater durability, for their everyday clothing.

BIDAYUH

The Bidayuh lived mostly on the middle and upper rivers of west Borneo, both in Sarawak and in Kalimantan. Their longhouses tend to be rather lightly built, often clinging to the sides of steep ravines. Unlike most other Borneo people, the Bidayuh did not depend on boats for transport. Their old name,

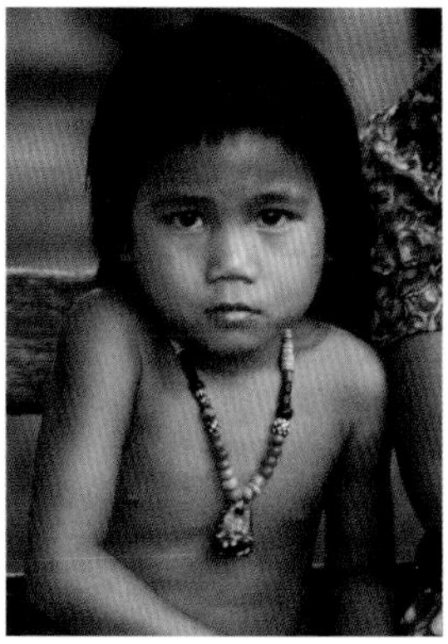

LEFT: Orang Ulu girl from the Ulu Mahakam, East Kalimantan, wearing a bead necklace.

BELOW: A traditionally-dressed Melanau bride.

Land Dayak, indicates their habitat and their skill as tireless walkers in steep mountain terrain.

Bidayuh longhouses were not decorated with enemy skulls. War trophies were kept in the men's house or "headhouse", separate from the main dwelling. This "guardhouse" served as accommodation for travellers, the venue for major meetings and festivals, and sleeping place for the tribe's unmarried young men and the occasional sulking husband.

IBAN

The Iban, once known as the Sea Dayak, are the largest indigenous group in Sarawak. They are an egalitarian society, mainly settled on the middle reaches of the major rivers. The Iban are thought to have moved northwards into Sarawak from the middle and upper Kapuas River, where related Mualang, Kantuq and Desa people are still living.

The Iban are hardworking rice farmers, until the end of the 19th century constantly moving in search of new lands. This restless habit, combined with the young men's need for spectacular achievement, contributed to the proliferation of feuds and inter-tribal warfare. They were known as Borneo's most inveterate headhunters. The Iban women are inspired weavers and artists, producing well-crafted mats, baskets and one of Borneo's most distinctive textiles, the dyed-in-the-warp *ikat*.

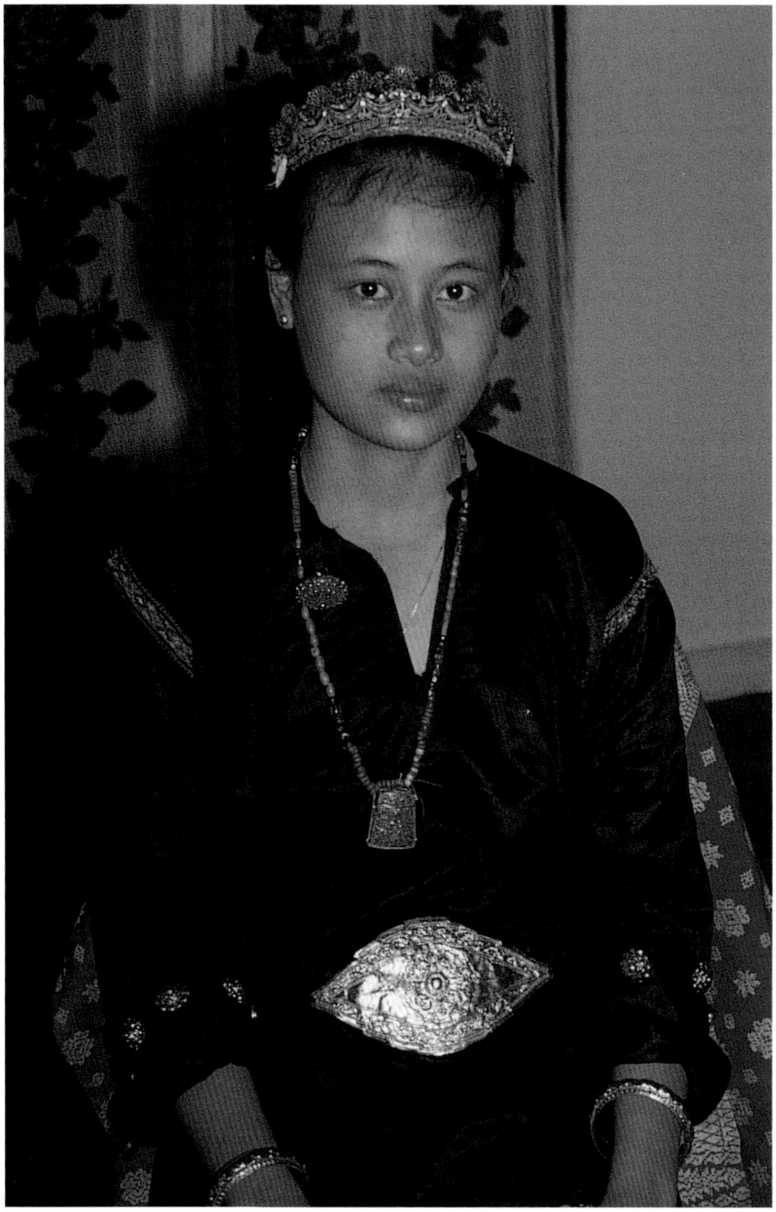

CLOCKWISE FROM BELOW, LEFT: Rungus girl in traditional attire, complete with bead necklaces, bandoliers and headband; Rungus woman from north Sabah wearing her beads; and Rungus house in Kudat, north Sabah.

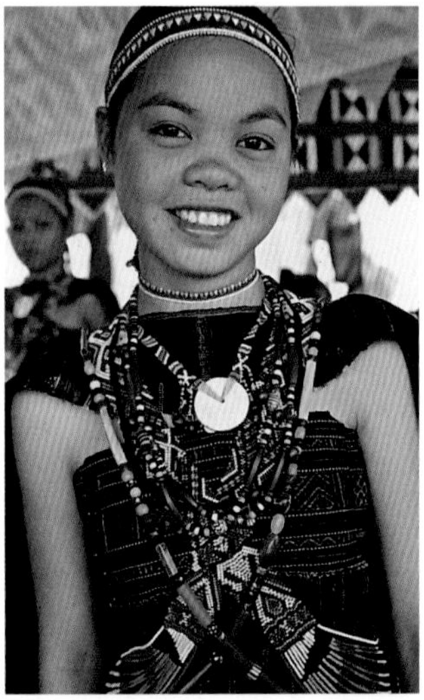

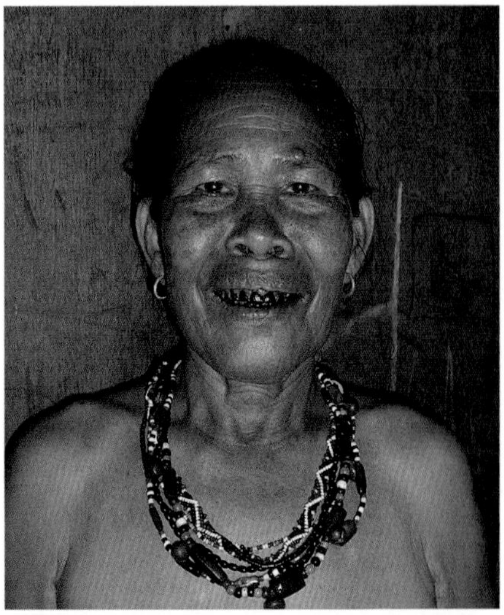

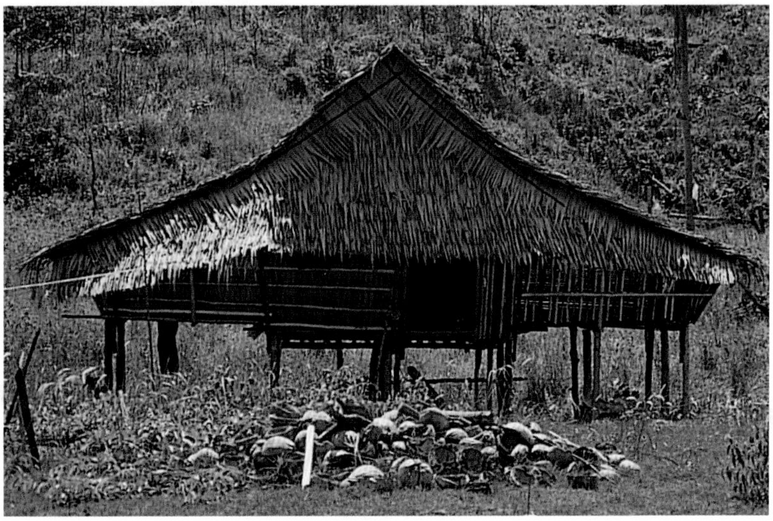

MALOH

The Maloh people live along the northern tributaries of the upper Kapuas River. Like the Orang Ulu in the vicinity, theirs is a stratified society. The Maloh are a very artistic people, and respected as such by their neighbours. Itinerant Maloh silversmiths could dare to travel the interior regions even in unquiet times, and were always welcome.

The distinctive beadwork garments made by the Maloh women can be found in many Iban and Orang Ulu longhouses, a testimony to their long-standing barter trade relationships.

MELANAU

The Melanau live in the coastal swamps of Sarawak between the Rajang and Baram rivers. Wetlands are the natural habitat of their staple food, sago, found in the trunk of a stately palm. The cultivation and trade of this commodity put the sago-growing districts into the spotlight of regional commerce in the 19th century.

The Melanau share a love of seafaring with the Malays, together with many aspects of material culture such as the weaving of gold brocade cloth. Today, most Melanau are Muslims or Christians, with only a minority still observing the religion of their ancestors.

KADAZANDUSUN AND RUNGUS

The main indigenous group in Sabah used to be

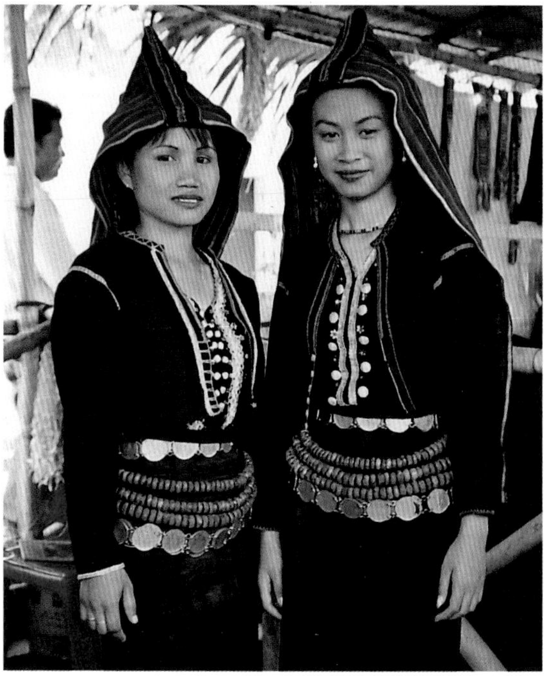

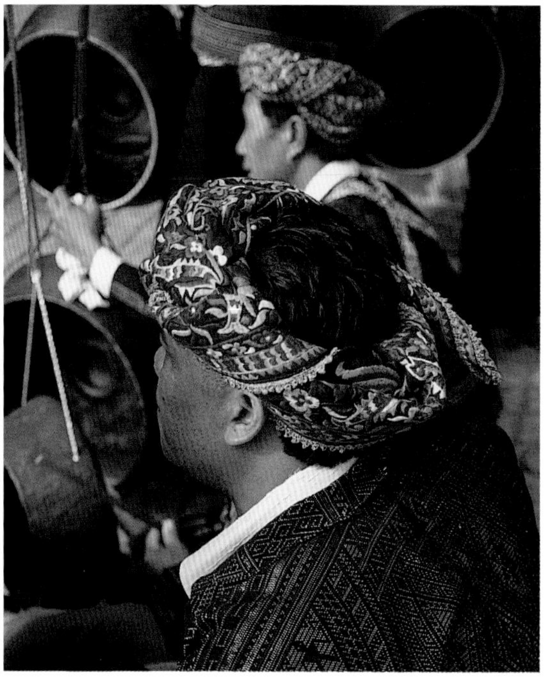

EXTREME LEFT: Kadazandusun women from the west coast of Sabah wearing their traditional hoods.

LEFT: Kadazandusun men of Sabah wearing their distinctive ornamented headcloth woven by their womenfolk.

called Dusun, supplemented by a geographic definition: The Ranau Dusun were the people living at the foot of Mount Kinabalu, the Tuaran Dusun those who lived near Tuaran. The name Dusun is still occasionally used for those who live in Brunei.

The Kadazandusun of Sabah have many linguistic and trading connections with the people of the southern Philippines. They grow rice in irrigated fields, tilled by buffaloes which are also used as beasts of burden and tokens of wealth. Some Kadazandusun women weave their menfolk's ornamented headcloths on backstrap looms. The coastal Bajau women also share this skill.

The Rungus people of Kudat on the northern tip of Sabah and adjacent areas have a highly developed bead culture which is still active, partly thanks to tourism.

NGAJU AND OT DANUM

The Ngaju live in Central Kalimantan, a province carved out to accommodate these war-like non-Muslim people after Indonesia attained independence. It is mainly due to their determined efforts that the animist cult, dubbed Kaharinga, has been accepted as an "official religion" by the Indonesian authorities. The Ngaju used to deposit the bones of their dead in artistically-decorated ossuaries. An elaborate death cult involved the use of carved "spirit boats" to send the souls of the departed safely to the other world. The Ot Danum are a related people, living in the upper reaches of the rivers of Central and West Kalimantan.

DAYAK RELIGION – THE SHAMAN

Before the advent of the world religions, the Dayak were animists. They respected and worshipped divinity in nature. Auspicious or warning omens were elicited from bird and insect calls, natural phenomena and dreams. Each society had its shamans and bards, men or women skilled in healing and the recitation of origin myths, songs and saga cycles. This oral literature celebrates supernatural heroes and enshrines the exploits of distinguished ancestors who, in time, came to supplement the tribal pantheon.

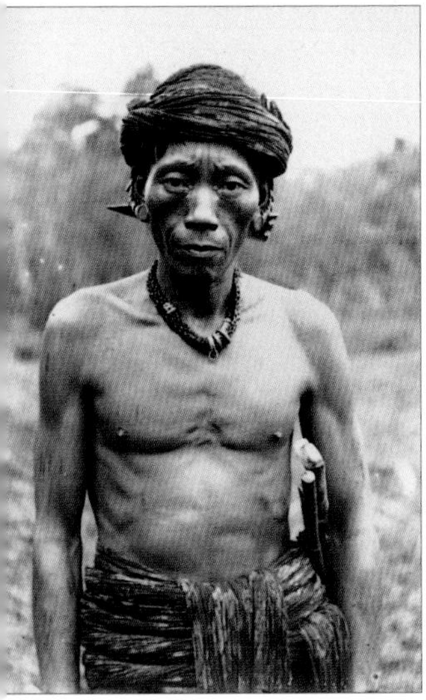

Murut man in everyday dress, circa 1900–1910.

In the past, outsiders routinely described the shaman as a "medicine man" or "witchdoctor", terms which carry pejorative connotations. In Borneo societies, the shaman, male or female, is indeed qualified to treat sick people or "prepare medicine", but the scope of his or her work is much wider and differs slightly from one ethnic group to another. Most importantly, the shaman is a mediator between the human and spirit worlds. It is his duty to cure illness, whether of a person, the all-important rice fields, or of a community. For example, a whole longhouse can become "hot" with phenomena such as illness, unexplained deaths or misfortunes, or a general feeling of unease and malaise, to the point where it has to be abandoned at least temporarily while the shaman and helpers carry out propitiation rites.

The shaman is skilled in interpreting omens. He knows the ceremonies involved in siting, building and inaugurating a new house, and is frequently consulted by individuals or groups who have a difficult decision to make, who feel threatened, or who have had a traumatic experience. In some Borneo societies the shaman/healer has a position beyond the usually quite rigid framework of gender-linked activity which confines ordinary people. As one Melanau lady put it: "Wearing beads is a womanish thing to do. For a *bomoh* I suppose that's all right ..."

A short digression on the popular image of shamans as creatures between the genders may be in order here. The healers are known variously as *manang*, *dayung*, *balian*, *bomoh*, *tukang tabor* or *dukun*. As found in classic Borneo literature, "witchdoctors" are perceived to be a dubious lot. Nineteenth-century Western writers especially portrayed the Iban *manang bali*, a man who adopted female dress and mannerisms, as a quack who duped sick people with his antics, an unashamed old queer who "even went to the extent of taking a "husband"!

The average Victorian longhouse visitor was not necessarily aware which one of the "fine dusky savages" was the shaman, or that the office could be filled by a woman as well as a man. The *manang* who invited comment was an obtrusive male who pushed himself forward, meddled, proffered unwanted advice and services. Any housemate could have behaved like this. If the busybody was also the *manang*, all *manang* were stigmatised as charlatans in the travel book that was designed to give armchair adventurers in genteel drawing rooms a few decorous thrills.

Professional rivalry comes into this. Much of early Borneo writing was penned by missionaries and administrators, both with their own agendas concerning the hearts and minds of the natives. Longhouse chiefs and *manang* were seen as opinion leaders. A *manang* who did not appreciate the blessings of civilization being bestowed upon his

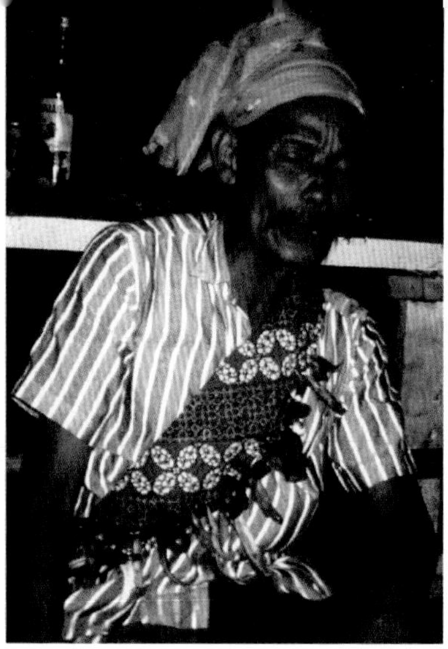

community had considerable resources for making himself troublesome. If this recalcitrant fellow could be shown up as a fraud *and* a rampaging homosexual, the Society for the Protection of Aborigines was in no position to say much if he was put, very firmly, in his place.

The majority of shamans were and are ordinary people with exceptional gifts. There is a healer in every longhouse and village. Many have followed the rural-urban drift and now perform their rites in the terrace houses or squatter huts of Borneo's major towns. The shaman's clientele is by no means confined to kinsfolk with longhouse connections. A traditional healer who gains a good reputation is much sought after by people of all races and religions.

IMPACT OF WORLD RELIGIONS

Since the advance of world religions into the interior of Borneo, much of the old healing and magic lore is beginning to disappear or go underground. Neither Muslims nor Christians are supposed to follow "heathen traditions". New converts are encouraged – and in some cases ordered! – to discard all vestiges of their old religion and to adopt the lifestyle, including the sartorial and dietary prescriptions, of the new.

In practice, most religious authorities are prepared to turn a blind eye as long as the pagan lapses do not become too frequent or too ostentatious. A researcher has to frame questions cautiously, and be prepared for evasive answers: Informants often say that "in the old days, our people used to do such-and-such", but sometimes they are not keen to discuss details at all, or point to somebody else, "the people upriver" for instance, who did or do strange and unusual things.

A few years ago, religious fervour prompted some Christian longhouse communities on the Baram River to toss their old beads and dragon jars, supposedly tainted with heathen magic, into the river – "and a few months later, the young men went diving into the water to try and salvage what they could!" to quote a snide neighbour from a community with less enthusiasm but, possibly, more common sense.

When it comes to the use of beads for healing or ritual purposes, some Borneans consider their beliefs vindicated by the strings of *tazbi* beads used by the Muslims, and the rosaries freely distributed by the Roman Catholics. Here are beads specially made for praying, and sanctioned by the highest religious authority – beads must be powerful! I have seen several Bidayuh healers' necklaces which have rosary beads neatly strung among blue glass, brass bells and bear claws.

ABOVE: A Bidayuh Jagoi shaman, wearing his protective beads, sings to the good spirits.

BELOW: A young girl wearing the traditional Bidayuh Jagoi costume and her grandmother's 'healing beads'.

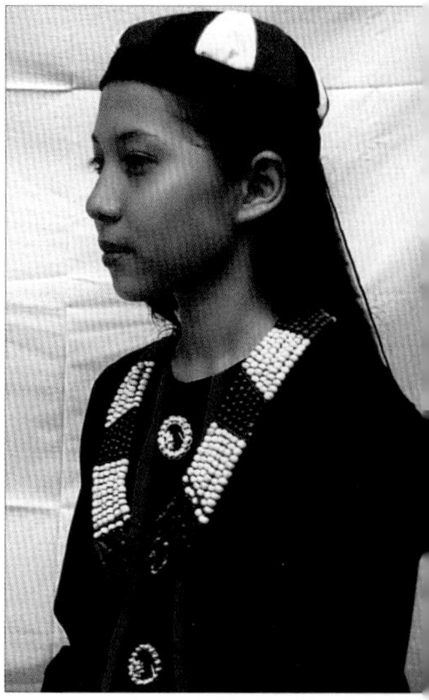

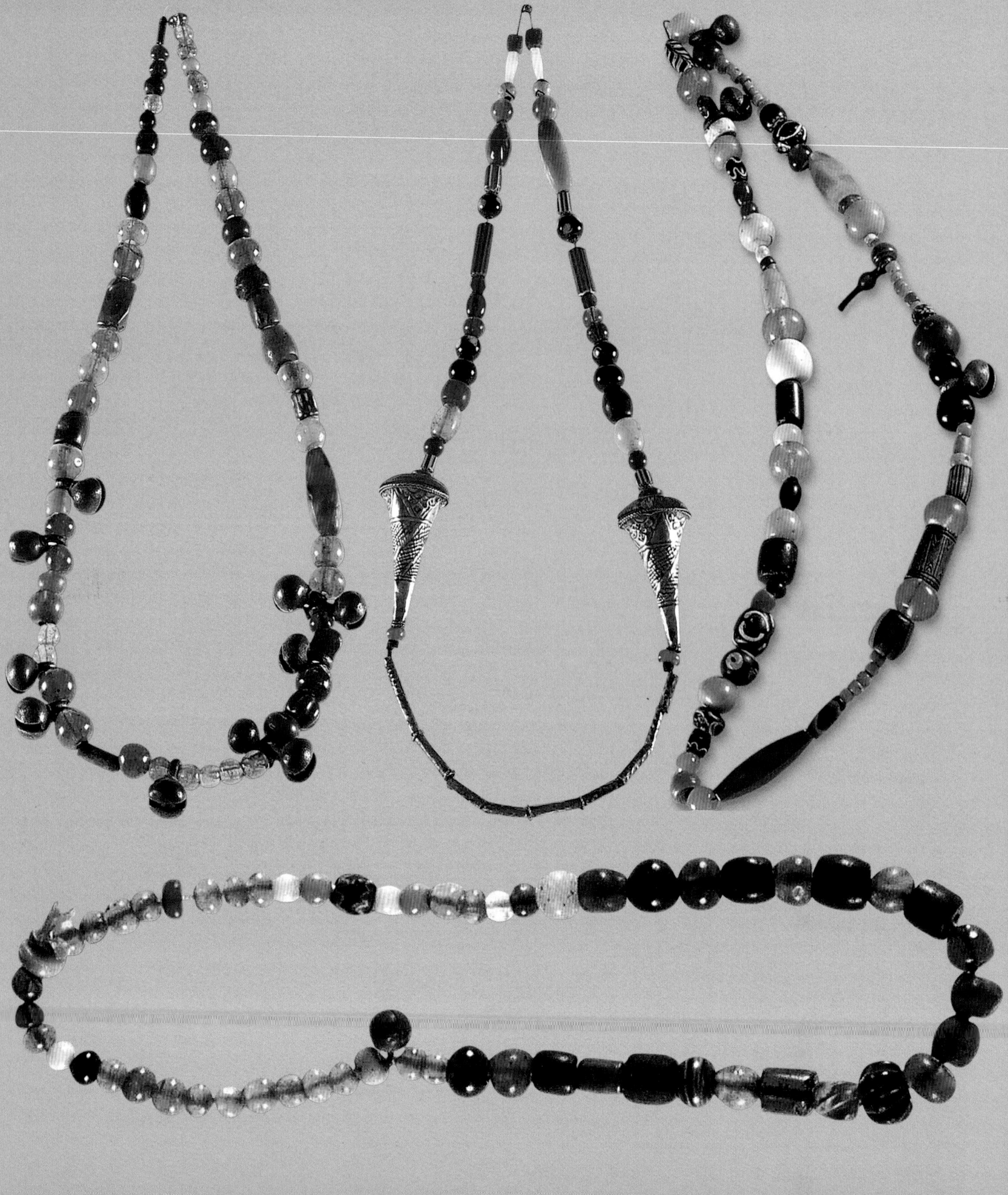

[CHAPTER 2]

BEADMAKERS, BEAD SELLERS, BEAD BUYERS

An overview of the kinds of beads found in Borneo, how they were manufactured, and where they came from.

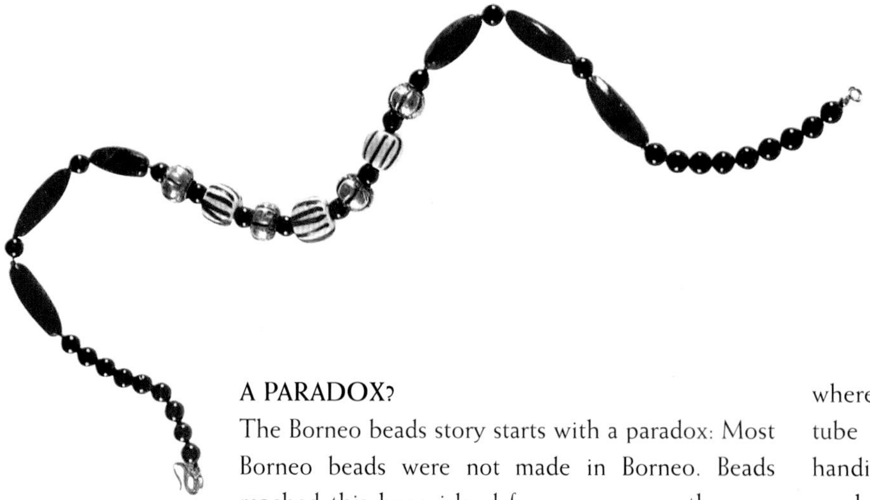

FACING PREVIOUS PAGE, TOP LEFT AND BOTTOM: Bidayuh bead strings with hawk bells.
CENTRE: Lotud beads with silver cones from Tuaran, Sabah.
TOP RIGHT: A string of typical Borneo beads.

ABOVE: Deep-red carnelian beads can be seen in this bead string. Carnelian beads were used and valued in the whole Indo-Pacific region and beyond. They came in many shapes, some plain, others decoratively etched.

A PARADOX?

The Borneo beads story starts with a paradox: Most Borneo beads were not made in Borneo. Beads reached this huge island from overseas – they are imports. This applies to nearly all the beads in circulation today. The main exceptions are beads of bone, tooth and pebble found in archaeological sites such as Niah in Sarawak, Madai in Sabah, and the shell discs and cylinders produced more recently in seaside locations such as Brunei Bay. Here is an overview of the kinds of beads found in Borneo and how they were manufactured.

BEAD MANUFACTURE

The methods of beadmaking have changed surprisingly little over the centuries. The techniques described below are still practised in many parts of the world. A 15th-century beadmaker would feel quite at home in a bead workshop in India, Indonesia, Pakistan, or any of the other places where beads are made by painstaking manual labour. Even the studios where "art beads" are produced for the boutique market employ the same basic techniques – only the sale prices differ!

The one significant innovation is the Prosser process, developed in the 1840s in Europe and finally patented in 1880. This process presses beads, buttons and other small items into the required shapes. Such beads often show a ridge or "seam" where the two halves of the mould met. Cane or tube beads, mainly the small gauges used for handicrafts and embroidery, are also produced by mechanical means, but the original technique of drawing a hollow gather of viscous glass remains the same.

STONE BEADS

The early stone and glass beads found in South-east Asia originated mainly in north-western India, where a lapidary industry has been documented as far back as the first millennium BC. Its products were exported throughout the then known world. The beads that reached Borneo were made mainly of carnelian, onyx and related semi-precious stones – hard durable material which could be perforated and ground to a high polish.

Chinese lapidary artists were making beautiful jade beads at the same time and even earlier. These superbly-finished artifacts were destined for the high-end imperial and aristocratic inland market, not the "barbarians of the south seas".

Carnelian beads were used and valued in the whole Indo-Pacific region and beyond. They were made in many shapes – some plain, others decoratively etched. The beadmaking process in the region of Cambay, India, still follows the traditional processes. Raw lumps of stone are sometimes soaked in honey and then carefully heated in pits of

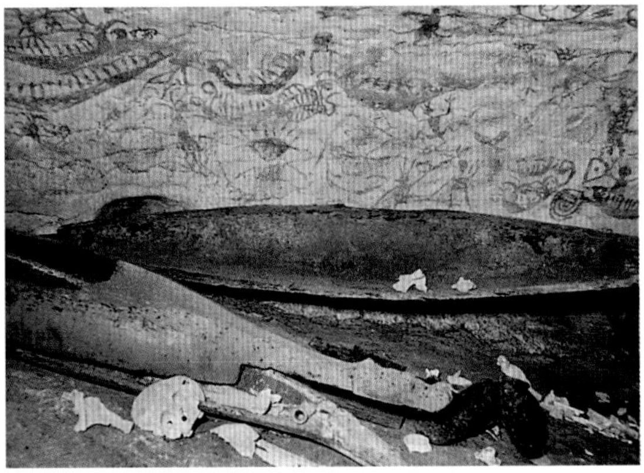

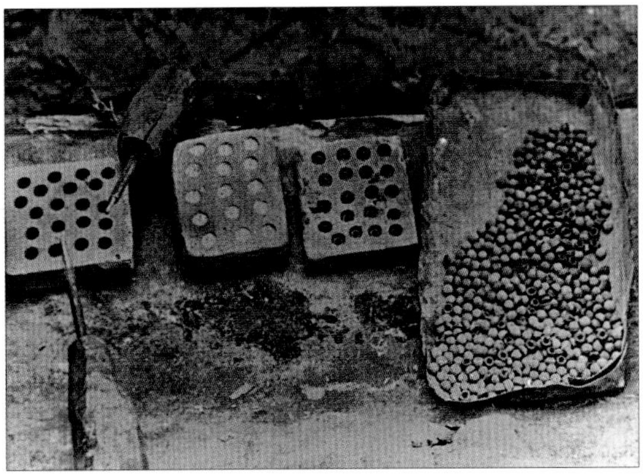

EXTREME LEFT: Prehistoric mural in the Niah Cave in Sarawak, an archaeological site. Decaying coffin-boats and scattered grave gifts lie below the mural.

LEFT: Moulds, awls and beads found in a backyard bead factory at Tanjung Selor, on the east coast of Borneo. Picture taken in the 1920s.

smouldering sawdust. This treatment enhances the sought-after, deep red colour of carnelian.

To make beads, the stone is chipped into "blanks", roughly shaped like the finished artifact – spherical, long or discoid. The blanks are perforated by drilling. It is interesting to note that even where electrical tools are available, many Indian beadmakers still use the bow drill of their ancestors – manual labour appears to be cheaper than electricity. After drilling, the rough beads are ground to give them their final shape and polished with fine abrasives. Today, most beadmakers use a revolving tumbler for the final polish. In the old days, a leather bag containing beads and diamond slurry was rolled up and down a hill, endlessly, until the right degree of lustre was achieved.

GLASS BEADS

The earliest glass beads found in the region of Borneo are fairly inconspicuous. Each bead is about the size of a peppercorn, made of opaque glass in muted shades of red-brown, yellow, white, black, light blue or light green. Such beads have been in production for centuries. Very brightly-coloured specimens of a similar type are sold today under the name "seed bead" or "handicraft bead".

Archaeological sites have yielded large numbers of these beads. Careful examination will show that there are two different types – one is like a tiny seamless ring, the other is coiled, sometimes in two or three twists.

Veteran bead scholar Peter Francis Jr has documented that the first type, which he called the "Indo-Pacific Bead", was made in southern India. At Arikamedu, where beadmaking dates back to the third century, craftsmen perfected the art of drawing tubes off a carefully-manipulated lump of semi-molten, coloured glass. These tubes were then cut into segments 3–8 mm in lengths, depending on the size of bead the market required. The jagged edges of the cut pieces were then smoothened by tumbling the finished product in hot ash.

The second method of making small glass beads was by winding one or two twists of viscous glass around a wire. The Chinese beads, which began to appear on the South-east Asian market around AD 1200, were made using this method, but it was not confined to the production of small beads. A rod of glass was heated in the flame of a blowtorch or "soldering lamp" (hence the name "lamp bead") until it was soft, but not melted. Then it was twisted around a mandrel (similar to an awl), usually with the help of fine pliers, and cut off. The resulting loop was held in the flame again to smoothen and round it. It was then shaped by patting or pinching into cubical, triangular, gadrooned "melon" and a variety of other shapes.

This basic glass bead, which was made from

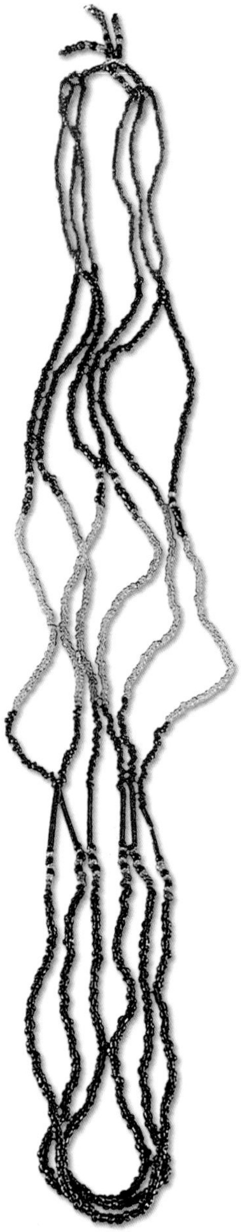

Peppercorn-size glass beads. These were the earliest glass beads found in the region of Borneo and came in various colours. Archaeological sites have yielded large numbers of these beads.

either of these two methods, is monochrome. To decorate such a bead, a second operation was necessary. Glass cannot be "painted". Even enamelling wears off beads after a few years of use. The only lasting decoration on glass is glass, and the only permanent glass pigments are metal oxides. Thin rods of differently-coloured glass were heated in the flame and skilfully applied to the bead in the shape of dots, stripes, flowers or whatever design was required.

The Indo-Pacific beads produced in southern India were basically glass tubes cut into segments. These beads pre-date the use of the blowpipe in glassmaking, generally believed to have originated in Roman Egypt. The glassmakers of west Asia and North Africa, and later Europe, used the blowpipe primarily to produce rounded vessels, but the same technique was also applied to produce "tube beads".

The process of making "tube" or "cane" beads has been described in reports on the old glasshouses of Venice and Amsterdam. A pocket of air is blown into a viscous lump of glass metal. Two workers each take up one end of this "bubble" and walk in opposite directions, thus stretching the lump into a hollow tube. Exact skill is needed to produce the right length and thickness of tube before the glass hardens. These tubes are then sliced to make beads. The finish may be achieved by tumbling in hot ash. Larger beads were spiked on a fork, and carefully "roasted" in the heat of the furnace to melt off jagged ends.

The chevron bead, still produced in various parts of the world, is based on a tube. The tube is decorated with inlaid zig-zag layers of contrasting colours, rather like the boiled "orange slice" lollies of yesteryear. When cut, the chevron cane or rod shows a star-like cross-section. After the ends have been ground diagonally, the layers appear as zig-zag or chevron bands around the end of the bead. The "true chevron" was a much sought-after bead, but the technique required special skill and was kept secret wherever possible.

A line of "fake chevrons" have appeared in the market at least since the 17th century. They are blue or black beads with a surface-applied band of red and white zig-zags. These fakes come in all sizes and colours and enjoy great prestige in Borneo.

MOSAIC/MILLEFIORI BEADS

Decorated lamp beads have an immediate collectors' appeal, as do the ornate mosaic and "millefiori" products of the glassmaker's art. Variously shaped and coloured glass rods are fused together to make "eye", "flower", "face", "bird" and other designs. When such a rod is cut into segments or thin slices, the identical design appears in each section, just as the "star" appears in a chevron rod, but without the central perforation. These canes are fused together

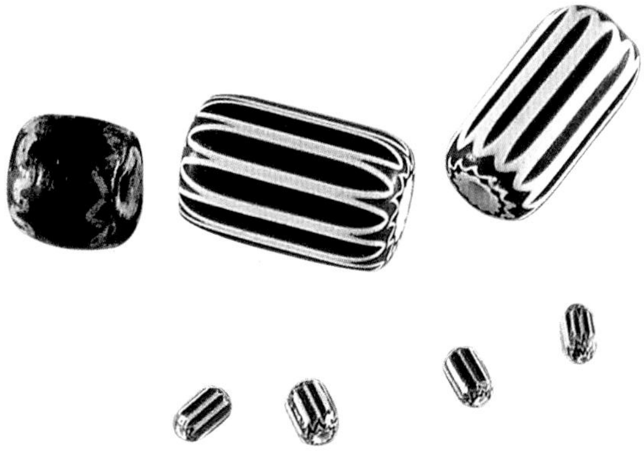

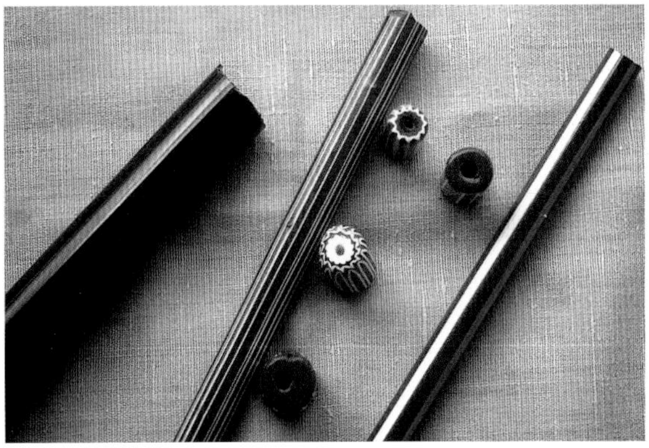

side by side to make a richly-ornamented plate which may be worked into dishes or vessels, or folded around a mandrel or a plain-coloured base to make a millefiori glass bead.

In South-east Asia, the earliest of these dainty beads were found at Sungai Mas, on the north-western Malay Peninsula. A similar bead, found in Java and called the "Jatim bead" (East Java bead) by collectors, was made by the more economical method of applying thin slices of "eye" canes on a round core of monochrome, opaque glass.

There is at present no evidence that the elaborate canes were actually constructed at Sungai Mas, though it is possible that traders brought them from the Islamic world, and the beadmakers in South-east Asia decorated an inferior base of glass with the precious imports.

EARLY HISTORY OF BORNEO BEADS

Beads, then, reached Borneo by means of trade. By the middle of the first millennium, Indo-Pacific beads were being made in Mantai in Sri Lanka, and along the eastern seaboard of the Indian Ocean by craftsmen of the Arikamedu connection. In the seventh century, beads were manufactured in Sating Pra in southern Siam and in Kuala Selinsing on the Malay Peninsula, major harbour towns which catered to the maritime India-China trade.

The earliest glass beads are not very spectacular to look at. They were about the size of peppercorns, in muted shades of white, brown-red, yellow, turquoise, blue and black. But they were bestsellers for centuries! Itinerant traders distributed beads on their journeys up and down the Malacca Straits and across the South China Sea. Beads were exchanged for jungle produce in the coastal markets of Borneo.

However, beads were by no means the only trade goods of the period. There was never a bead trade per se with flotillas of sailing boats laden with beads only. The country traders who dispersed merchandise from the regional emporia carried a wide range of goods, including beads. But when modern archaeology assembles the evidence, beads are among the best-preserved witnesses of those far-off times. Foodstuffs and organic materials were sold for consumption, textiles and matting have left few, barely distinguishable traces, and metals have corroded. Some of the ancient trade ceramics have been preserved, but sherds are a lot more common than whole pots. Beads, small and hard, have, on the other hand, withstood the ravages of time.

It would be fascinating to know how beads were worn in the last 2,000 years. A 14th-century Chinese mariners' handbook comments that "the people of Pahang and Kelantan keep their hair in order with bead rings of five colours" when describing profitable merchandise for the "barbarian nations". Many beads were recovered in funerary contexts, probably as

TOP LEFT: Chevron beads. The blackish-looking bead on the extreme left is a 'fake chevron' – the decoration is surface-applied. The large blue-white-red beads are 19th-century Venetian, the small ones at the bottom were purchased by the author in Kuala Lumpur in the 1980s.

TOP RIGHT: The chevron canes or rods from which the chevron bead is made.

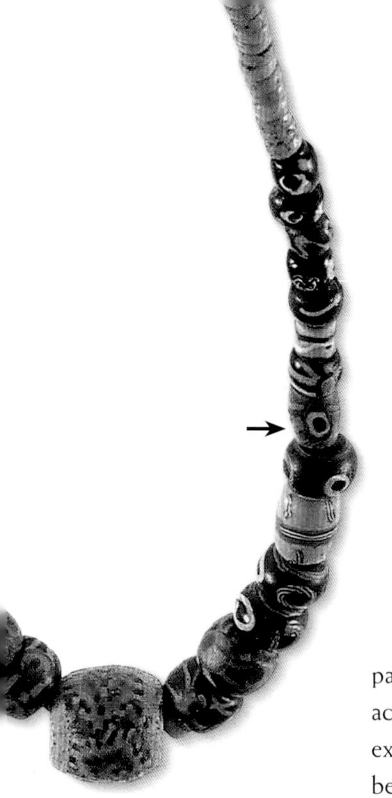

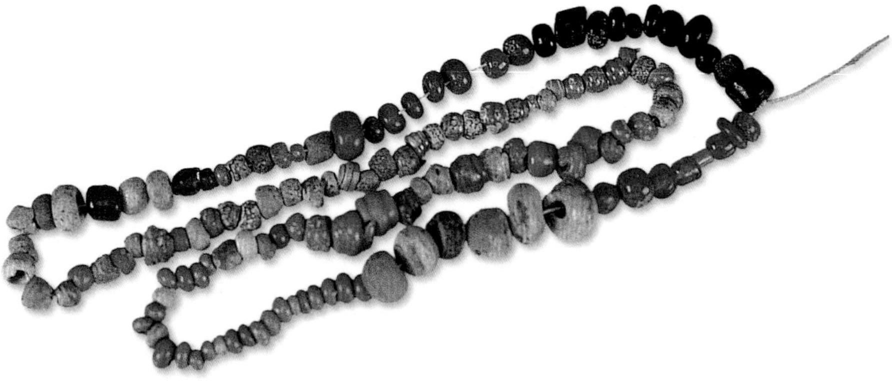

ABOVE: Eye bead (arrowed) in Orang Ulu necklace. This kind of bead was found at the Sungai Mas historical site in West Malaysia, and is still worn by the Orang Ulu, who call it 'palm leaf bead'.

RIGHT: Early examples of 'peppercorn' and larger beads recovered from the Niah Cave in Sarawak.

part of grave clothes and jewellery worthy to accompany an ancestor into the other world. In excavations of burial sites in some Borneo caves, beads were found scattered among the remains.

As mentioned earlier, the earliest beads – of semi-precious stone and glass – were of Indian origin, and by about the 12th century Chinese beads began to enter the South-east Asian archipelago market. The latter usually show striations in the coiled bead, while the former drawn type is more homogeneous but may show air bubbles pulled along the bead's axis. End users seldom bothered to distinguish between the two, however. They wanted a bead suited to their purpose, and in some regions were slow to change preferences.

Western travellers in the 16th and 17th centuries commented that some of the "natives" were not interested in multi-coloured beads. It was necessary to lay in stores of small reddish-brown beads in India, known as mutisalah in the eastern Indonesian islands, and readily bartered for exotic produce there.

If some South-east Asian archipelago bead users were conservative in their tastes, most of them eagerly accepted what traders brought from Europe and West Asia. The rise of Venice as the glass capital of the world coincided with Western exploration and colonial expansion from the 16th century onwards. The Beadmakers' Guilds of Venice protected glass recipes and manufacturing secrets with severe penalties. For a variety of reasons, however, skilled craftsmen occasionally left the confines of their island republic and helped to set up or revitalise glass industries elsewhere in Europe. In South-east Asia, the traditional producers continued their business. Many travelled a long way from home and settled near their prospective customers.

In pre-industrial societies, beadmaking was essentially a backyard industry. Locally-collected broken glass was recycled in one crucible with probably imported glass metal. No two batches of glass were of exactly the same composition and even the most painstaking spectrographical analysis cannot accurately determine the manufacturing site or period of many of these beads. A Dutch East India Company merchant's servant would most likely have sold his master's empty genever bottles to the local beadmaker in Batavia or Bantam, in Java.

Few of these beadmakers left any trace of their activity; it is by sheer chance that one is documented in the transactions of the English East India Company.

In a letter dated 1608, an English merchant described Chinese beadmakers in Bantam, west Java, who turned out a bean-sized, barrel-shaped translucent blue bead destined for the market of Sukadana on the south-west coast of Borneo. This Javanese manufactory was one of the sources of the "blue barrel" beads (see Chapter 7) much valued in Borneo.

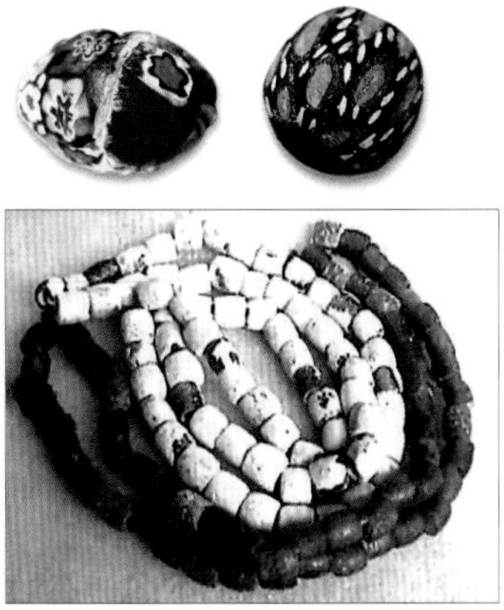

CLOCKWISE FROM TOP LEFT: Millefiori bead circa 19th century; the Jatim bead; and blue barrel beads recovered from the 'Xuande' shipwreck site off Pulau Tioman in West Malaysia.

Recently-discovered shipwrecks off the east coast of the Malay Peninsula add yet another twist to this story. One site, called the "Xuande" site, contains a wreck of a ship which was sailing from China. The site yielded, besides 16th-century trade ceramics, a pot full of blue, barrel-shaped, bean-sized beads, apparently for sale to the archipelago.

The Chinese craftsman in Bantam, described in the English merchant's letter years later, was producing the same type of bead *in situ*, thus cutting out the middleman. Potters did very much the same thing. While the stoneware jars imported from China and Indochina were known and valued by consumers in the South-east Asian archipelago, there was a steady market for the slightly inferior, more economical "country-made" product.

LOCAL AND IMPORTED BEADS

The Bornean cave dwellers of prehistoric times made shell, bone and tooth beads, and their descendants continued this production in a limited measure. Animal teeth and claws, and sometimes even human teeth, are perforated and worn as talismans, necklaces and earpieces, or to embellish hats and baby carriers.

Shell bangles were made in many parts of Borneo, often for use by traditional healers. Small, flat shell disc beads were produced north of Brunei Bay until the mid-19th century. These were mainly worn as belts or incorporated in the sides of Kelabit ladies' caps. Filed-off cowrie shell beads, produced here and elsewhere, were also used to embellish hat tops and textiles. The Kadazan women of the Sabah seaboard used bead discs to embroider their skirts and the sack-like hoods which they wore for ceremonies or during mourning. Today these garments are still occasionally worn for traditional displays.

One of the few instances of indigenous stone beadmaking was recorded in the late 19th century by the Dutch traveller A. W. Nieuwenhuis. In the Ulu Bahau, north-west East Kalimantan, he saw people producing discs, ear weights and beads from green-flecked serpentine. Today, locally-made stone beads are rare to the point of being non-existent, vaguely recollected by a few, now very aged, people.

Was there ever local production of glass beads? In Kalimantan, especially in the region of the upper Kapuas and in the central highlands and west Sarawak, a bluish-green, translucent bead with surface-applied squiggles of red glass is occasionally found. The glass is bubbly to grainy (see Plain Bubbly Glass, Chapter 7), suggesting an unskilled but motivated artisan who tried his best with the resources at hand. The colour of these beads resembles that of case bottles, of which any Dutch or English "outstation" in Borneo would have yielded a plentiful supply. No backyard glassworking site has been found in this area yet.

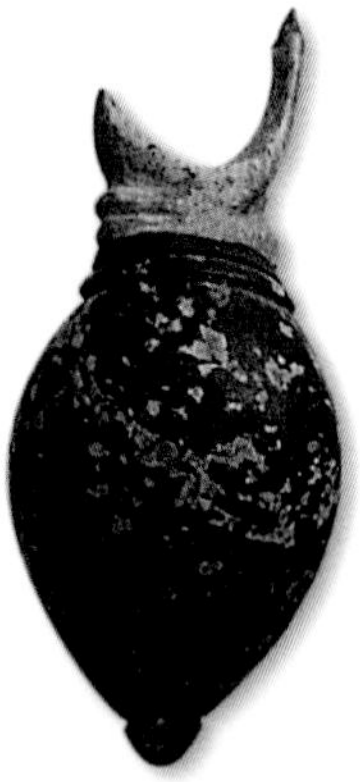

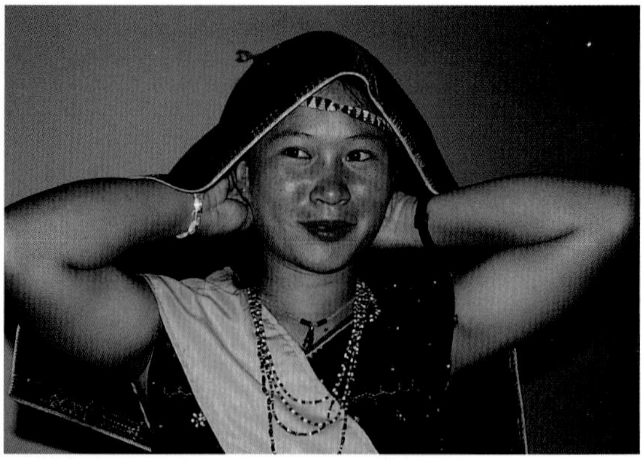

TOP LEFT: Stone ear weight made by the people of the Ulu Bahau until around 1900.

TOP RIGHT: A Kadazandusun girl of Sabah adjusts the hood which is typical of her ancestors' costume.

Some obviously home-made beads include segments of brass, such as ammunition shells. These would usually be worn as amulets. A cylindrical wooden bead roughly covered in silver foil belongs to this category. Bidayuh healers hesitantly classify it as "very rare, probably a cooling bead" (i.e. to cure fever). It is found mainly in the west Sarawak-Kapuas region, but its maker knew more about magic than silvercraft.

By the 19th century, the trickle of imported beads had become a veritable flood worldwide. The wave of "new beads" washed over Borneo too from about 1850. With an increased Dutch and English presence in the area, there was more trade of European goods, and many of the pretty Venetian and Bohemian beads got into the Borneo market during this period. Chinese consumer wares, including beads, were also freely traded throughout the South China Sea. However, some native groups preferred Indian textiles and the Indian or Chinese beads they were used to, to the "foreign" stuff.

The products of European glassworks, notwithstanding some conservative attitudes, are found in all parts of Europe, in the Americas, in mainland Asia and South-east Asia, and Africa. Production was nothing if not consumer-oriented – the larger Czech glasshouses sent "sample men" into the main trading regions of Africa and Asia with orders to buy samples of the beads most highly valued by the native traders.

These specimens, which included semi-precious stones, amber and even lions' teeth, were skilfully copied in glass (see Carnelian Spindle, Chapter 7). Beads were, and still are, trade goods.

International trade deposited these beads in the coastal ports of Borneo, but that was by no means the end of the road. Beads were traded up and down the rivers and mountain paths of this island and beyond. In the 19th century, Kenyah from Central Borneo occasionally travelled to Sumatra to buy beads which the Batak had by then considered "old-fashioned".

A North Borneo Company administrator in Tempasuk, on the west coast of today's Sabah, commented that shell disc beads were bought up by traders, who took them to "the Dayaks" of Sarawak. As recently as the 1950s, ancient tombs in Sumatra were looted of small brick-red mutisalah beads (see Chapter 7) for re-sale to Timor. Beads are among the most mobile of trade commodities. This is one reason why it is very difficult to date a bead collected in any but an undisturbed archaeological context.

THE BEAD TRADE

A visitor to the Moluccas records that "trade is carried on by barter, the most prized article of exchange being a species of bead, by no means plentiful, called by them lakkai, of an ochrous red colour, evidently some sort of soft stone. Whence these beads come is quite unknown ... no imitation

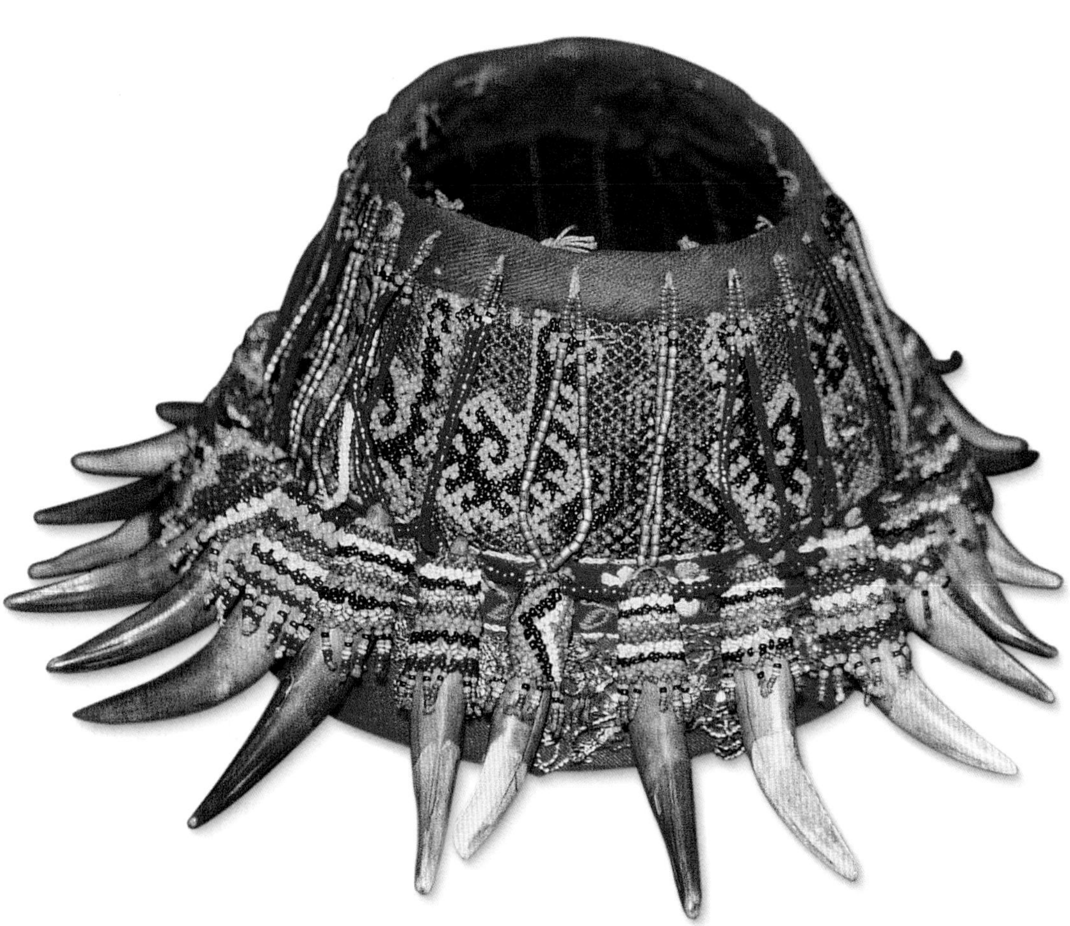

Bead, tooth and bear claw hat used by the women of the Ulu Bahau. The Bornean cave dwellers of pre-historic times used animal claws and teeth, and sometimes even human teeth, to embellish hats. Their descendants have continued this practice in a limited way.

yet made in Birmingham or elsewhere has been found to be sufficiently exact to deceive the native ..." This was written in the 1880s.

Today, we have a fair idea where most of the beads came from, and we know that the "lakkai, of an ochrous red colour", are a widely-distributed opaque glass bead known elsewhere as mutisalah. But this explorer's cursory remarks record the trend: Explorers and administrators carried beads, to be used as a serious medium of exchange, or as gifts to purchase goodwill and cooperation.

All traders carried beads among other merchandise. In 1848, *The Journal of the Indian Archipelago and Eastern Asia*, a Singapore journal, published lists of regional trading ports with information as to what merchandise could be obtained and what currency was most useful in each – Dutch, Portuguese, English or Spanish coin, or beads.

Most beads got to Borneo in the vessels of "country traders". From the coast, they were carried up the big rivers, under sail as far as the tides reached, then under paddle power. Some Chinese and Malay traders made their way far upriver. In fact, one handsome black rosette bead takes the name *lukut barong* or "boat bead" from the vessels of these daring merchant-adventurers. They were daring – in 19th-century Borneo, an interloper risked losing his head in a very literal sense!

Beads and other merchandise passed to the Dayak barter-traders who brought "jungle produce"

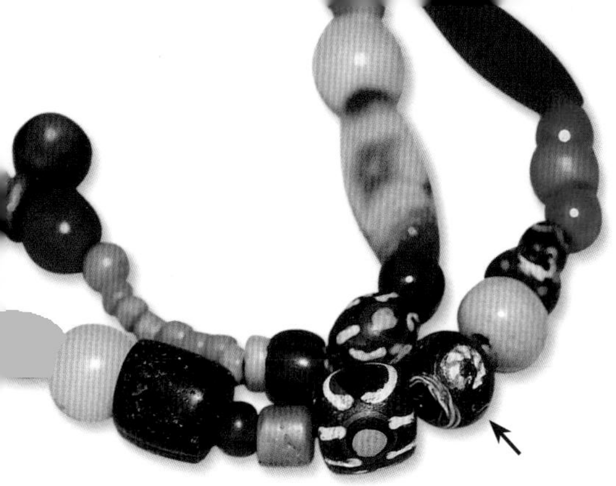

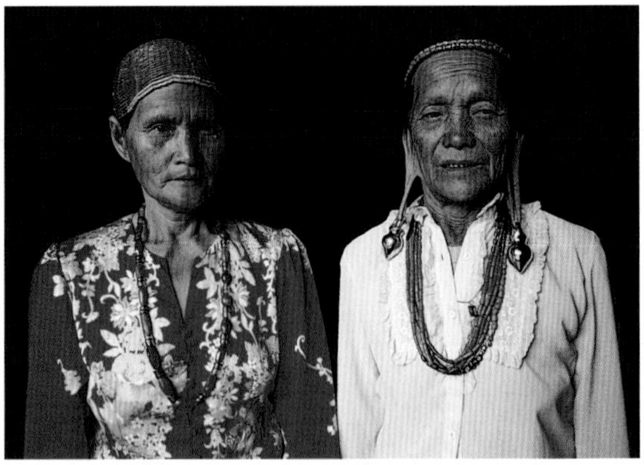

TOP LEFT: The *lukut barong* bead or 'boat bead' (arrowed) was brought by Malay and Chinese traders far upriver into Borneo.

TOP RIGHT: Kelabit ladies. In 1999, the Kelabit matrons of Sarawak told tales of a brave Brunei Malay who went to Bario, the main Kelabit settlement, around 1900 to sell beads.

such as rattans, resins, birds' nests and assorted *materia medica* in exchange. The interior trade moved in dugouts of shallow draught; skill and brawn pushed and pulled the light craft over gravel beds and rapids, and finally portaged them across watersheds.

The villages of the interior did not have a designated trader, but most men went off on trading or raiding expeditions once in a while. The women fended for themselves and the farms without complaint while the successful raiders replenished the community's stock of head trophies, or the traders brought back highly esteemed valuables from their trips to the coast.

Most beads passed through many hands before they reached the high plateau of Central Borneo, where the bead culture is still very strong. Occasionally, a trader "from the rivermouth", as strangers are called in the highland plains, carried a consignment of beads all the way to the end consumers.

Such a brave traveller was long remembered! In 1999, the Kelabit matrons of Sarawak still told tales of an Awang (a Brunei Malay) called Jali, or maybe Jalil, who made his way up to Bario, the main Kelabit settlement, around 1900.

"My grandfather bought this string of opaque yellow beads from the Awang, and these translucent blue ones," they tell visitors, proudly displaying their now 100-year-old treasures. A Kelabit headhunting song describes the structure erected to hang freshly-captured head trophies in this manner:

> *...the high ulung which strangers can see from far away*
> *strangers who come to sell beads*
> *and buy pigs, and deer with long horns...*

WHERE ARE BEADS FROM?

Only a person from the rivermouth would ask this sort of question! The Bornean bead owners' reactions typically range from "don't know and don't care" to polite bewilderment. One very common answer is: "We got the beads from our mothers, our grandmothers, our great-grandmothers." Only a few, usually aged persons are prepared to say that beads "grow", that is they have been told that the well-known male and female varieties of some beads can actually reproduce in some mysterious way, though nobody has claimed to actually own "new-born" beads.

To the Bidayuh of west Sarawak and West Kalimantan, some beads grow in the ground – that is where a person, guided by a dream, may occasionally find them. There is no way of planting beads, however; the cultivation of such mystical plants is in the hands of the good spirits. The same donors may also decide to flush a bead into the catch-net of a woman fishing in a mountain stream.

Most people are aware that beads reached them by way of trade, from "far far away". To many

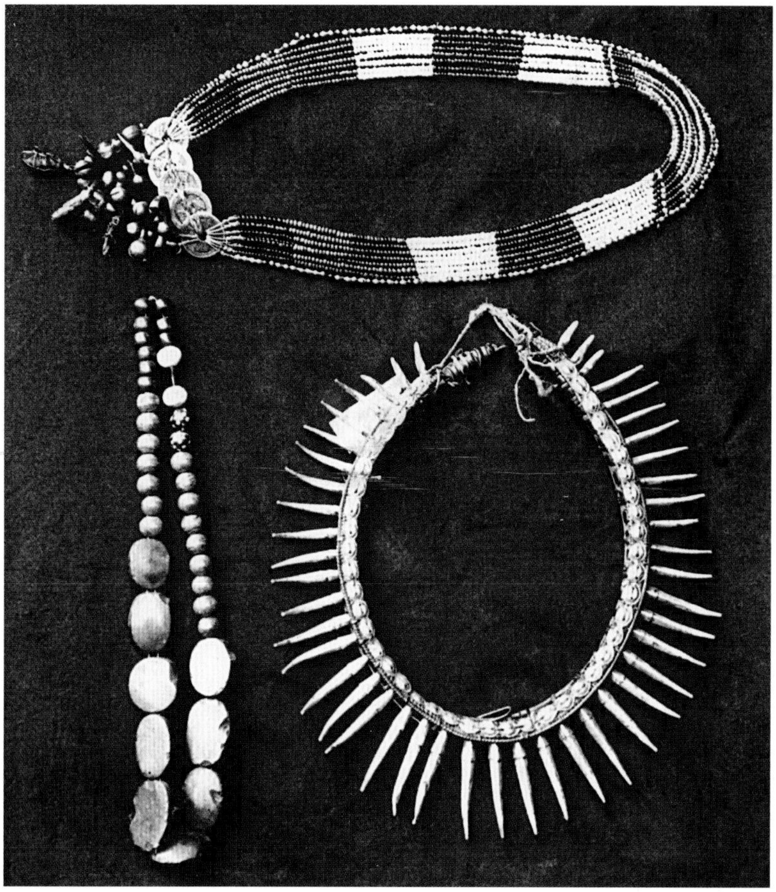

Bidayuh necklaces. CLOCKWISE FROM TOP: Female healer's necklace strung in blocks of red, white and black; warrior's neckpiece of beads and boar tusks; and necklace containing carnelian discs. Photo circa 1900.

Bidayuh, "far far away" is Brunei, source of beads and any other strange and inexplicable things such as *buah Brunei* (Brunei fruit) or the pineapple. There is a widespread tradition, probably from Kalimantan, of holding the Dutch, i.e. the foreigners, responsible for what are perceived as freaks of nature, such as *ayam belanda* (turkey), *tikus belanda* (guinea pig) and *durian belanda* (soursop), *belanda* meaning "Dutch".

Education widens the scope of possible bead sources: One woman, whose daughter had studied overseas, told me that her value beads were from Egypt, the sort of thing King Solomon gave to the Queen of Sheba. No doubt about it, her daughter had seen some beads exactly like hers in the Victoria and Albert Museum in London.

One knowledgeable Melanau elder informed me in 1998 that "beads always come from outside, from far-away countries. Our ancestors went trading to Brunei, to Sambas (West Borneo), to *selat* (Singapore). Some of the sago trade was conducted in beads, brass and similar items. Brass bells from Brunei are very popular, they were traded together with beads. Pilgrims used to bring beads back from Mecca, especially the banded agate which is still available there today. One type of agate has stripes of gold inlay instead of the white bands. These are very potent beads, and were made by the *jinn* [spirits]".

An elderly gentleman now living in Marudi, Sarawak, also told me: "Our people used to make beads with fire." His family was part of a group migration from the Ulu Bahau in Kalimantan to the Kelabit highlands when he was still a small boy. Nobody has made beads since the community settled in Sarawak. But his assertion is tantalizing.

Was he referring to a very roughly-made "bubbly" glass bead which is mainly found in the middle and upper catchments of the Kapuas River, near the Bahau homeland, and which might be of local production? The Bahau, or Saba'an as their neighbours call them, certainly made stone beads in the late 19th century, though nobody seems to have kept the rather clunky artifacts. A pair of ear-weights are currently preserved in the Sarawak Museum, but I have never seen this kind of ornament worn by anyone in Borneo.

A BEAD ORIGIN MYTH

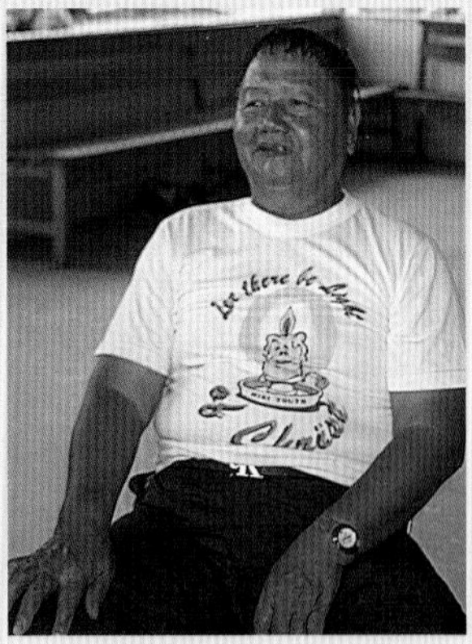

The late Tuai Rumah Lah Wan, headman of Long Laput on the middle Baram River, told me this elaborate bead origin story in 1998, which, interestingly, tallies with a Melanau tradition.

Today's new beads come in from Java, and a few smaller manufactories on the southern coast of Borneo. In the third millenium, beads are still part of life. The "sample men" are at work again, this time from Indonesian glass works which turn out "new old" beads, some of them beautifully finished, by the bushel. The itinerant bead seller is back on the scene, carrying his wares to fairs and markets and longhouse festivals. Local owners of heirloom beads buy the new products for "everyday wear", to preserve their antique treasures.

"Once upon a time, there was a Kayan man who lived in a longhouse. He was the son of a chief, and was a hard-working, intelligent young fellow, a skilled hunter and a good farmer. This story happened a long time ago, when there were no guns. Instead, people used spears for hunting.

One night this man went to hunt. He put flint and tobacco in a bamboo box tied to his belt, and he took a strong spear. He wanted to kill whatever animals were constantly disturbing his tapioca plantation. He waited behind some bushes and sure enough, some animals came in the darkness. They were wild boars. He managed to spear one but the creature struggled so hard that the spear handle broke. The animal ran away with the spearhead still in its flank.

The man decided to follow the wild boar. He followed it for a great distance. For two days and two nights he searched, until he lost his way. Then he came to a huge lake. Looking across the lake, he saw a longhouse on the other side. The man walked around the side of the lake until he reached the other side. He said to himself, "I'd better be careful, these people might be enemies."

So he removed the bamboo box from his belt and buried it at the foot of a *mawang* tree. He then went to the house. He saw several people; they all had a distinctly different smell from his own people. He was sure they were not Kayan. They asked him where he had come from, saying: "You are not of our race."

He replied: "You're wrong there, my friends. I belong to the same people as you do. In fact my grandparents came from here. My grandfather never failed to remind me of the *mawang* tree that he planted. He said he buried his bamboo container underneath a stone at its foot."

"Let us go and see," the people said. They went to the tree and dug near its roots, and behold! A nicely ornamented bamboo box was found. So they said: "He is really one of us, and not an enemy."

The longhouse leader did not take much notice of the young stranger initially because he was worried about his daughter. She had been hurt. He said: "I don't know how to treat my daughter, all the wise women have tried in vain. Let us ask this stranger if he knows how to heal wounds."

So they called him in. He said: "Very well, let me have a look." They led him to where the young lady lay on her sleeping mat. But he had a shock – the broken-off end of his own spear was stuck in the wound! He said: "All right, I will try to treat her since you ask me to."

He went into the jungle to obtain a young piece of bamboo. He cut it off below the node. Then he asked that an enclosure be made from mats so he could treat the sick girl in privacy. When they were alone, he pulled out the spear head deftly and placed a little bamboo in its place to stop the blood from gushing out. Then the girl began to recover.

When the young lady was fully recovered, the stranger wanted her for his wife because she was of noble birth. Her father said: "Since you have cured her when none of us could help, it is right that you should marry her."

They had been married for some time, but did not have any children,

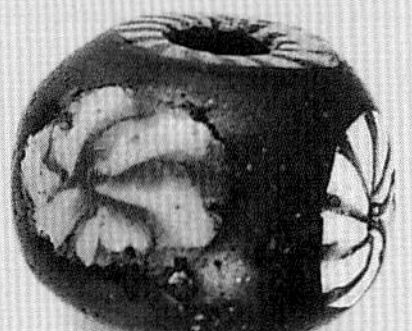

before the young man began to feel homesick. "I want to return home to see my parents," he said to his wife. "If it is possible, let us go together."

"No, that will not be possible," she replied. "As soon as I cross the lake, I will be transformed." Then he remembered that the first time he had seen her and her people, they had all been wild boars. "If that is so, then I will have to go back alone," he said, and started to make preparations for his journey.

Before he left, his wife said to him: "Now listen carefully to what I tell you! Sometime soon, my people will start crossing the Baram River. When that happens, watch out for me. In all that herd, I will be the white one with a ring through its nose. That is the mark on me. When you see a very fair wild boar, I want you to kill it with your own spear. Then you have to take it and bury it in a grand tomb, just like the ones you make for high-ranking Kayan people. Leave the body there for one year, then come and check it again, to see how everything is changed."

The man was amazed to hear his wife speak like this. "This is what I want you to do," she repeated. "I want you to promise me that you will do it." Her husband merely nodded, unable to speak. Then he left. He walked around the lake and through the jungle, a long way. When he reached his own longhouse, his people commented that he had been away for a long time. "Well, yes," he said. "My journey took much longer than expected."

After some time, news came that a large herd of wild boars was crossing the river. People went out in their boats, waited for the animals to cross, and killed as many as they could catch swimming in the water. The man went with his friends, but did not kill any boars. He was waiting for her only. He did not want to kill any other wild boars. Every day he went out in his boat.

Then, one morning, he saw a very fair boar. "This must be her!" he thought. He paddled rapidly towards the animal and plunged his spear into its flank. "It is only because of our promise that I am doing this," he said. "You know I love you very much."

Sad at heart, he killed the white boar. Despite everything his friends could say to stop him, he placed the body in a beautiful tomb hut which he had ordered built beforehand. There he left it.

After one year he climbed up to the tomb hut to see what had become of the body. He could hardly believe his eyes! Inside the tomb was a mound of beads where the body had been. Where the head had been, there were *lukut sekala*. Other value beads lay where the chest had been, the less important ones lay further down. All the people of the longhouse came and took some beads.

This is the story of the origin of the beads that we have today. The first, original beads were formed from the blood of a magic animal. All the other beads since were made by people, in imitation of the real ones.

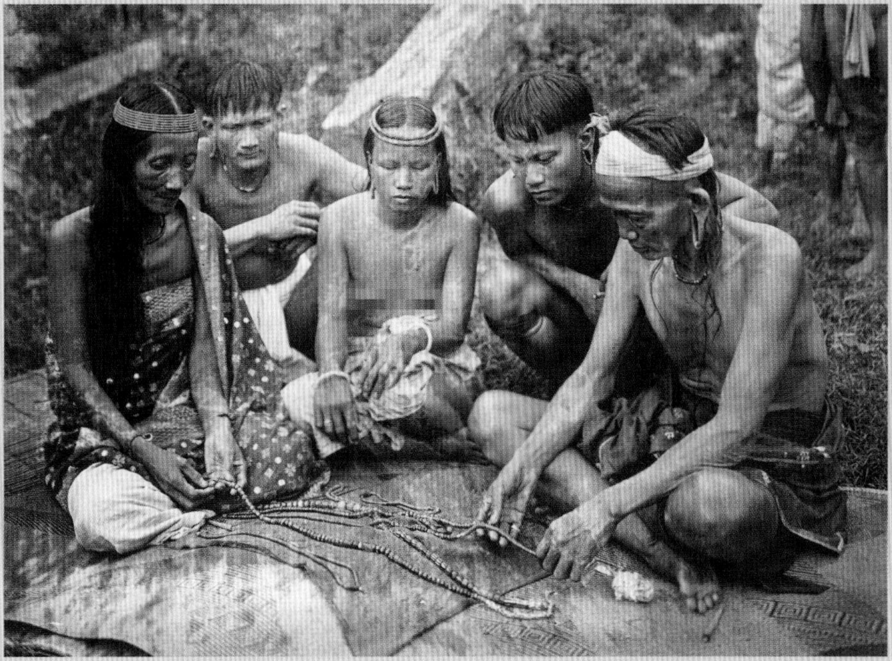

Sulau, a Kayan chief's wife, displaying her collection of valuable beads. Photo taken in the late 19th century.

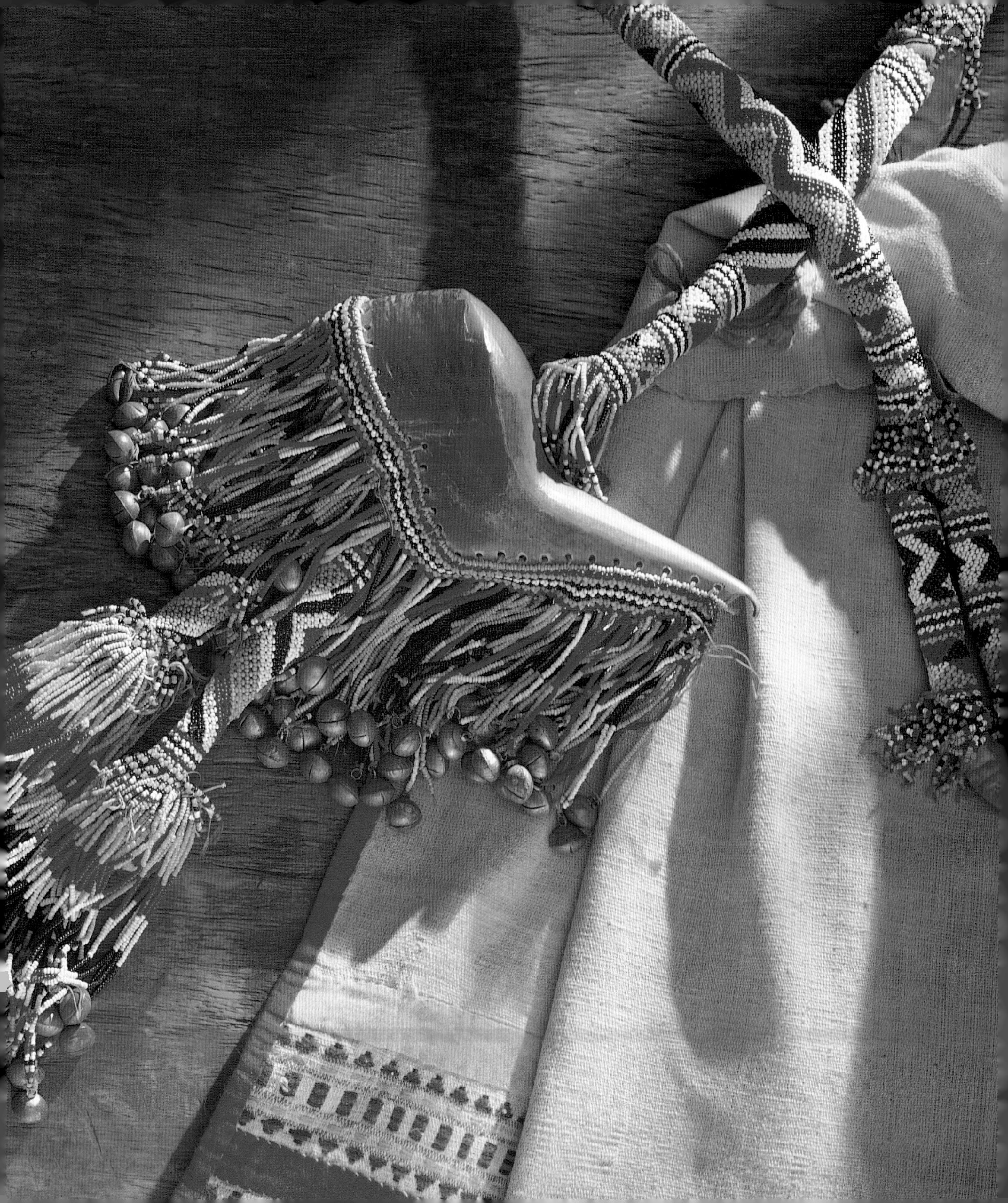

[CHAPTER 3]

BEADS OF POWER

How beads are used for ritual and spiritual purposes, for ceremonies and in rites of passage.

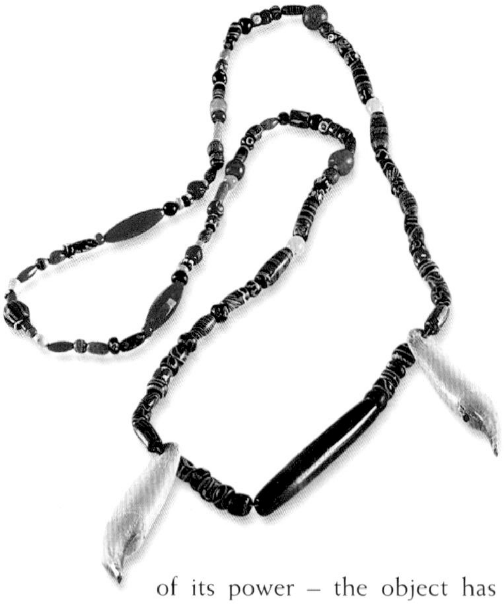

THE POWER OF BEADS

Compared to other things of value such as textiles, metals and ceramics, beads are physically strong. They are made of durable materials such as stone or glass, and are comparable to ceramics although they seldom break the way ceramics do. Burials, shipwrecks and enemy raids dispersed but did not destroy beads. The people involved in secondary mortuary rites also noted that beads retained their texture and colour long after corpse, burial clothes and assorted grave gifts had decayed and corroded.

An individual bead's reputed age is an indication of its power – the object has lasted a long time because it is strong, both physically and spiritually. The rightful owner of such an article can thus draw strength from it.

There is general agreement that "good" beads are ancient, and were bestowed upon the present owner's forebears by ancestral deities. The office of healer tends to run in families. Inherited ritual beads thus reinforce his or her power both by their physical durability and by the accumulated virtue of a succession of shamans.

Some beads are considered powerful because they were found in significant circumstances such as at the base of a tree uprooted by a storm, in the soil after a landslide, while clearing land for farming or while preparing a house site.

A mountain stream in west Sarawak occasionally washes a bead into the Selakau women's small fishing nets. The rational explanation is that earth movement or water erosion further upstream exposed burial sites so old that the current inhabitants of the area know nothing about them. But to the finder, such a bead is even more precious than one inherited from a long line of ancestors – it is a direct, personal gift from the spirit world. The finder's descendants will treasure this bead and link it to her name forever.

A bead or talisman found by chance is finally validated by a dream – the recipient either dreamt

FACING PREVIOUS PAGE: A bead-ornamented sword belt with hornbill casque worn by Iban warriors.

ABOVE: A string of Melanau healing beads.

BELOW: Ritual beads and bronze bell of the Aoheng people, an Orang Ulu group.

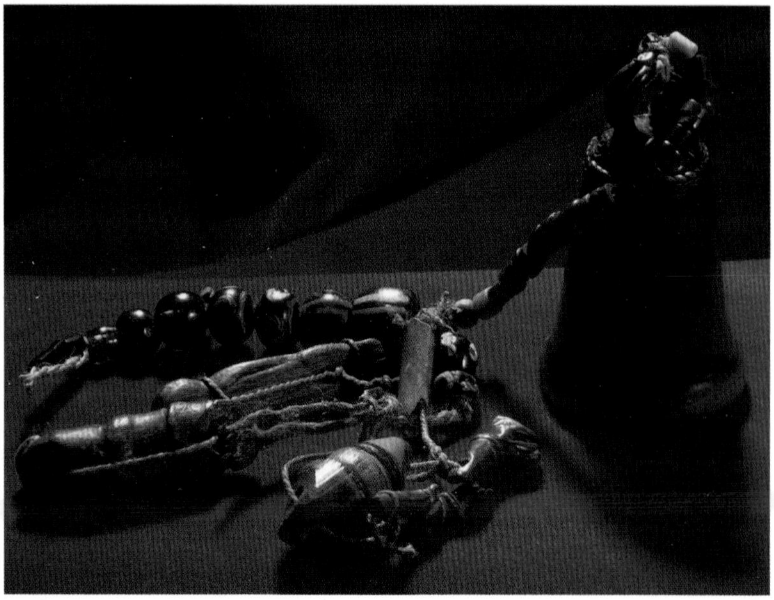

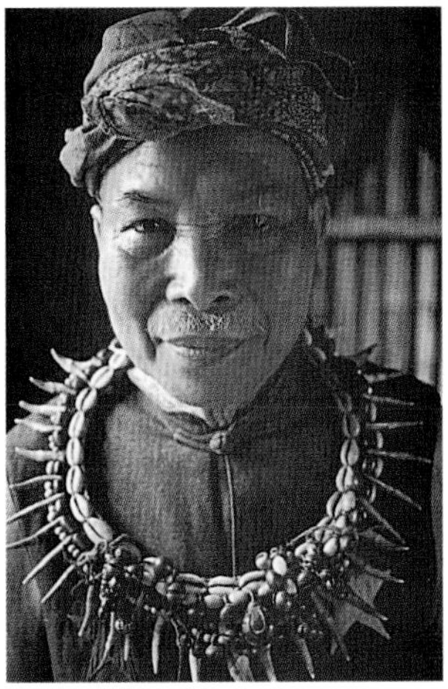

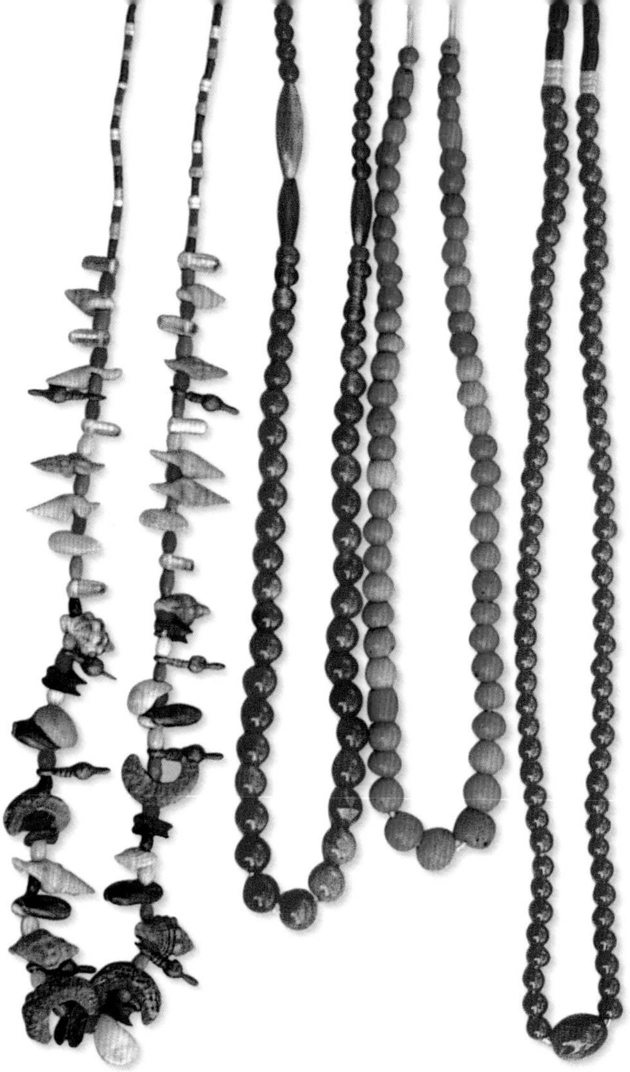

something unusual beforehand or will dream thus within a few days of finding it. However, he must have the strength of soul to retain this gift, otherwise its power might harm him. In aristocratic societies, a special bead found accidentally by a commoner had to be surrendered to the chief of the community for the finder's own protection. The chief, by virtue of his exalted descent, had the requisite "strong soul" to own a potent talisman.

The opaque blue beads used by the Kayan people in Sarawak and Kalimantan in their housewarming rites strengthen not just an individual owner, but also the house itself and its inhabitants. According to one elder, these beads bring "discipline" to the community as well as prosperity. The chief who holds them in his hands has a good reputation "by virtue of these beads", and he will pass them and his good name to his children and grandchildren.

'MAGIC' BEADS

Special beads are kept by many shamans and healers, often in conjunction with rock crystals or unusually-shaped pebbles. Shamans have beads which nobody else may touch. Some communities own beads which only a few initiates ever get to see. Even today, healers keep sets of beads which cannot be shown to a researcher "just to look at".

"I only take my beads out if they are needed, otherwise I myself will get sick!" one Bidayuh lady who lives in a suburban village near Kuching told me. She keeps her healing beads in the bottom of a rice jar.

What exactly is the power of beads? Are beads magic? While Borneo societies have different ideas about the ritual function of beads, none consider them "magic" in the popular meaning of the term – there is no bead that will turn a prince into a frog.

The Bidayuh of west Sarawak and Kalimantan, for example, see a shaman's beads as "strengthening". The Orang Ulu of central and east Borneo, on the other hand, see beads as supernaturally attractive. They frequently add beads to ritual offerings, or display them during important ceremonies. Rare and beautiful objects serve to charm the spirits and induce them to support the human activity in

TOP LEFT: The late Bidayuh elder T. G. Oto wearing his warrior/healing beads.

TOP RIGHT: Various healing and protective beads.

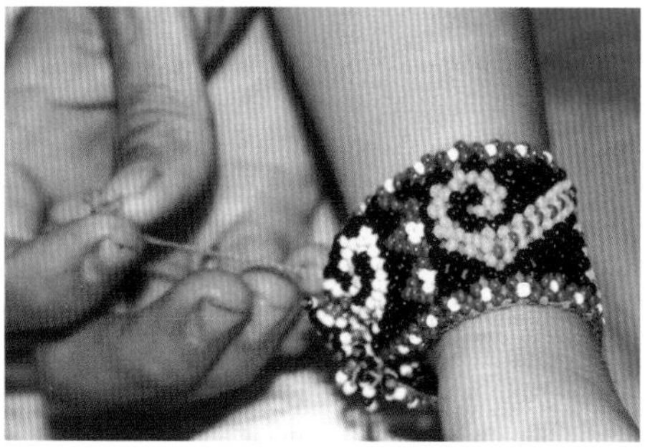

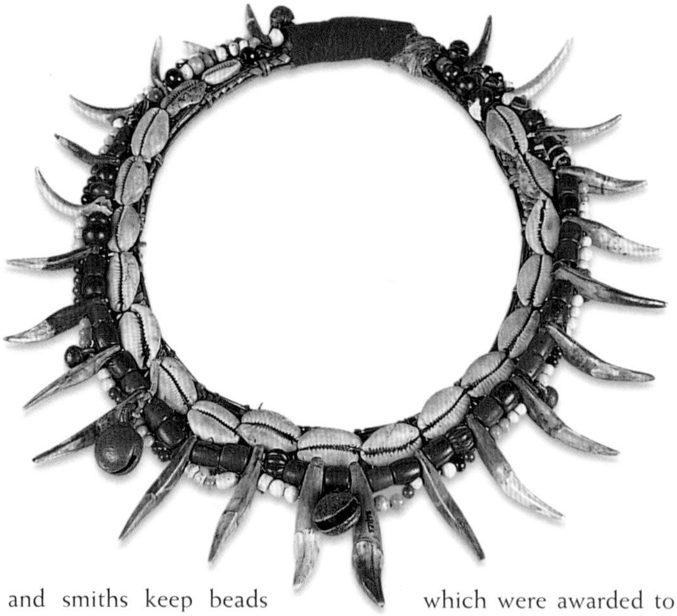

TOP LEFT: A bead bracelet is fixed onto a child's wrist. Sickly persons sometimes have beads tied to their wrist in order to 'strengthen' their soul and improve their health.

TOP RIGHT: Bidayuh warrior neckpiece of glass, shell, claws and brass bells, strung on rattan. It is worn during ceremonies.

progress. Artist, carvers and smiths keep beads among their tools for the same reason – to propitiate the tutelary spirits of their craft. The intermediary between the human and spirit worlds needs beads "to strengthen his or her soul" in the risky work of administering rites. According to a Melanau *bomoh*, the spirits recognize his beads, like a badge of office, and tolerate the shaman's forays into their realm because he is protected.

WARRIOR BEADS

Properly used, the potency of a bead can be transferred to its human owner. One way of using protective beads is to wear them around the neck, a particularly vulnerable spot in the land of headhunters! Indigenous warriors in all parts of Borneo wore or carried beads. The Biatah men of West Borneo have a distinctive neckpiece of boar tusks, bear claws, cowrie shells and barrel-shaped blue glass beads fastened on a circular rattan frame. This *taya bubut* was passed down from father to son, together with information as to which ancestor had worn it in which skirmish. Today the shaman wears it when performing his rites.

A Bidayuh Jagoi man's string of beads is worn over one shoulder, bandolier-style. It consists of large spherical blue, green and amber glass beads, perhaps a few very old fake chevrons, boar tusks and bear claws, "frog head" brass bells, and some items which were awarded to past owners by the helpful spirits – a ceramic medicine jarlet, a perforated chunk of brass, a spent rifle shell. This string is not used to count prayers like a rosary, but the owner can describe the special power or use of each item on the string.

A Tuai Gawai or elder in the ancestral cult was quite happy to show his beads to an outsider during a headhunting festival in a village near Kuching, but he warned that no woman could touch them. He explained that one bead on this particular string enabled its owner to fly "in the old days", another could render him almost invisible, small enough to hide behind a blade of grass. The Tuai Gawai himself has never made use of either of these beads, however.

"We live in peaceful times, so there is no need," he told me. "Also, you'd have to know the right word," which he either did not know or did not want to reveal. And then he was off to join his fellow celebrants in a wild sword-waving dance around the central hearth of the headhouse. The days of headhunting are past, but some Dayak members of the Armed Forces and paramilitary police still wear amulets and beads. Such talismans, often presented to the young man by his mother, are discreetly worn under the uniform, but they are there to bolster the wearer's courage and protect him from danger.

BEADS AND RITUAL

Before male shamans perform their religious ceremonies, most put on a covering to give added spiritual protection to their head. This may be a roughly-draped cloth, a more carefully folded turban or a brimless plaited hat. The black velvet cap known as *songkok* in Malaysia and *kopiah* in Indonesia is sometimes worn, especially in Kalimantan. Many Bidayuh shamans wear a string of beads wound around the head, covered with a head-cloth.

Some female shamans do their work bare-headed. But where female headgear is worn, it tends to be eye-catching. During ceremonies or festival times, the officiants of the ancestral cult can be identified at a glance. The Kadazandusun priestess of Penampang in Sabah, the *bobohizan*, wears a half-hat which can be as tall as 46 cm (18 inches) in height, and which is embellished with colourful strips of cloth, bunches of cock feathers, and long streamers of beads. This remarkable structure is open at the back. It does not sit on the head like a hat, but is firmly tied on over small pillows so the tight string would not hurt the wearer's head.

In the course of performing her ceremonial duties, the *bobohizan* priestess leads her followers in a dance. However, her movements have to be very slow and dignified on account of her top-heavy hat. The usual reason given for the disproportionate size of this hat is "so the spirits can see the priestess –

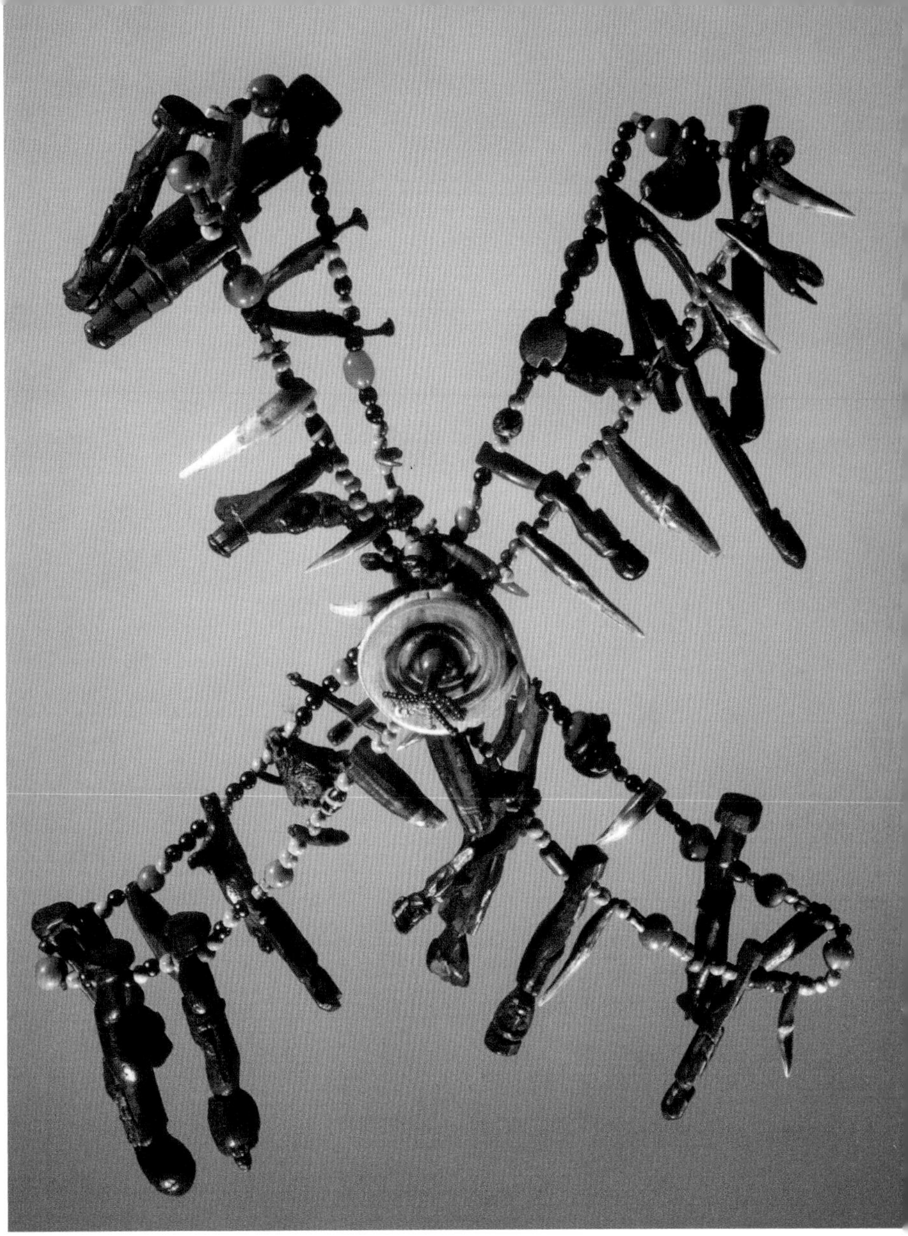

ABOVE: Ritual beads of the Tanjung people, an Orang Ulu group in Kalimantan.

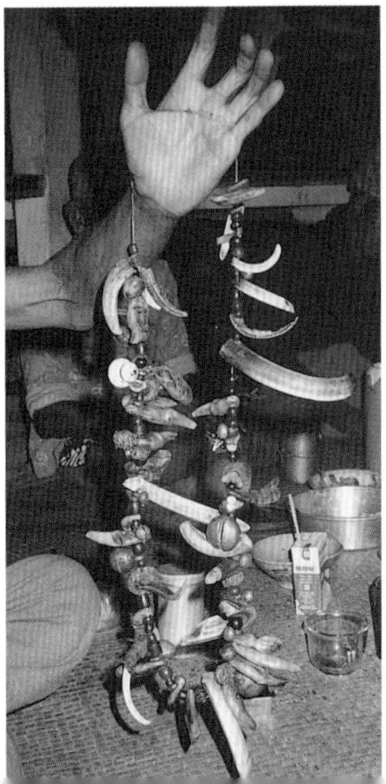

LEFT: A Bidayuh Jagoi Tuai Gawai displays a spiritually powerful necklace which contains spherical glass beads, boar tusks, bear claws and 'frog head' brass bells.

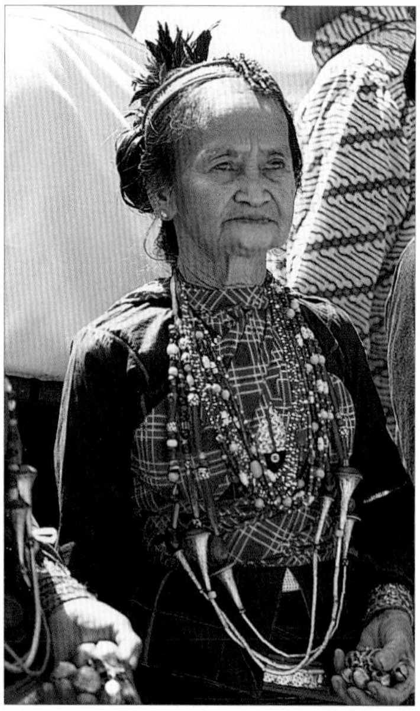

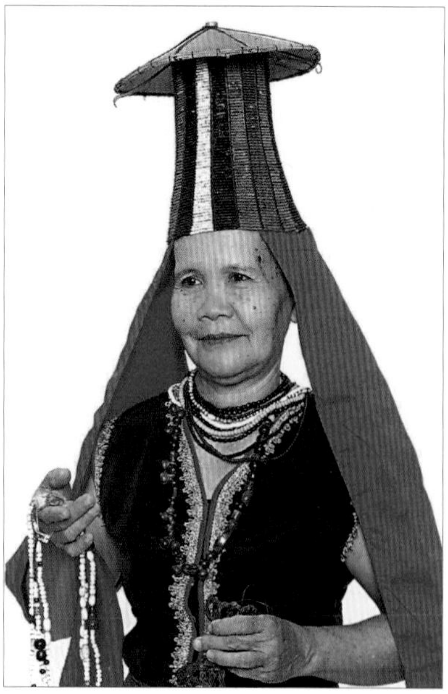

TOP LEFT: Lotud priestess wearing bead necklaces containing embossed cones of silver foil worked over wooden cores.

TOP RIGHT: A *dayung baris*, a female traditional healer of the Bidayuh.

BOTTOM: Close-up of Lotud priestess' necklace.

Kadazandusun women tend to be short".

The Bidayuh priestess in Sarawak wears a truncated cone of seed beadwork strung on a framework of fine rattan strips, sometimes topped by a flat conical palm leaf hat. The beads are strung in blocks of black, blue, red, white and yellow, symbolically-important colours in the Bidayuh rituals. A now obsolete variant of this hat is described as a "Hapsburg Crown" in the old Sarawak Museum catalogue. It is a headband topped by an arch, worked in the same technique and in the same colours as the tall cone. Another rare style is a hat shaped like a skullcap.

In societies where headbands are generally worn by women, the ritual specialist's status is indicated by a comb embellished with beads and metal, usually in the form of brass bells. This accessory, tucked into the headband, gives more spiritual protection to her head because there are now more beads.

The Kadazandusun of Sabah's west coast, the Rungus of Kudat and the Murut/Tagal of west Sabah wear different variants of this ornament: One or more long-handled combs or hairpins strung with long dangles of cloth ribbons and bead strings are stuck into the back, or at the sides, of the headband. In south-west Sabah, the headband consists of one or more strings of long glass or large, chunky carnelian beads. Tall combs with bead fringes are tucked into the back or sides.

The Maloh priestesses of the upper Kapuas in West Kalimantan, which is a considerable distance away from coastal Sabah, use dark blue or black scarves to cover their hair. The scarves are edged with silver coins or antique beads. Into the back of these head-coverings they stick bamboo skewers, split into forks at the top end, which are decorated with streamers of cloth and long bead strings.

The healer wears beads, first and foremost, to keep his soul safe. He needs to communicate with the tutelary deities face to face, and is often called upon to cajole or fight the spirits which are making

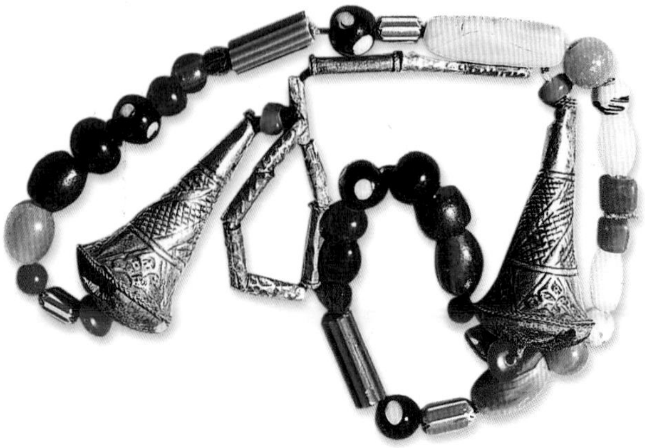

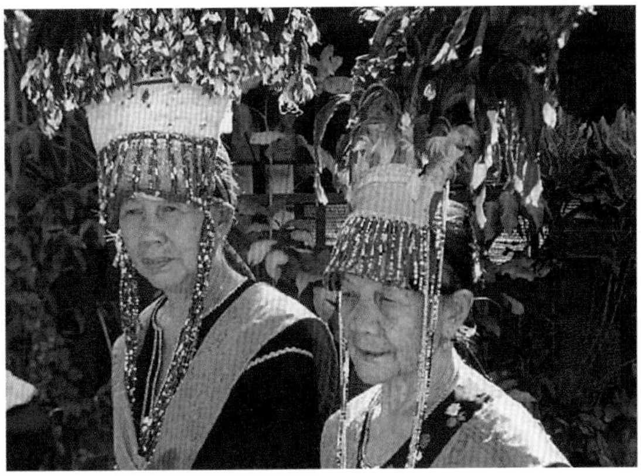

Kadazandusun priestesses wearing their half-hats, which are decorated with colourful strips of cloth, cock feathers and seed beads.

the patient sick. To do this, he needs spiritual strength and protection. In a trance, the shaman follows the patient's soul to the abode of spirits and omen birds, in the underworld or on a tall mountain. In this place he has to deal with, and often trick or outwit, a whole array of supernatural foes. The beads around his head and neck, on top of his charm box, or held firmly in the palm of his hand, fix soul and body together. Their hardness is *strength*, while the sparkle of polished stone or glass is *light*, which helps him find his way back to the human world after he has accomplished his mission.

At the end of the healing ceremony, when the healer has emerged from his trance, the patient's soul is restored to him by pressing a bead – often a long carnelian – on his head.

Sickly persons sometimes have a string with a few beads tied to one wrist for the purpose of strengthening their souls and thus improving their health. The Iban of Sarawak occasionally tattoo a bead wristlet on a chronic invalid's arm. This is more permanent and thus considered more effective.

A Lotud priestess of Sabah wears sets of three or more bead necklaces, enriched at the front with embossed cones of silver foil worked over wooden cores. The beads are mixed, mostly of European origin, and are pea-sized or larger. The silver "trumpets" are said to originate mainly from Brunei. The Rungus of north Sabah cross two or more long bead chains over the chest. The "strong" ones are of old carnelian beads and their 19th-century imitations, both considered equally potent. Colourful large beads make up the strings. Large shell discs are worn on chokers "for keeping cool", i.e. healthy.

The Bidayuh Jagoi priestess of west Sarawak wears a rather elaborately worked neckpiece. It is made up of four to six strings of pea-sized red, white or yellow and black or blue beads, the blocks of colour separated by wooden or brass wire spacers. The front part consists of coils of brass wire or little silver rings. The back part, covered with old Chinese coins, ancient blue beads, animal claws or teeth, and small hawks' bells, protects the nape of the wearer's neck and thus her head. Each time she is called to a sickbed, the patient's family ties a set of two blue beads and a small brass bell to the shaman's wrist. After the healing ceremony is over, this wristlet is attached to the side of her necklace. A rich tally indicates a successful healer. All Bidayuh necklaces contain a few pieces of brass, usually bells. The elders agree that this addition is necessary "to keep the peace among the spirits of the powerful beads".

MANIK BERAWAN: THE FIGHTING BEADS

The *manik berawan* of the Bidayuh people are exclusively healing beads. They are never worn for ornamentation, but are carefully hidden away when not in use. The name literally means "fighting

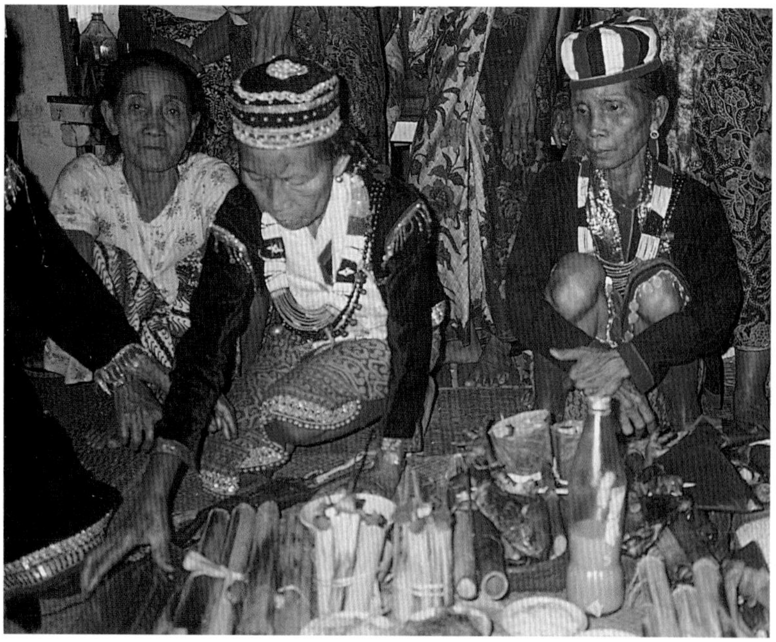

Bidayuh Jagoi priestesses of west Sarawak presiding over a ceremony. They present spirit offerings on behalf of their womenfolk, who can be seen standing behind their leaders.

beads". In competent hands, they *fight* sicknesses in humans, crops, livestock, houses and communities.

Seen as artifacts, they are not impressive – a collection of pea-size opaque red, black or blue, and white or yellow glass beads, supplemented by a few long carnelians, animal teeth and claws, roughly-perforated rock crystals, brass bells, old Chinese coins, silver rings or coiled brass wire, and any other items that were awarded to the shaman by dreams or spirits. Unlike other necklaces, the *manik berawan* are strung in an apparently haphazard fashion without regard to pattern or symmetry.

The power of *manik berawan* lies in their mystique. These beads are kept secretly and only taken out when needed. One prominent priestess of the Bukar-Sadong people of south-west Sarawak and the adjacent area of Kalimantan agreed, after much persuasion, to allow me to look at and even photograph her treasures. To appease the beads' spirits, however, she had to sing them a long, detailed invitation to the special feast which had been prepared for them. Two male elders assisted her, sometimes playing the bamboo zither, sometimes striking a snail-shell rattle. The ceremony lasted most of one night! The priestess also explained to me that the spirits are very small people dwelling on the jungle-clad hills, therefore the food offerings had to be put into special, small dishes.

The healing properties of these beads reside in their power to invoke the spirits, each bead having its own specific function. At a healing ceremony, the priestess sings an invocation to summon her spirit helpers, but to treat her patient she wraps a selected bead in a little piece of cloth, dips it in water, and anoints the affected part. The colours are important. Blue or black is used to cure a child who has fits, "its eyes turned upwards because an owl flew over the house", as the worried mother or grandmother explains. Red will "keep away the devils" or calm a hysterical patient. By extension, red will also keep the rats away from padi store-houses. In fact, the beads' services are often employed to protect the vital rice crop from pests. Yellow or amber beads are carried through the rice fields to cure crop disease. Green or blue beads are used to maintain health.

Healing beads may be owned and used by a male or a female shaman. Generally, individual cases are treated by a woman, while a man ministers to the whole community. At a time of epidemic or persistent bad luck, a longhouse community may hold a cleansing ceremony which involves the sprinkling of the whole building and its inmates with a string of

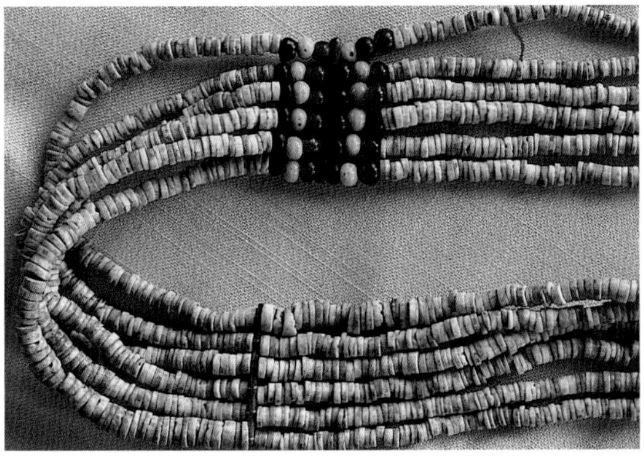

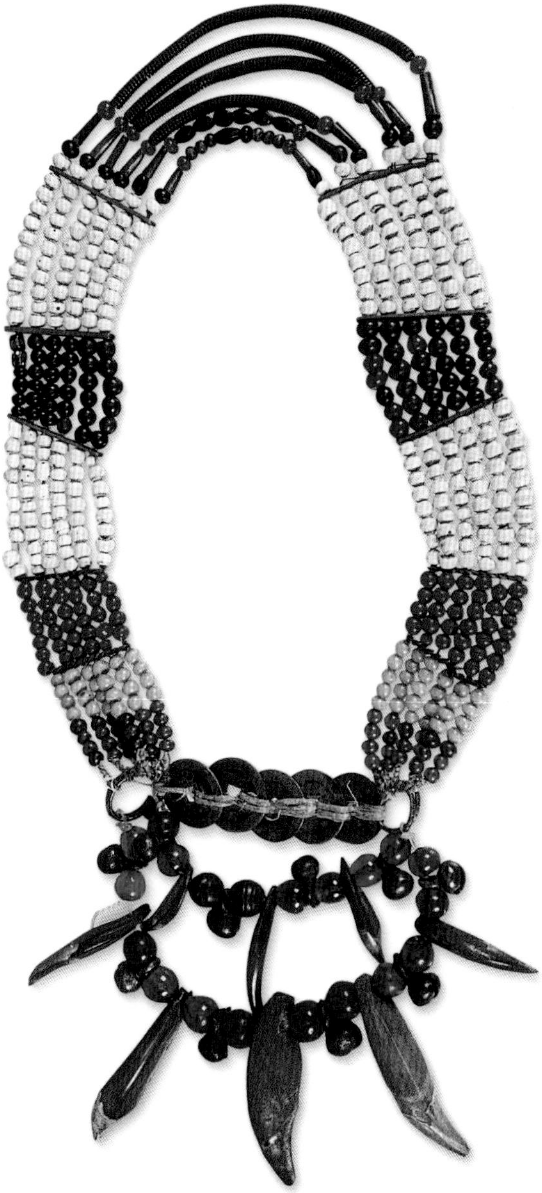

manik berawan dipped in water or coconut water. As the liquid splashes the heads of the assembled multitude, the eldest priest chants: "One, two, three, four, five, six, seven! Answer us, oh guiding spirits of Perintang Sijingkan ... come here and dribble diamond water, sacred bead water, the most precious of all waters, Gimah and Gumagi water, silver water, gold water, yellow root [turmeric] water. Let us pour it out on the heads of all, old and young, little children, to make them healthy and fresh and free from all sickness. Let those who receive this holy berawan water be always in good health."

EXTREME LEFT: Shell disc bead belt with vertical rows of monochrome glass beads or *manik berawan*, worn by a Bidayuh priestess during healing, agricultural or general ceremonies.

LEFT: Bidayuh Jagoi priestess' necklace of opaque glass beads and translucent blue glass beads, strung with bear claws, brass bells, ancient Chinese coins and brass wire coil.

BEADS TO INVOKE THE SPIRITS

In the old days, the Orang Ulu hung strings of antique beads in the open roof windows — i.e. parts of the roof that can be lifted up with a long pole to let in air and light — to call back the wandering soul of a seriously-ill person, or to attract the good spirits who are known to be partial to beautiful, valuable things. The shaman protected his patient from the strong spirits he invoked by tying plain red and yellow beads around his wrist. If the case was considered serious enough to call for a sacrifice, the chicken or pig would be draped with strings of opaque light blue beads.

The same type of blue beads could be put on a convalescent patient to hasten the recovery process, or on small children as a general protection. At the end of the ministrations, the *dayung* was paid in beads, especially the opaque yellow "doughnut" type (see Yellow Doughnut, Chapter 7).

The Kayan priestess had a little pouch decorated with strings of beads to keep her ritual paraphernalia. She would bring along a red bead and a yellow opaque bead whenever she was asked to perform a rite. The yellow bead was to strengthen and calm her soul. She used it especially after coming out of a trance by holding it tightly in her palm until she felt strong again.

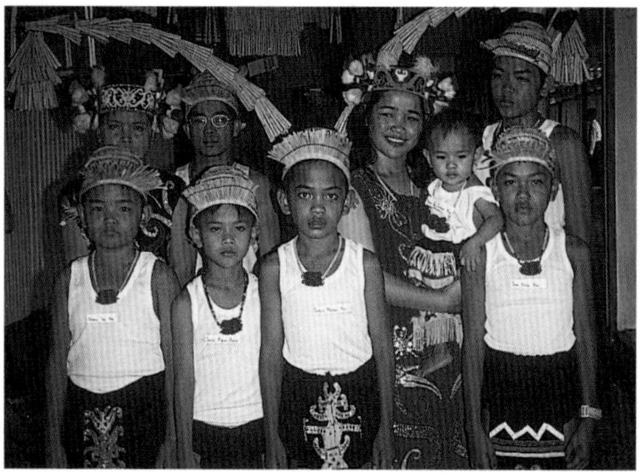

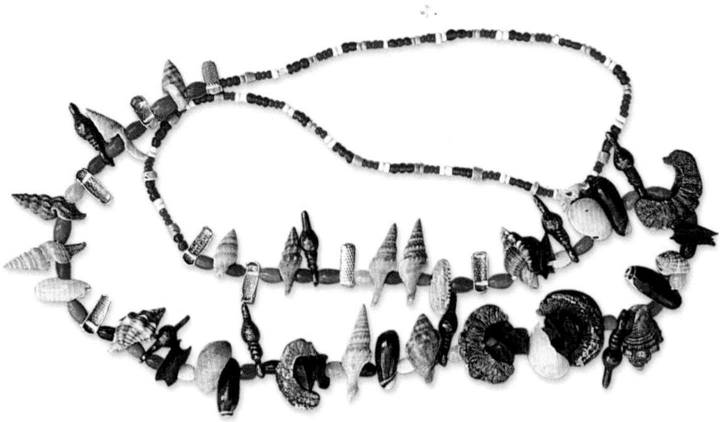

TOP LEFT: Kenyah children all lined up for their name-giving ceremony. Each candidate wears his family's best beads for the occasion.

TOP RIGHT: Kayan protective beads for the baby or nursing mother. It is sometimes hung above the cradle.

OPPOSITE: Orang Ulu baby carrier with beaded mask motif and three rows of leopard fangs.

BEADS IN CHILDBIRTH, INFANCY AND CHILDHOOD

Childbirth is strictly women's business. In most cases, not even the baby's father is present. Normal deliveries were attended by the mother's elder relatives. A shaman was called in only if problems arose. At the moment of delivery, the child's new, still very tender soul was believed to be in danger from lurking spirits; so was the mother's. The midwife, whose work hovers on the fringes of this world and the next, also needed special protection. In many Borneo societies, she tied beads to her wrist while she performed her duty. Opaque yellow and translucent blue beads appear to have been commonly used for this purpose. A Bidayuh priestess assisted the midwife's work with her ritual beads, the *manik berawan*. The priestess wrapped a white bead in cloth, dipped it in water, and wiped the labouring mother's crown and forehead with it.

A child's earliest years are believed to be fraught with danger. His soul is only loosely attached to his body, and an army of malevolent spirits is believed to be trying to snatch it in a variety of ways. To mislead this predatory horde, new-born babies are called "worm" or other similar deprecatory terms. Today, a child is registered a few weeks after birth, but in the past, infants were not named until they could at least crawl or toddle. A healthy child should be "cool" (free from fever) and sleep without sudden starts or shudders. He should not roll his eyes up or suffer fits and spasms. He should not cry excessively, and should have a good appetite. Beads are believed to help get him through this difficult time of life.

When she had completed her duties, the traditional Orang Ulu midwife was paid in cloth, food, a knife, and beads. Before she left her patient's room, she made sure the young mother wore a string of carnelian, blue-black, amber and red spherical glass beads to keep the baby "cool". Ideally this was not taken off until the baby could walk.

Young Selakau mothers in west Sarawak wear strings of translucent blue "barrel" beads (see Chapter 7). The baby touches these beads while nursing; the beneficial contact keeps him "cool" and healthy, and helps to fix his soul firmly to his frail body. These blue beads are the only ones the women care to wear, although another variety is kept by most families. To dispel the effects of a bad dream, one cherry-sized opaque brick red bead is tossed out of the window.

When an Orang Ulu baby is taken to his relatives' rooms for the first time, he is given beads of the colourful lukut-type, and at least one yellow *lavang* "to keep him cool" (see Chapter 7). During the child-naming ceremony – which may not be held until the youngsters are in their teens! – each candidate is decked in his or her family's best beads for the grand occasion.

A variety of beads are used to keep a baby cool – fevers used to regularly afflict the young and the

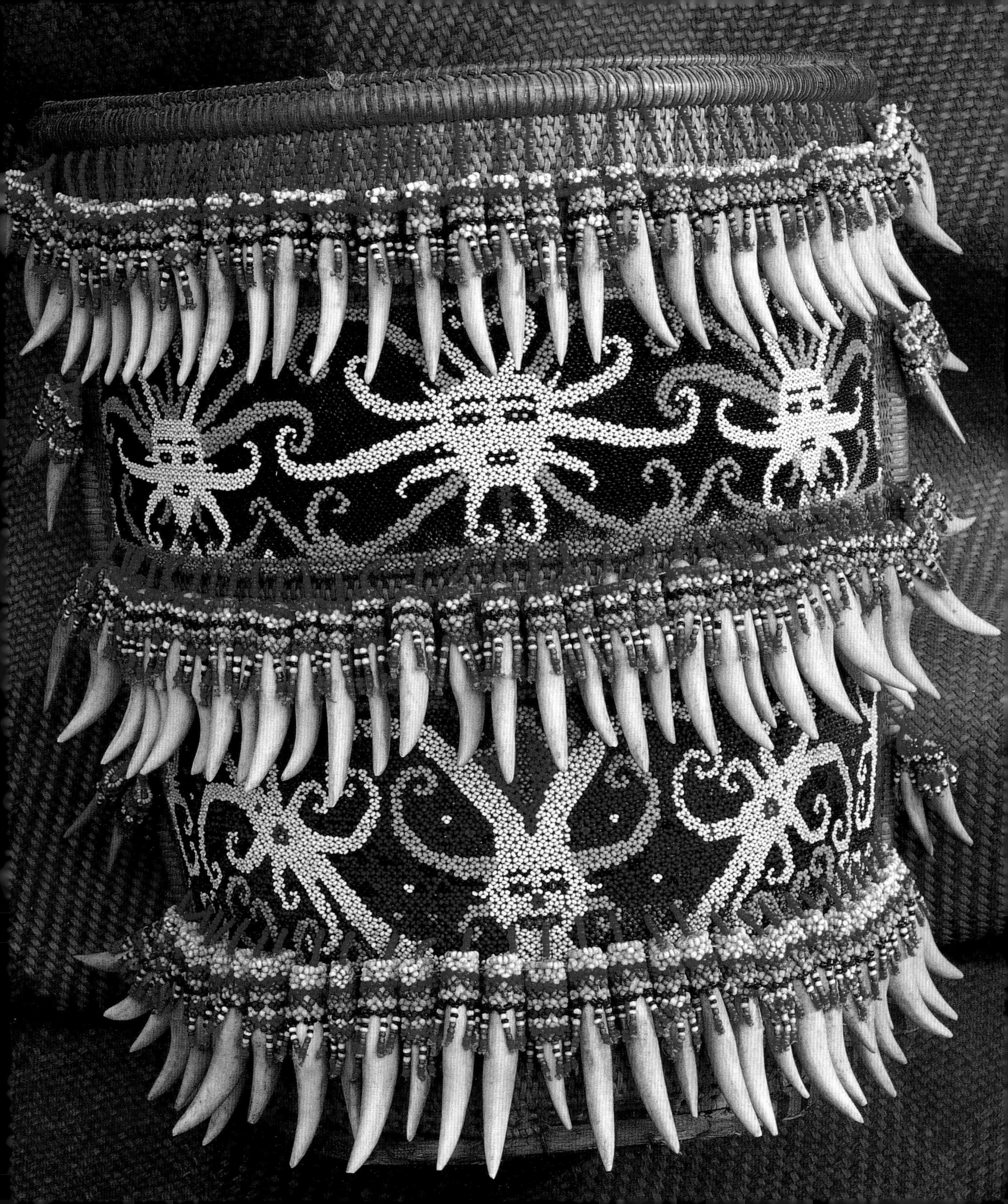

BABY CARRIERS

The beaded baby carrier has become something of a Borneo icon. It is a reedwork basket, open on one side, which is used to carry a baby. Young infants tend to be carried at the front, to facilitate breast-feeding for the first few months. After that, the baby rides on the mother's back as she goes about her work; toddlers seek the security of the carrier even after they can walk. While travelling in boats or visiting the nearby market, mothers may carry two- or three-year-olds in their baskets, mainly for safety.

Many baby carrier baskets are embellished with fine beadwork. The symbols in this beadwork used to be of utmost importance: They demonstrated and preserved the user's status. Within Orang Ulu society, rank and its associated symbolism were serious considerations. A breach of these taboos brought disaster to the community – illness, bad harvests, unseasonable weather and resulting famine.

An Orang Ulu baby carrier embellished with a tiger, a dragon or a full human figure sheltered a tiny sprig of the aristocracy. The tiger was the ultimate symbol of the high-class *maren* or aristocrat, despite the fact that the creature does not exist in Borneo. The Clouded Leopard is the largest member of the cat family found on the island. A leopard tooth could be lent within an aristocratic family to decorate a baby

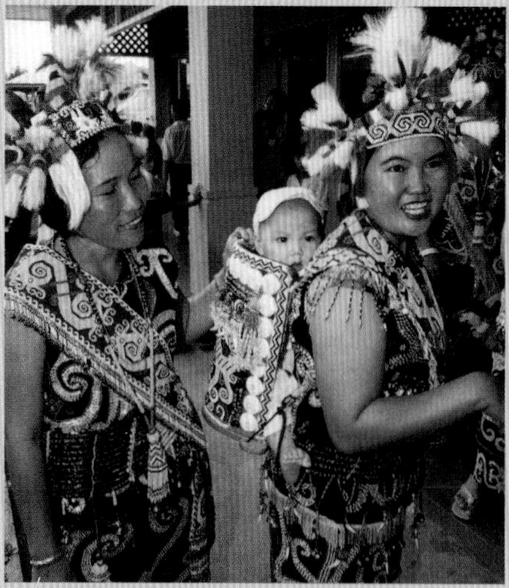

carrier, but it had to be returned after the baby had outgrown its use.

Larger beads, hawks' bells and animal teeth were sometimes attached to the upper rim of the carrier, a tradition that probably originated with the Kenyah but which has been adopted by their neighbours, the Kayan. These beads and bells served to soothe the baby with their tinkling, and to document his or her status. The use of high-value beads and leopard teeth was restricted too.

A middle-class baby peeped at the world from a basket decorated with a human face, stylised animals and scroll designs. The family might be wealthy enough to cover the whole object edge-to-edge in beadwork, but they still could not use the "reserved" designs. The Basap, a small group in lowland East Kalimantan almost absorbed by their neighbours, confined their beadwork mainly to abstract, geometrical designs. Down the social scale came the baby carrier of fine basketry with just a panel of beadwork, or a plain basket of split rattan or bark.

Ornaments, particularly ornamented personal belongings, were associated with their owner and user. They declared and protected a person's rank, but at the same time some of his or her vitality was lodged in them. In the case of a baby basket, part of the child's still tender soul adheres to the article. After a child no longer needed to be carried, the basket was carefully stored away for the next baby in the family. The beadwork panel and other decorations of an old baby carrier were detached and kept for future use, possibly to be passed on to a close relative. A 19th-century Borneo traveller found that he could not buy baby carriers except a few which had been the property of persons long dead.

The bulk of very pretty beaded baby carriers, now available in the bazaars of Sarawak, Sabah and Kalimantan, are brand new, made for the tourist market. No infant has nestled in them, and the "leopard teeth" dangling from the rim are carved of deer horn or made-in-Java fibreglass!

OPPOSITE: Mother bringing her child in a baby carrier to an Orang Ulu festival in Marudi, Sarawak.

THIS PAGE: Baby carrier beadwork panels.

LEFT: Basap carrier from East Kalimantan.

BELOW: 19th-century Kayan carrier with 'slave' motif from the Ulu Mahakam, Kalimantan.

BOTTOM: 19th-century baby carrier with tiger head and 'slave' motifs, also from the Ulu Mahakam.

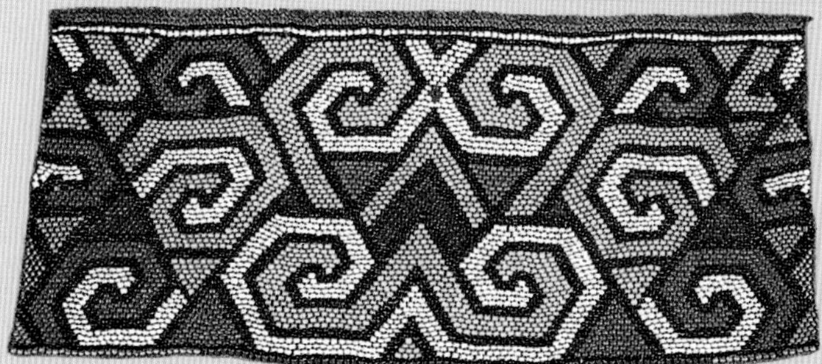

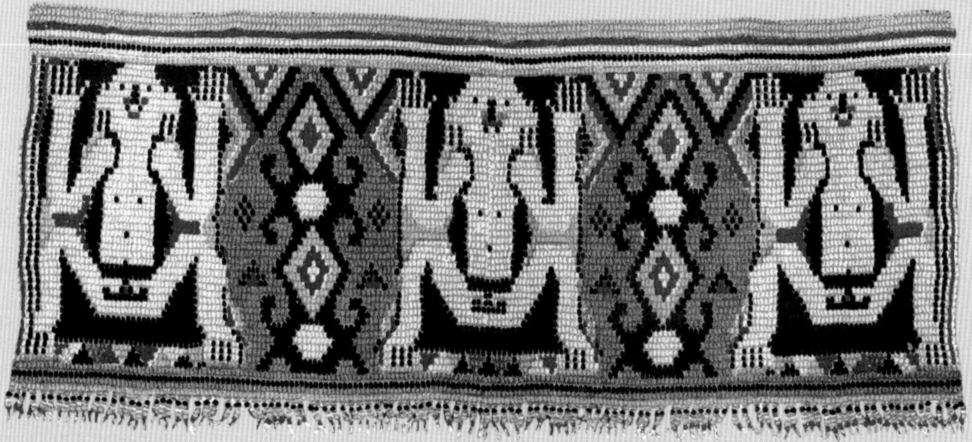

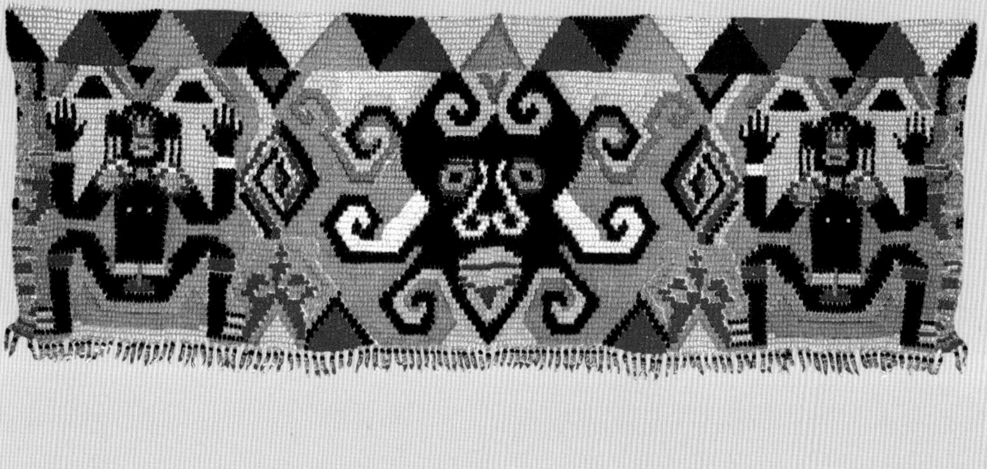

MORE BABY CARRIER PANELS

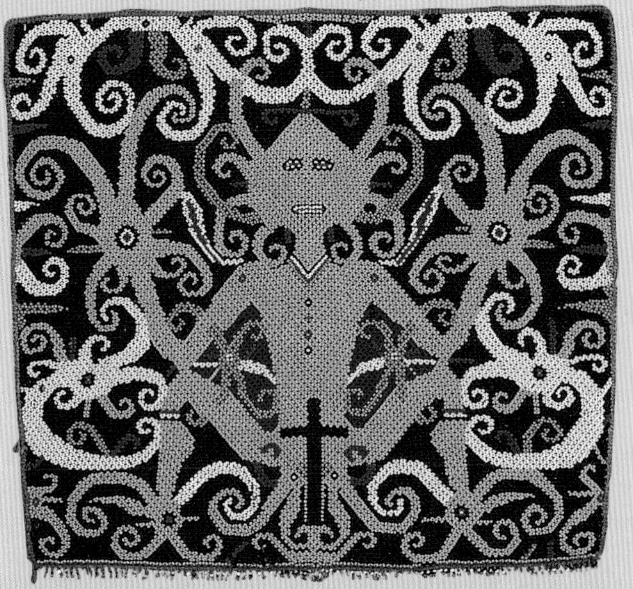

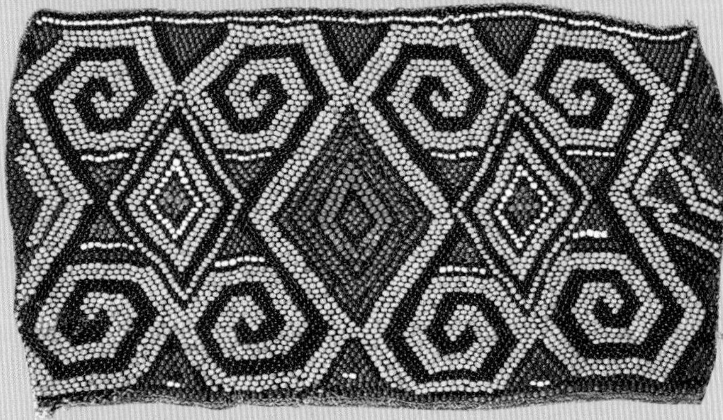

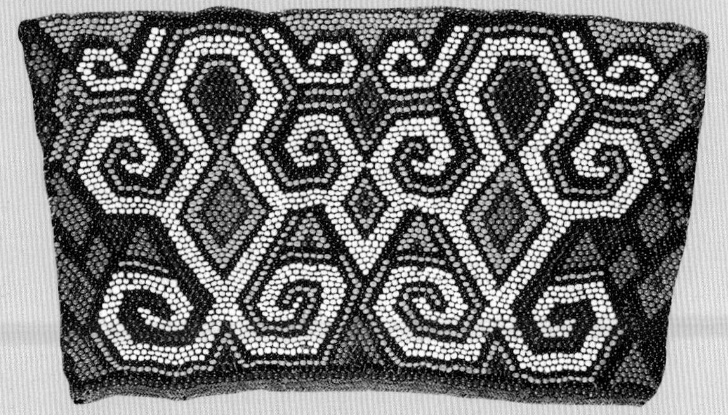

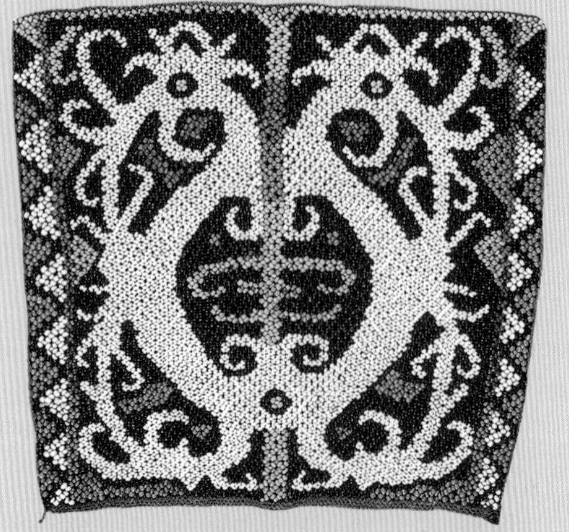

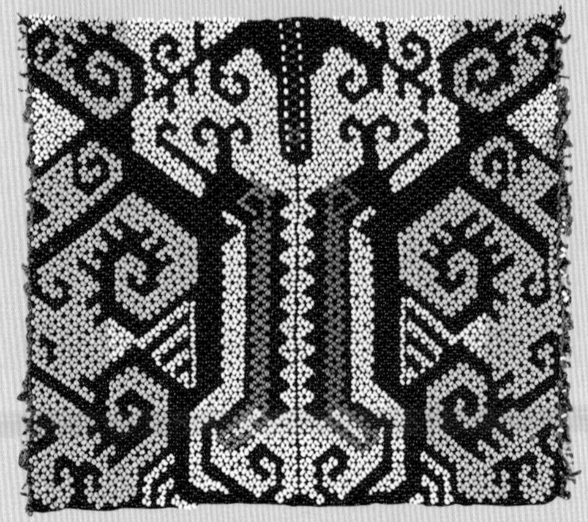

Baby carrier beadwork panels from different ethnic groups.
ANTI-CLOCKWISE FROM LEFT:
Kenyah, made in the second half of the 20th century; Basap with diamond motif; Basap with geometrical motif; Kayan with abstract design; and Kayan with 'forest face' or two dragons motif.

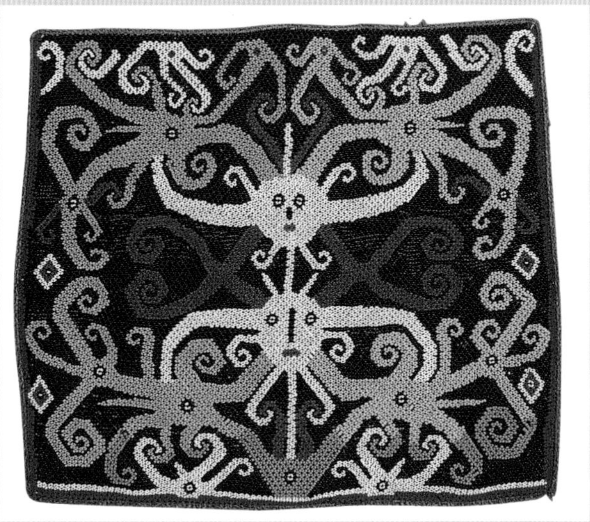
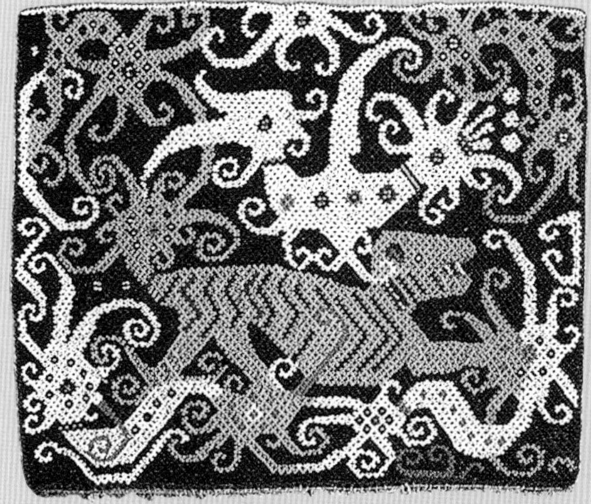
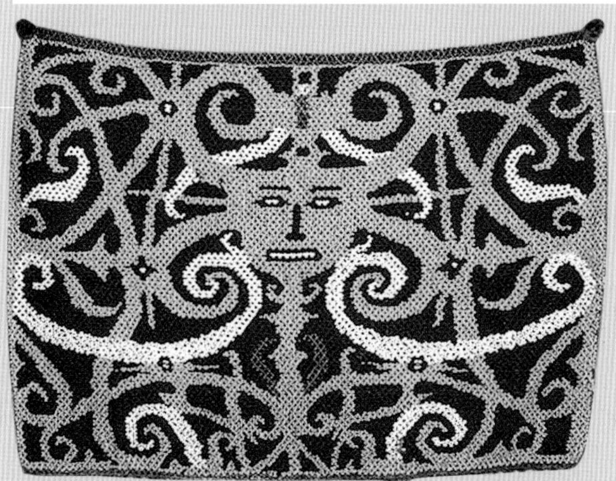
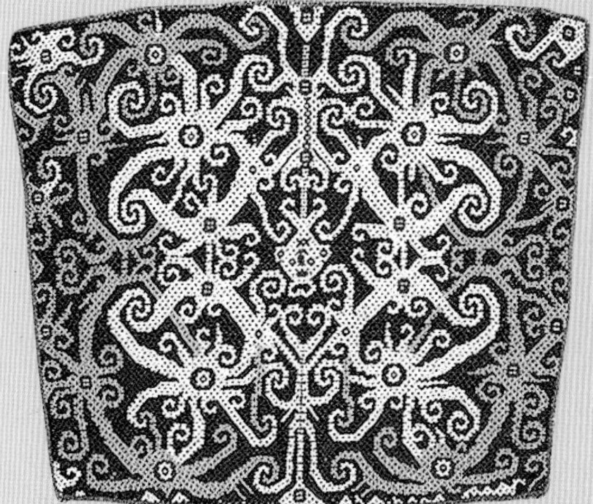
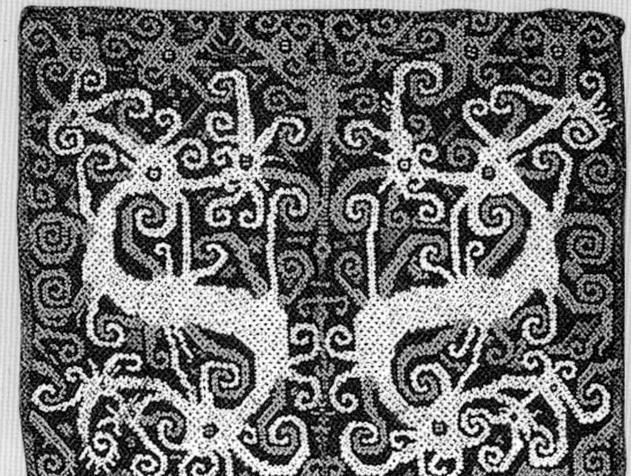

CLOCKWISE FROM TOP LEFT: The first four baby carrier panels are Kenyah. The first is fairly new, made in the second half of the 20th century. The second features the tiger and hornbill, while the third and fourth have dragon motifs. The last panel is Kayan featuring a 'spirit face'.

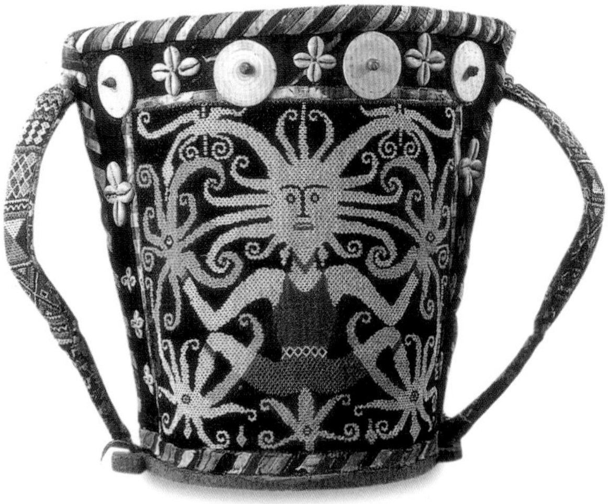

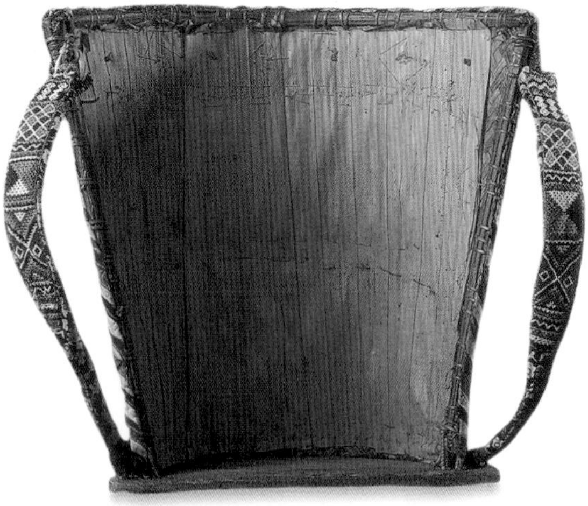

Orang Ulu baby carrier seen from both the outside and inside. This 20th-century design features the traditional human figure arrayed in singlet and breeches. Some woodcarvings of this period even wear wrist watches!

old of every community. Among the "cooling" beads used are the dried perforated seeds of a jungle plant, tied to the infant's wrist. Melanau mothers put white beads on a teething baby, and grandparents still tie one or two blue beads and a silver button on a grandchild's wrist the first time he is brought to their house.

These blue beads are ancient and becoming scarce, so how is it possible to keep up supplies? Simple, a proud grandmother of many told me with a smile: "I tell my son or daughter that I want those beads back in a day or two to use for the next grandchild!"

Cooling beads maintain health. Protection beads, on the other hand, keep away the horde of wicked soul-eating spirits. The mother is advised to wear a string of protection beads as long as her baby is being breast-fed, or suspend it over the infant's cloth cradle. One such string, seen recently on the middle Baram River in Sarawak, contains a number of colourful glass beads, and the following items – sea shells to frighten troublesome spirits, perforated seeds of the *aya* tree which is believed to be the origin of human beings, pointed brass skirt weights and rattan seeds for their pricking qualities (rattan has sharp thorns), and a few small pieces of twisted metal foil to pierce or cut intruders. This string repels and, if necessary, wounds any spirit that tries to come too close to the baby.

The Kayan laid strings of opaque light blue beads over the back of the pig which was sacrificed at a baby's first, provisional name-giving ceremony. One or more of the beads were tied to the baby's wrist. Some weeks later, when the child was considered likely to survive, the *dayung* who performed the naming ceremony got these beads as payment, together with a head-cloth.

The Iban used to toss offerings, including beads, into the river when a baby was taken for its first bath in the open. They occasionally used beads for child-naming, particularly if a surfeit of names was proposed by all and sundry. A chicken was offered a handful of beads while an older member of the family recited the suggested names one by one. The fowl would eye the unfamiliar food for a while and eventually try to peck at it. The name enunciated at that moment was the name picked.

The Iban, like many of their neighbours, tied a few translucent beads to a toddler's ankle. These served as his "eyes" so he would not stumble in his first attempts at walking, fall into holes in the ground, or tumble into the river.

BEADS AND THE LONGHOUSE COMMUNITY

A longhouse is built on a clearing wrested from the jungle, of materials cut and gathered from the forest. The sylvan spirits were duly warned and appeased at

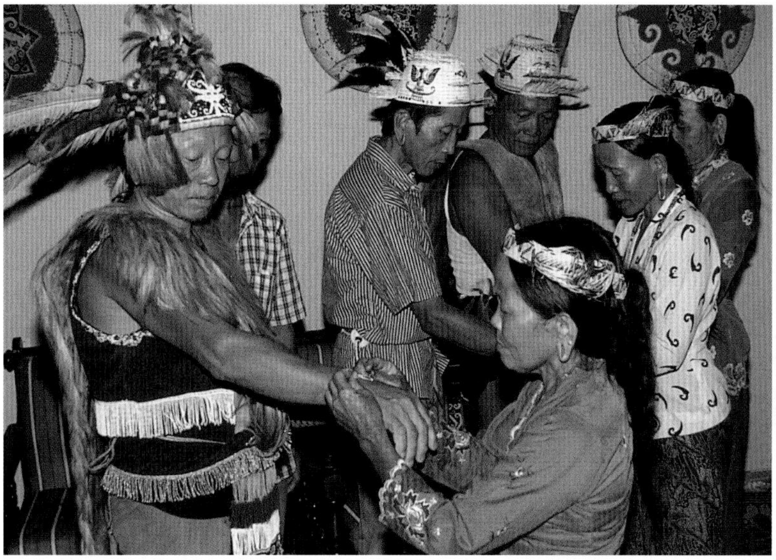

Orang Ulu women in Sarawak tying protective bead bracelets to their menfolk's arms before the start of a ceremony.

all stages of prospecting the site and collecting the building materials, but a few might have lingered. The new house needs to be cleansed and inaugurated before it is fit for human habitation. Four strings of blue beads were carried into a newly-completed Kayan house by the community's elders. They invoked the blessing of the goddess Bungan:

> *Whoever enters this house, let them have a good life by virtue of this string of beads*
> *These beads of bone, these beads of stone, these are the beads of life*
> *Go then, beads, and tell Bungan Malan Paselong Luan that we are ready to enter our house.*

At the completion of the housewarming ceremonies, the beads would be suspended from a tall pole on the verandah of the house.

Agriculture is a chancy business over which the farmer has little control: His fields are very much at the mercy of the weather, pests or crop diseases. No farming operation could be started before appropriate omens had been taken into consideration. The calls of birds and wild animals were interpreted by an elder specially appointed for the task. Ritual gifts were offered to the rice spirits at various stages of the farming cycle. In many rural communities, all or some of the old rites are still observed, together with the use of pesticides and chemical fertilizer.

The offerings prepared by Kenyah priestesses during the harvest festivities included five special, old beads – one to represent unhusked rice, one for polished uncooked rice, one for cooked rice, one for water, and one for fire. If the priestess feels faint or ill, which may happen as she comes out of a trance, she holds a yellow bead tightly in the palm of her hand until she has fully recovered.

Such beads were normally kept hidden. An initiated priestess had a "ritual box", a bamboo tube which contained a miniature ladder, a catch-net like the ones used for fishing, a hook, a fine piece of string, a small scoop or spatula, and one bead. During an agricultural ritual she gently "caught" the rice spirit with her net or hook, tethered it, and scooped it into the container where it would take up its seat on the bead. This box was brought out only for farming ceremonies. At other times, it was wrapped in several layers of calico and put away in some secret place.

The comparison of beads with rice grains is obvious; the "rice spirit" is an old lady in most cultures, and she uses or wears beads. In Kelabit and Lun Bawang mythology, she inevitably dresses up in all her beaded finery before setting out to grace planting or harvest festivities with her presence.

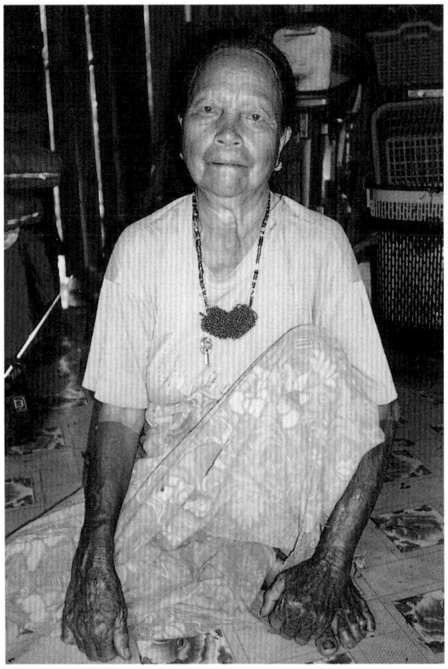

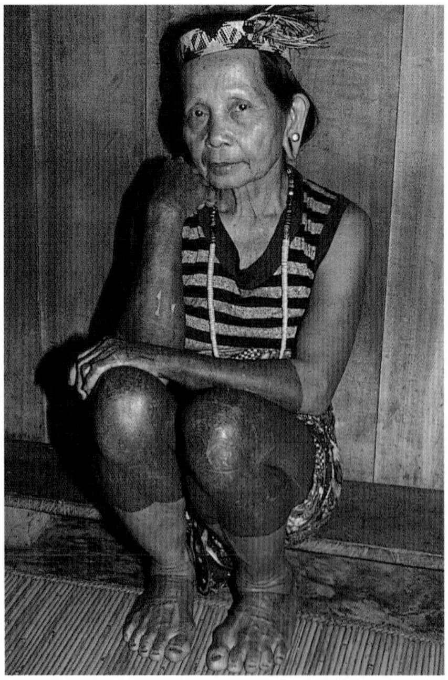

LEFT AND EXTREME LEFT: The tattooed arms and legs of these two Kayan ladies indicate that they are of high social rank. Payment for the tattooist included value beads.

OPPOSITE: An Iban woman's bridal and festival overdress featuring glass and carnelian beads and brass bells. It is sometimes worn with a bead headdress.

The Bidayuh of west Sarawak use beads of the *berawan* type to protect their vital crop at all stages of its growth. During the harvest festival, a group of priestesses selects the next season's seed grain which is carefully guarded by them, either in a small hut or in a room in the longhouse, and hung about with rushes and strings of blue beads.

Before sowing, beads are dipped in water and used to sprinkle the seed. When faced with pests or crop disease, the same remedy is applied. Beads and brass bells are also hung in the padi stores to make the rice spirit happy and to keep rodents away.

BEADS TO PAY THE ARTIST

The Orang Ulu, unlike most of the other Borneo groups, tattooed their womenfolk. Only ladies of high rank were eligible for the privilege of having their forearms, thighs and feet covered in fine lacy designs. A proficient tattooist, usually female, was well paid for her work – she received up to five beads of the *lukut* class per day, her keep and extra rice to take home.

Tattooing could involve other bead transactions as well. A full tattoo took several months to complete and, according to a now elderly lady, was a very painful process. "My mother gave me my first string of really good beads after the ordeal as a reward for my courage to lie still through it all!" she told me with a smile, as she reminisced about her experience.

The tattooist was a skilled artisan but not a shaman. Talented Orang Ulu artists who worked for the aristocrats, such as the painters of murals and carvers of tombs, belong to this class. They were also presented with special beads "to protect their eyes" while they fashioned designs above their own social level. Carvers who worked on funerary monuments for an aristocratic family needed the same protection.

WEDDING BEADS

Beads figure in most wedding traditions, whether as engagement tokens, bridal gifts, dowry or part of the splendid clothing worn on gala days. The fast-changing social and cultural scene of Borneo has

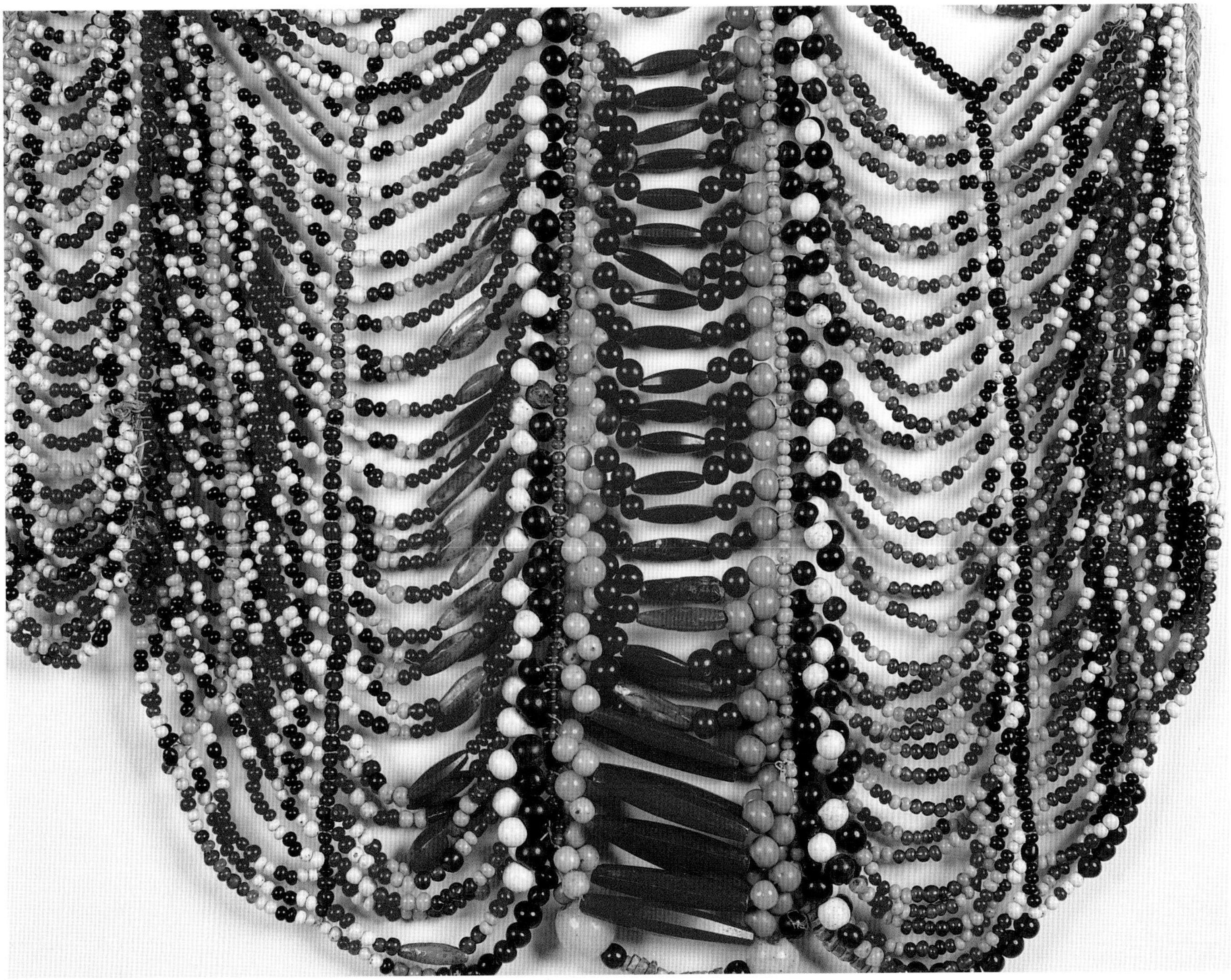

pushed many old customs and costumes into oblivion. Since World War II, many brides have worn white, while the male members of the wedding party swelter in starched shirts, neckties, pin-striped suits and well-polished shoes.

These sartorial effects would suggest a church wedding in other parts of the world; not so in Borneo. A Malay bridal couple of the 1950s and 1960s often wore Western dress, supplemented by a head covering for the groom. Today, Muslims might opt for Malay wedding outfits of gold brocade, but brides are still fond of white tulle veils over a delicately-worked headdress.

The 1980s have seen the start of a new trend. It is becoming chic, particularly among urban Dayak, to celebrate at least part of the wedding festivities with traditional rites, adapted for town use. A Muslim or Christian religious ceremony may be followed by an abridged traditional one, or at least the more picturesque parts of it. For example, the

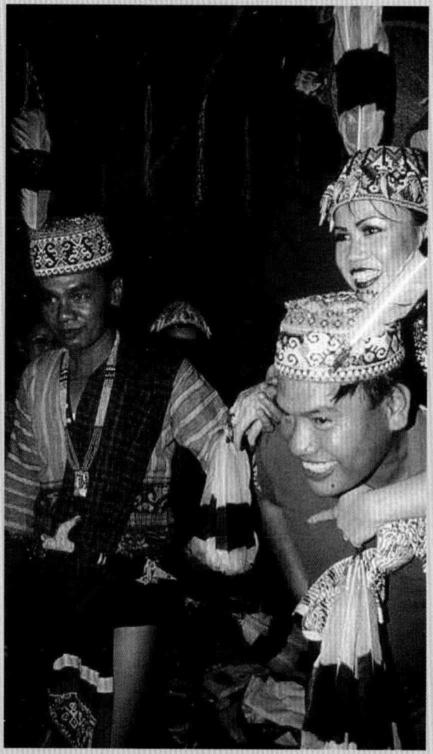

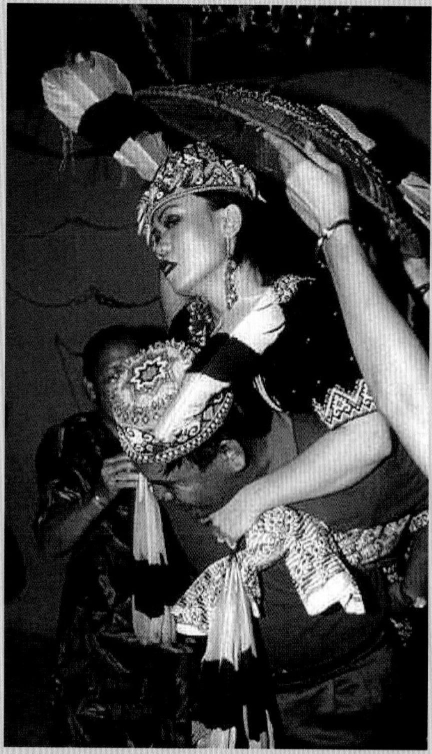

Various stages in a Kayan wedding ceremony.

TOP LEFT: The bride is carried to the ceremony by her brother. The groom is on the left.

TOP RIGHT: Sun hats are held over the bride as ritual protection from evil.

BELOW, LEFT: The officiating shaman ties the couple's hands together with a string of beads and a bunch of hornbill feathers.

BELOW, RIGHT: The groom circles a tray containing a set of ritual objects including value beads, ceramics and iron.

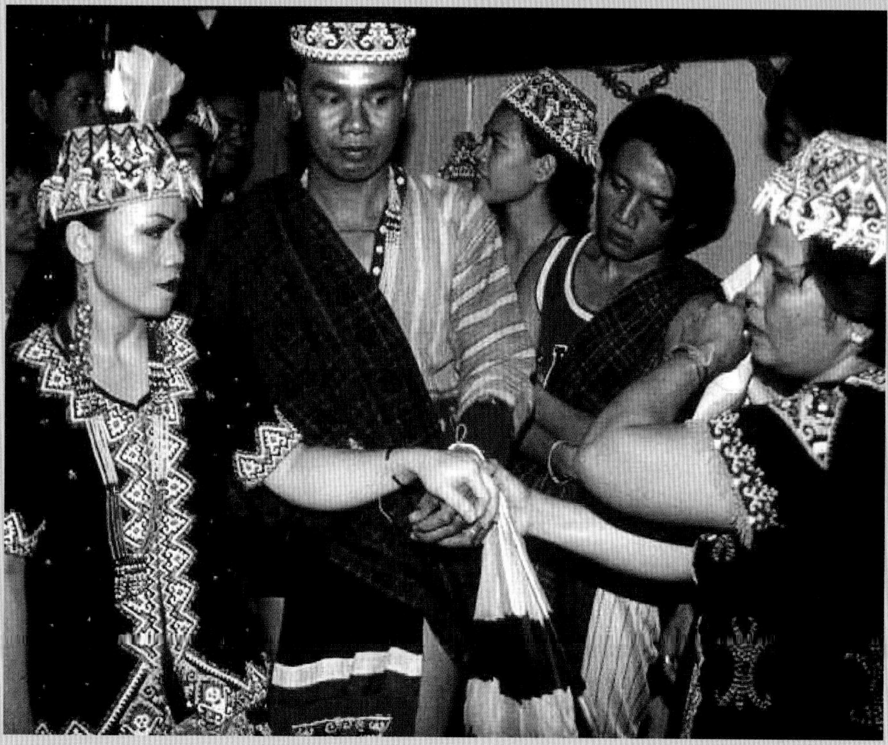

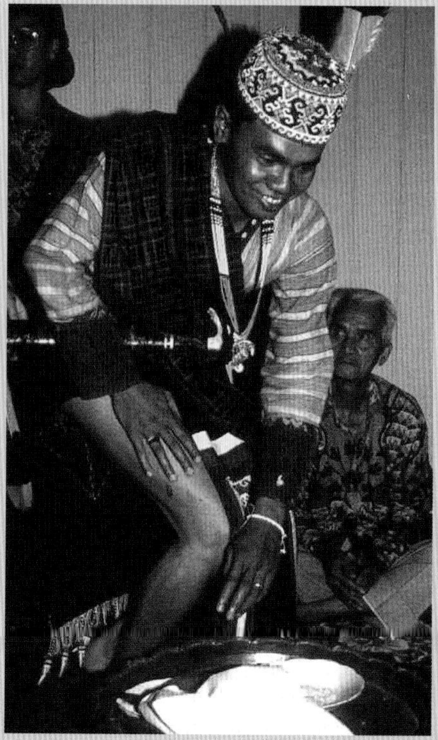

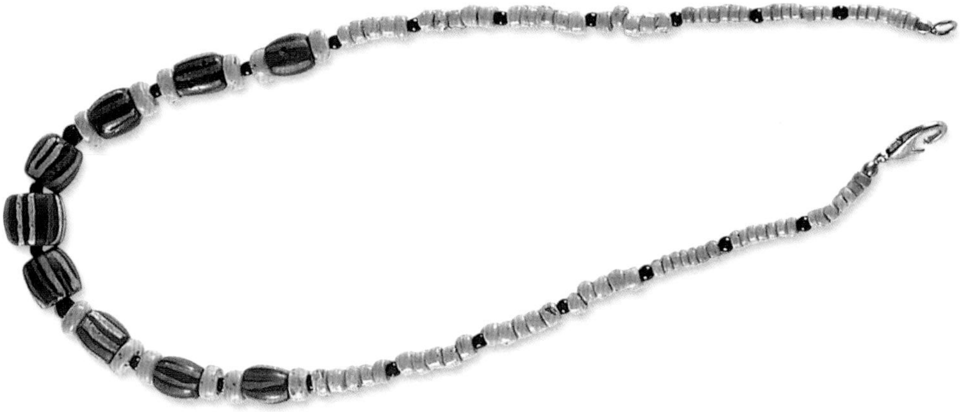

bride and groom may be dressed in gala costume and seated on a pair of gongs while a chicken is waved over their heads; the bridal procession walks up and down the house steps eight times "to collect firewood"; and a canopy of bead-embellished hats is held over the bride's head.

ORANG ULU

Courting and marriage involve the exchange of gifts in every culture. Among the Orang Ulu of Borneo, valuable beads play an important role. They are tokens of rank as well as value; they attest to the future daughter-in-law's eligibility to marry into the family.

Typical engagement beads would be polychrome *lukut bela* or *lukut sekala* for an aristocratic bride, and "pyjama beads" or deep blue barrels with white pinstripes for the bourgeoisie. Whatever the social rank of the couple, two opaque yellow "doughnuts" are part of the set. These plain beads are considered very old and are used in many ritual contexts. Engagement beads belong to the young lady until her marriage, after which they become matrimonial property.

At the time of the marriage, a Kayan groom in Kalimantan gives his bride a "wife's belt" which should contain at least a few really ancient beads in addition to the less important pieces. The marriage is solemnized by a shaman, male or female, who ties the couple's right hands together with a string of beads. During the wedding feast, two valuable beads are placed on the plate of rice offered to the bride "to season the meal".

On the Apo Kayan plateau, family members contributed a string of beads which had to be the length of the bride's height, from head to toe, while she is seated on a mat. Depending on the family's wealth, these might be very valuable, or more ordinary beads. A mother may decide to give her daughter valuable beads on the occasion of her marriage as a form of dowry. This is a family matter more than a prescribed tradition, and such beads remain the personal possession of the young woman. "Good beads will give the bride respect in her new in-laws' family", one Kelabit matron told me.

Not every family observes all the old marriage customs any more. If a respectable Orang Ulu family gives beads as bridal presents over and above the agreed "engagement beads", however, such gifts must be genuine. Only the lower classes could use new, Indonesian-made beads for this purpose.

How much longer will the bead tradition survive? In July 1999, a young mother on the middle Baram River proudly opened a little cloth pouch to show me a few *lukut*-type beads. She was starting to collect engagement beads for her son, then only three years old!

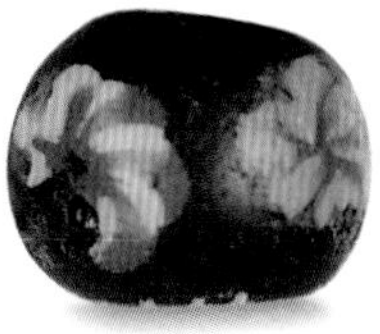

Striped 'pyjama beads', seen in the curve of the necklace (top), and a *lukut sekala*-type bead (above). These two kinds of beads are typical engagement beads for the Orang Ulu bourgeoisie and aristocrat respectively.

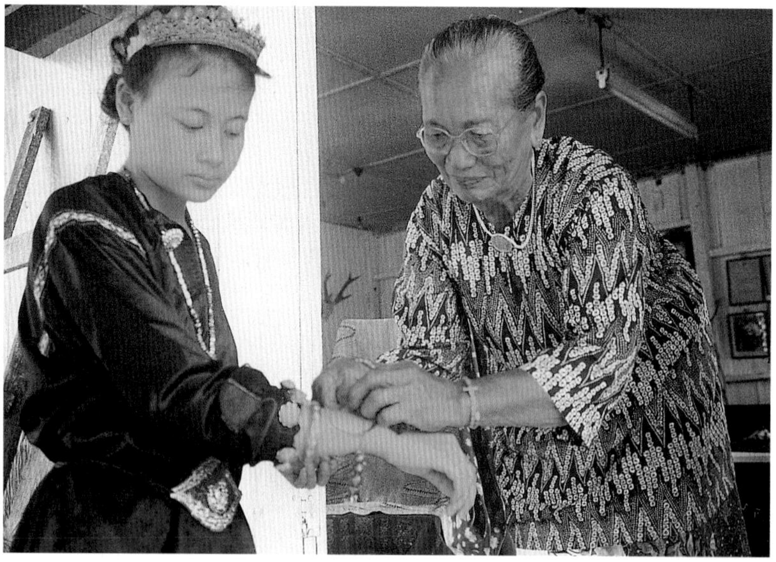

A Melanau woman tying beads to her new daughter-in-law's wrist on the threshold of the latter's new home.

MELANAU

The Melanau of coastal Sarawak used to be a strictly aristocratic society; rank was defined in terms of picul. A picul is a unit of weight of about 60 kg. A 9-picul bride, however, did not weigh 540 kg. She was entitled to a dowry of brass cannon of that amount. Not many families have brass cannon nowadays, but many still insist on the presentation of "wedding beads" which are linked to picul status.

A traditionally-dressed Melanau bride wears a silver or silver-gilt head comb decorated with small beads. This Naga Nikah (Wedding Dragon) is almost obsolete, as is the beaded headband, resembling that of Central Borneo people. A silver or silver-gilt comb is worn instead. The bride wears a black or maroon tunic hemmed with beads, over a brocade sarong held by a silver belt buckle with or without the matching belt; the buckle can be attached with cloth tapes. A silver filigree box is suspended by a string of old beads around her neck.

When the bride enters her matrimonial home for the first time, the mother-in-law gives her a set of wedding beads. It is important that these beads be of the correct kind, and the number corresponds with the bride's picul status or, if she is marrying into a higher social class, the groom's. The wedding beads are of two kinds, used almost exclusively for ritual purposes. The *manik tilek* is large (up to 2 cm in diameter), roughly spherical or biconical, of translucent blue glass, often rough and pitted. Visually it resembles the blue beads of the Bian Chiang excavations in Vietnam.

The *manik kabet* is a long tapered cylinder of brown or black agate with white bands. It may be a 19th-century glass imitation, but this does not appear to detract from its ritual value.

A 9-picul bride requires nine banded agates and seven blue beads. The numbers decrease with the picul status. If the right beads are not available, money might be accepted as a substitute, but many families, especially grandmothers, insist on beads. They can be borrowed from relatives or neighbours for a small payment "to appease the spirits of the beads".

Wedding beads are tied to the bride's wrist by her mother-in-law, usually on the threshold of her new home. They may be attached to a brass bangle, together with a chip of a broken iron cooking pan wrapped in black cloth. Even if a family no longer follows the old religion, when there's a wedding, some elderly ladies will bring some beads out of hiding and place them on a bride's wrist. The correct number is not an issue in a Muslim or Christian community, the protection offered by the beads is.

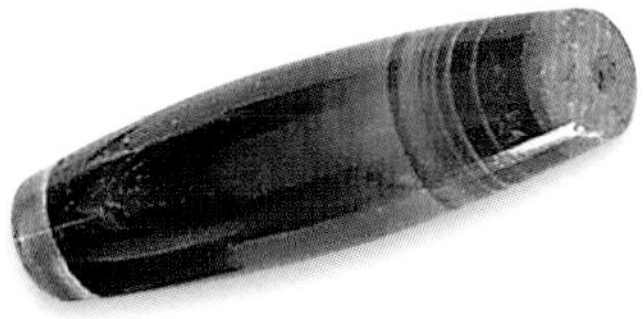

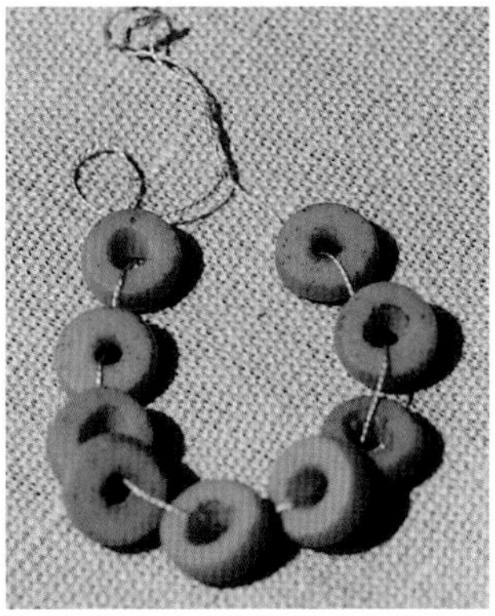

ABOVE, LEFT: A Melanau wedding bead, the banded agate known as the *manik kahet*.

ABOVE: Opaque yellow *lavang* beads. These were tied to a forefinger of a deceased Kayan member to 'replace' that part of the body, which was lost through death, in this instance, the hands.

A young girl, entering into her new life as a wife and eventually mother, needs the strength the beads are supposed to give to her spirit. This is as important as the acceptance into the family, which is symbolised by a welcoming present of valuable and powerful old beads. These beads are usually worn for three nights and three days. During this time, the bridal couple is under numerous traditional restrictions, and practically confined indoors.

MOURNING BEADS

All indigenous Borneo people put aside their personal ornaments after a death in the family and during a set mourning period. While some use special mourning clothes, others simply dress plainly. Some communities hang their best beads and silver on the walls of the bereaved's apartment to show respect to the dead, and to demonstrate the family's, and thus the deceased's, wealth and status.

Beads may play three different roles in death rituals – as part of the grave clothes, as "grave gifts" for the deceased's use in his passage to or in the underworld, and as supernatural protection for the bereaved family. There is usually a distinction between beads owned as personal property and heirloom beads. Only the former are used for grave clothes. Heirloom beads belong to the family rather than the individual. After an owner's death, they are divided among the descendants according to the community's custom.

Grave gifts are items that the deceased would need either as provision on his way to the underworld, or as wealth when he settles down to the afterlife. The very elaborate traditional accounts of a soul's passage to the underworld generally describe some test which the traveller has to pass. In one account, an ogre guards a vast hoard of beads at a narrow pass. The wayfarer tosses it the two beads which pious care had placed in her mouth. While the ogre is examining these, the soul slips past. In another version, the beads serve to illuminate the dark passages of the underworld "like torch-lights!" an elder explained to me.

The Kayan of the middle Baram River share with their cousins in Kalimantan a belief that a person buried without beads would be blind, lame and deaf in the underworld, and in this helpless condition, fall prey to evil spirits. Beads are provided not only as passage money, but to replace the deceased's "lost" body. The women who dress the body recite a rhyme to make sure the right kind of beads are used for the right function. There is some regional variety, but the women of Long Laput, Sarawak, confirmed for me in 1998 what Nieuwenhuis had recorded in Kalimantan a hundred years earlier:

> *A string of fine seed beads laid on the bridge and wings of the nose "to replace the breath".*

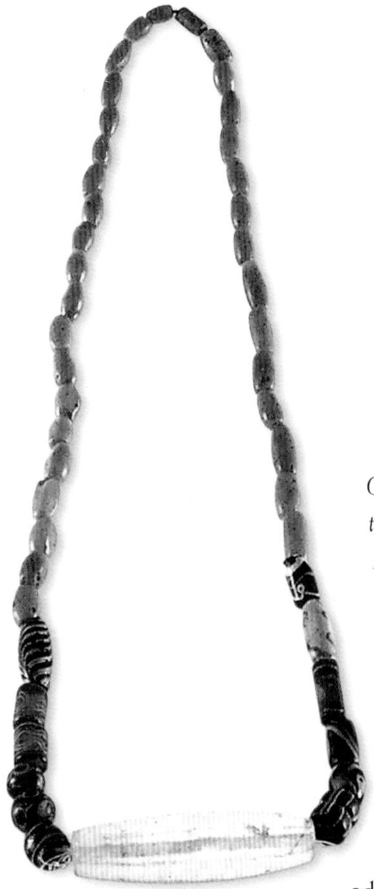

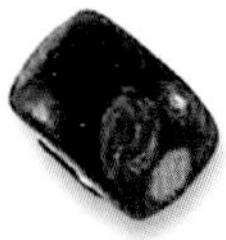

TOP: 'Yellow peanut' beads, seen in this string, are used to tie into position the lower jaw of a deceased Melanau.

ABOVE: The *lukut bela daha*, a bead used as a 'grave gift'.

Opaque blue beads are put on the eyes "to replace the sight".
A black, red and yellow lukut belah daha is laid on the chest "to replace the blood".
Lukut iyan are put between the toes "to replace the footsteps".
Opaque yellow lavang are tied to the forefinger "to replace the skill of the hands".
Strings of seed beads circle wrists and ankles.

One black bead with red and green eyes is added so the deceased would forget his family. If this item is omitted, he may not leave his habitation but stay and haunt people. This is sometimes cited as a reason for dressing a bereaved family in unattractive clothing, such as bark cloth or unbleached calico. The lingering spirit of the departed would recognize his family members if they were wearing their usual clothes and beads, especially if these normally denoted an individual's rank and standing. If he recognized them, he would entice one of them to accompany him on his journey.

At the time of the funeral, gifts of beads can be "sent" to an ancestor by placing them with a body about to be buried. The recently-deceased would then deliver them in the other world. In the old days, mourning lasted one year or more, depending on the family's status. The mourning period for an aristocrat could only be concluded when a fresh head was brought home by the warriors. A man who remarried before the end of the stipulated period had to pay a fine of gongs and valuable old beads to his children, or to his late wife's relatives.

MELANAU

The Melanau custom differs – special beads are worn at the time of bereavement. After a death, immediate family members put heavy, translucent blue *manik tilek* on their wrists for spiritual protection. After the body has been washed and laid out, its lower jaw is tied into a seemly position with a string of small beads. Mourners and helpers note if this string was long enough to pass twice or thrice around the head, or only once. This tells them whether the family has a good stock of disposable beads or not. The "yellow peanut" bead (see Chapter 7) is preferred for this purpose, but any common beads including seed beads can be used. Beads of the *manik tilek* type may also be tied to the wrist of the corpse.

After the body has set, the string of beads holding the chin is taken off and laid on the pillow. Antique plates are placed under the neck, hands, knees and heels, depending on local custom and the family's ability to furnish such valuables. The beads may be laid in the coffin and buried as "passage money", laid beside the coffin but put aside after the wake, or left on the coffin in its final resting place.

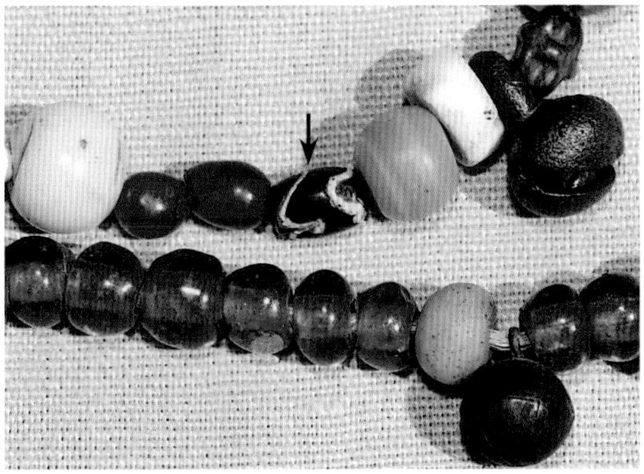

Opaque black glass chevron bead with red and white surface-applied decoration (arrowed), worn by bereaved Melanau families in the Matu area, Sarawak. A leaf-plaited bird was made to 'peck' at this bead to protect mourners' souls.

The last option refers to the time when the Melanau deposited their dead above ground, on wooden scaffolding or in tall carved pillars depending on the deceased's social status.

In the Matu district by the mouth of the Rajang River, bereaved family members wore one opaque black glass chevron bead with red and white decorations on a string while the body was still in the house. A bird shape, *manok siau*, was plaited from sago palm leaves. Friends held the leaf bird and pretended to peck the mourners' beads with it. The bird, having been sufficiently "fed", was then placed on the new grave or discarded in the cemetery. It protected the departed from graveyard spirits. The widow or widower was also considered to be at risk.

The real danger is not that the spirit of the departed might come back to haunt the living. It is the ghouls which haunt the graveyard, evil (generally considered "dirty") wraiths which menace not only the soul of the newly-buried corpse, but also the living who invade their space when burying a body. Beads, which are spiritually "clean", can ward them off.

The custom of wearing mourning beads is still observed, sometimes surreptitiously, by some Muslims and Christians, especially those living in the villages. The beads are worn – usually one or two tied to the wrist – until the funeral party has returned from the graveyard. The family then leads the mourners in taking a bath in the river. This may be an occasion for horseplay of a kind not usually seen among the Melanau.

A Melanau lady from Oya on the Sarawak coast told me, "After my grandfather's funeral, the mourners returned to the house. Then they put on blue *bomoh* beads and everybody took a bath in the river, with all their clothes on. We poured water over ourselves with antique plates. Some of the young fellows threw mud at the girls. There was a lot of splashing and screaming. After this, the beads and plates were kept in a sago leaf basket called *jabai*, that's a basket used for important things of this sort" (i.e. ritual purposes).

Some aspects of the old culture may appear unobtrusively in Muslim or Christian funerary rites. In the 1990s, the coffin of a dear friend and distinguished bead expert was carried through the streets of Mukah, Sarawak, under a canopy of umbrellas tinkling with beads and bells. This structure was left in the church porch during the Requiem Mass, but later re-assembled over the grave. "*Adat* [customary law] is *adat*, religion is religion," an authority on Melanau traditional law said on the occasion of the funeral. "There's no reason why they should disagree. Just don't mix the two!"

BEADS AS GRAVE GIFTS

Grave gifts of jewellery, beads and other valuables used to be the norm among all Dayak groups. This

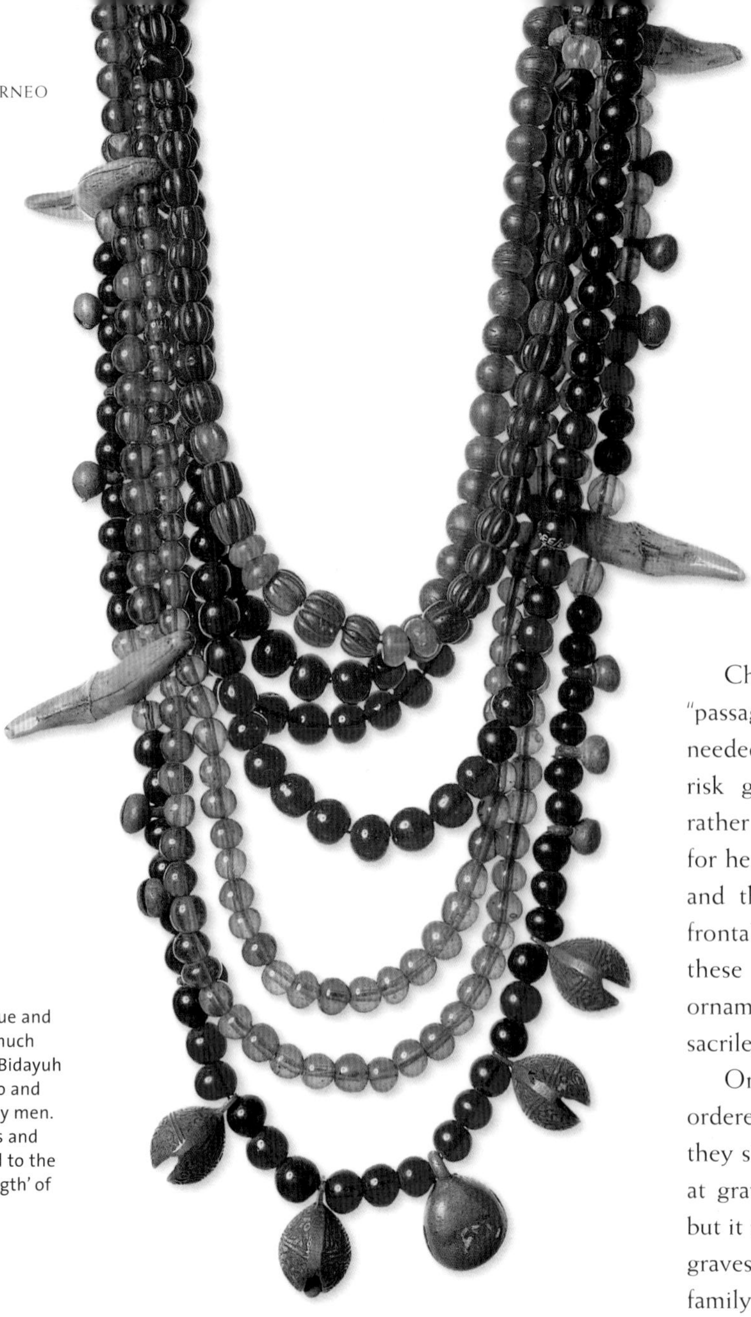

Translucent blue and green beads, much valued by the Bidayuh of west Borneo and worn mainly by men. The bear claws and brass bells add to the spiritual 'strength' of these beads.

custom is now all but abandoned. The generally-stated reason for burying the dead without traditional provisions is the danger of tomb robbery. There have been such incidents, especially in older graveyards, where the looter could count on finding genuine antiques 100 years old or more. The fact that graveyards tend to be lonely, ghost-ridden places in the dense jungle usually delays the detection of the theft until it is too late to even attempt to catch and punish the offenders.

Christians and Muslims maintain that the "passage money" to enter a pagan paradise is not needed by members of their faiths anyway, so why risk graveyard desecration? One Kayan matron rather proudly showed me the burial beads destined for herself and her husband. This was in the 1990s, and they were new beads, nicely strung, with a frontal bobble of red seed beads. A body wearing these would look respectably dressed, but the ornaments are not valuable enough to tempt a sacrilegious thief.

One Lun Bawang lady with no close relatives ordered that all her beads be buried with her but that they should be pounded to grit to foil any attempts at grave robbery. This seems an extreme measure, but it may be mentioned that ceramics deposited on graves are often cracked or smashed by the mourning family for the very same reason.

Deliberately looting a grave is one thing, "finding" items from very old burials is another. The Orang Ulu and Melanau used to deposit their dead above ground in the past, in massive tomb-pillars, tomb-huts or elevated coffins. With time, these monuments collapsed or crumbled, but the site around them is often rich in beads and similar small value items. The "finder" might know very well where to look, or he might stumble upon treasures quite innocently while tilling the soil or digging holes for some building project.

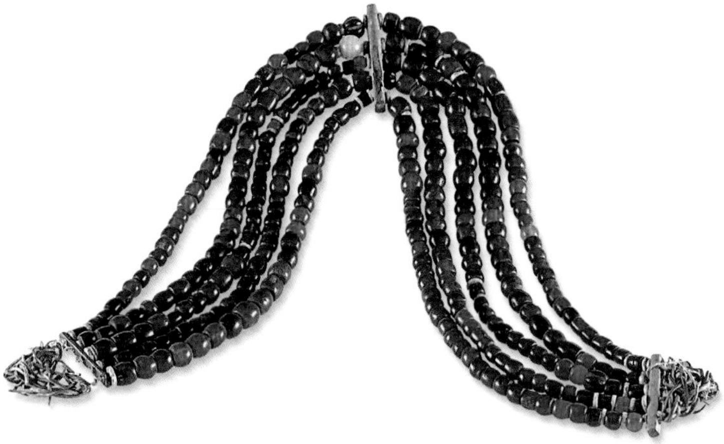

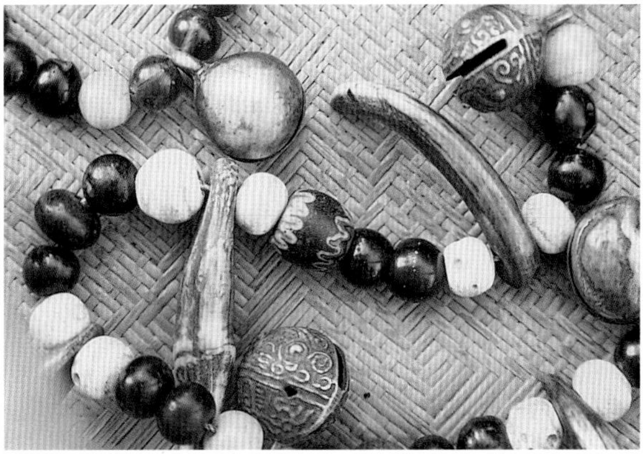

TOP LEFT: Blue-barrel bead belt worn by the Selakau women of west Borneo.

TOP RIGHT: Detail of a Bidayuh Jagoi man's necklace of glass, claws, tusks and brass bells.

Should such items be collected or reverently re-buried? The ethics of this question are complex; personal feeling comes into it. One highly-educated Melanau lady rejected the proffer of a few very worn-looking blue glass beads of the wedding/ mourning type because the seller could not account for them to her satisfaction. I encouraged her to add them to her collection but she shook her head. "I think he got them from an old tomb site," she explained. "I wouldn't want to own them. They're beads of the dead."

HIS AND HER BEADS

To the Orang Ulu, individual beads can be either male or female. The distinction is obvious to a Kayan or Kenyah matron, and is usually explained in terms of shape or colour. To the Uma Jalan Kenyah in Kalimantan, one type of black bead with compound white-yellow-green eyes is male; if it contains traces of red it is female. The high-value *lukut sekala* and the ritually-important *lukut bela daba* may be male or female, depending on whether the shape of the bead is considered "long" or "flat". Sometimes even the longhouse experts disagree about an exact classification.

Bead ownership may also be defined by gender. Among her ritual paraphernalia, the Kayan priestess has a little pouch or pillow decorated with strings of beads, a red and a yellow bead dangling separately, and a button. This container is normally kept out of sight, used only for major ceremonies such as those connected with the rice farming cult, and handled only by women.

Among the Bidayuh of west Borneo, not even a priest or priestess could wear or use the beads belonging to a person of the opposite sex, though beads do succeed from an older shaman to a younger one. This might be from father to son or from mother to daughter, to another relative, or to a "novice" recruited from outside the family, but it must be to a person of the same sex. Violating this taboo carries the serious punishment of "a slap in the face from a devil" – the offender is likely to fall ill or go mad.

One prominent Bidayuh shaman, after having explained his beads to an interested outsider, stated categorically to all present that "women don't have beads". Female relatives present at the time protested vociferously and brought some very pretty beads out of a storage basket. But the shaman, Raseh, was not impressed. To him, "beads" meant "power beads", and there was no female shaman in his village in the 1980s. The beads owned by his wife and sister were only personal ornaments to him.

The Selakau men of west Borneo may not wear any beads at all, ritual or otherwise; only women wear beads, especially as brides and young mothers. The spirits of the beads would rebel against such a

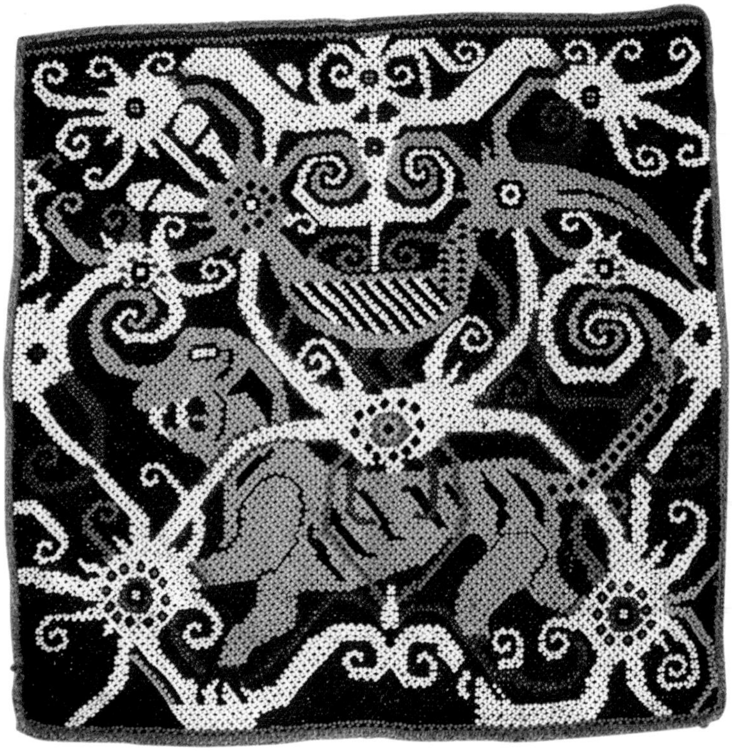

Orang Ulu beadwork featuring tiger and hornbill images. The tiger, for the Orang Ulu, was a favourite high-class design in painting and beadwork, symbolic of power.

confusion of genders. If a man wore beads, he would fall into a hole next time he went hunting in the jungle. Considering the rugged terrain inhabited by the Selakau, or Kendayan as they are known in Kalimantan, this sanction is taken seriously. An injured hunter could well die of blood loss or starvation before search parties from the village manage to find him.

DANGEROUS BEADS

A number of top-value beads are actually considered dangerous for a low-class person to wear. What about simply *owning* a few valuable beads? A hundred years ago, there would have been no question – only an aristocrat could own *lukut sekala*, for instance. The Orang Ulu carefully refrained from using symbols inappropriate to their social stratum. The tiger was a favourite high-class design in painting and beadwork, symbolic of power, though Borneans know this creature only from hearsay – there are no tigers on the island. Around 1890, Nieuwenhuis promised to bring a high-ranking Orang Ulu chieftain a stuffed tiger head from Sumatra. No Dayak boatman or bearer would touch the crate containing it on the long journey from the coast to the Apo Kayan highland. The project had to be abandoned!

A tiger tooth had to be kept secret until Nieuwenhuis could hand it over to the recipient, a chief of sufficiently high rank to own such a potent charm. The use, even the touch of a tiger tooth was inappropriate and dangerous for a commoner, though leopard, bear and, rarely, rhinoceros teeth were perforated and worn with or as talisman beads, depending on a person's rank and "strength of soul".

And what happens if this strength of soul is lacking? An informant in Marudi on the Baram River told me the tale of a Kayan girl whose family was of very high rank, and owned a tiger tooth, perforated so it could be worn as a bead if anybody dared. This girl married "beneath herself", against her mother's very bluntly and publicly-expressed wishes. The extended family got on after a fashion, but later the two women quarrelled acrimoniously. Everybody in the longhouse heard the older woman cursing her daughter: "If you ever come in here again my tiger tooth will burn your heart!" The young woman lived entirely in her in-laws' family rooms from then on. Years later, when all parties thought the quarrel was forgotten, the daughter entered her mother's room

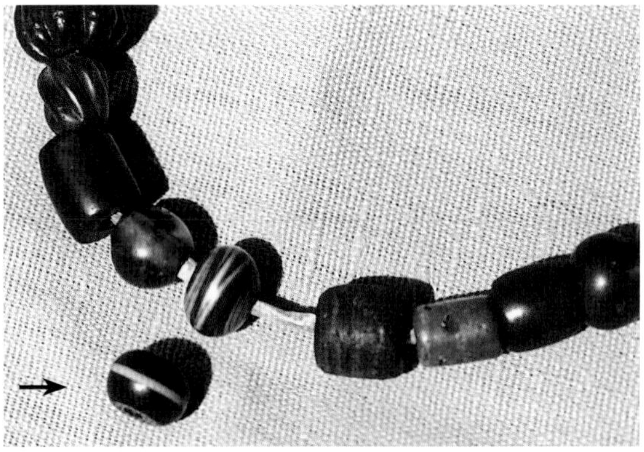

The Kayan shaman's *manang* bead (arrowed) was regarded as extremely sacred and was hidden in a small receptacle called the *kawit.* Women were not allowed to see the *kawit*, let alone the *manang* bead.

for some reason. Within a few days, she fell sick and died. The tiger tooth had done its work.

Anecdotes of this kind abound in all Borneo societies. In west Sarawak, I heard the story of a Bidayuh lady who owned a number of beautiful and potent beads, which she stored in an ancient jar in her rice barn. After her death, these heirlooms were taken care of by her daughter, but after that lady's death, the family decided to divide up the treasure. Some of the beads should have gone to a young grandson, but nobody spoke up on his behalf. An uncle took possession of beads and jar. Later, when he wanted to put rice into his newly-acquired treasure, it cracked in his hands – an extremely inauspicious omen.

The Kayan shamans or *dayung* conceal their ritual paraphernalia in a small receptacle called the *kawit*; these effects inevitably include a special bead or beads. One of this kind, a black cherry-sized bead with a white zone around the middle, has been dubbed the *manang* bead by some collectors. Such a bead was considered very sacred; it was hidden and jealously guarded. In the really conservative societies, no woman was ever allowed to even lay eyes on the receptacle, which belonged to a male shaman, let alone the bead.

When a new *dayung* was initiated into the occult practices, a bamboo box was made for him. Inside were a special bead, a ladder carved of wood (symbolic of access), small hooks (to catch spirits), and a length of rope (to bind things). The "spirit", which was to assist the shaman in his work, resided in or "sat on" the bead. This was what gave power to the whole set. The small receptacle was put into another, that into another, each neatly fitting. Then it was put into a cloth bag, and finally into a basket. This was kept near the headman's door as a sacred symbol of power. An unauthorized person who dared to see or touch this bead was threatened with illness or madness.

In one instance, when one Kayan *dayung* decided to become Christian, he took farewell of the spirits and opened his secret container at a public meeting. The people sat around, looking at it in silence, but no ill effects followed. This bead, which was seen to have lost its "magic", thus has no special rank within the Kayan bead value system – it is just a plain, ordinary piece of glass. The debunking of mysteries certainly paves the way for social changes.

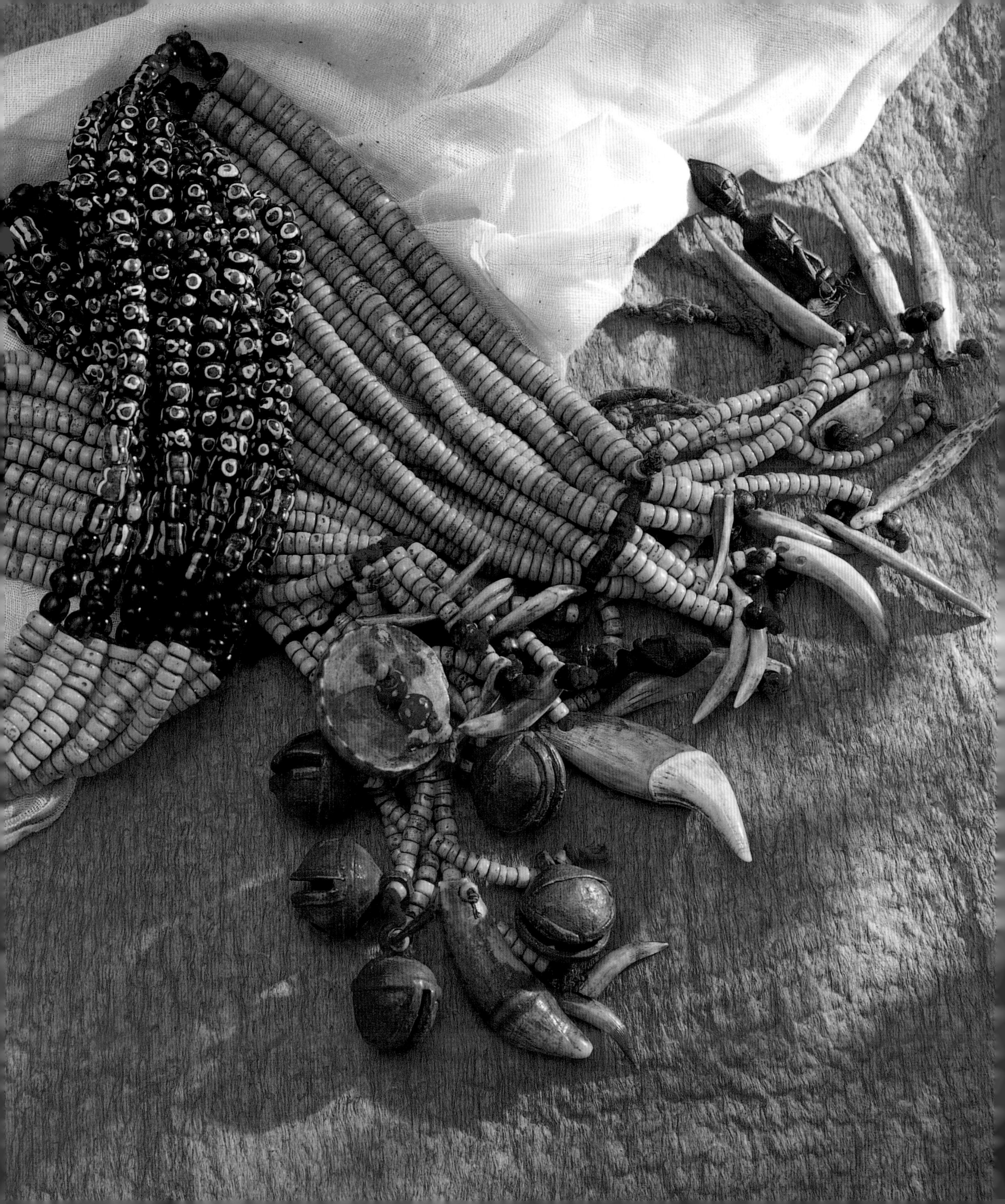

[CHAPTER 4]

BEADS AS WEALTH

Beads used as investments, wealth and status symbols, and in fines.

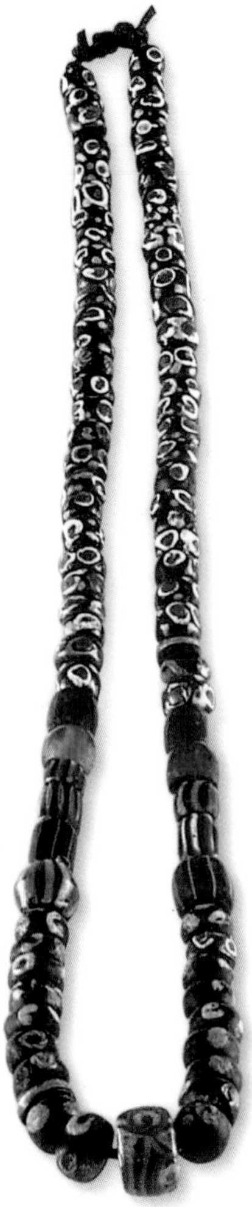

FACING PREVIOUS PAGE: Belt of Orang Ulu value beads, complete with animal teeth and claws, and brass hawk bells. Value beads reveal the owner's social status and are carefully kept.

ABOVE: String of Orang Ulu value beads including (from top) eye beads of various kinds on the sides, two blue barrel beads, 'Amsterdam-stripe' beads, and a front section of *lukut*-type beads.

STRATIFIED SOCIETIES AND BEAD VALUES

In the past, the Orang Ulu and related societies were strongly stratified. There was a top level of aristocrats, a fairly well-to-do middle class, an economically- and socially-demarcated lower class, and the slave class. A person could be a slave by birth or as the result of captivity in war. The advent of education, world religions, and an indigenous cult revival at the time of World War II (based on a *commoner's* dream revelations, it should be noted) have changed many of the once-rigid distinctions, and drastically simplified the complicated system of rituals and taboos that used to shore up the position of the upper class.

The aristocracy had close ties with the spirit world. A high-class individual had a tutelary deity which protected him and, by extension, his tribe. Disobeying a leader was equivalent to disobeying the spirits. No wonder a chieftain could and did order the common folks around! Such arrogance is mainly a thing of the past, though people may still mutter, "He's got a ghost!" when fulfilling as a courtesy requests which would have been unceremonious orders 100 years ago.

School has served as a great leveller in this respect. The poorest man's child can top the class, school children wear the same uniform, ambitious young folk can move "downriver" if they feel so disposed. Gone are the days when the lowest class could neither marry nor leave the longhouse without the chief's permission. A "runaway marriage" for instance would have been quite impossible under the old dispensation. The longhouse could not offer shelter to a couple guilty of breaching the traditional law. A neighbouring community could not take them in and risk divine displeasure. Once they ventured too far away from their chief's sphere of influence they were free of *adat* restrictions all right, but it meant that they were also in enemy territory.

Today, many school leavers from the villages join the rural-urban drift, where they will be absorbed into a much larger society. Nobody knows them here, or cares about status as defined in the longhouse. A young man of low birth may join the police or the army. Within this framework, he has the opportunity to rise to a high, universally-recognized rank by his own efforts.

But when he takes his family back to the longhouse for a visit, his wife may carry their baby in a well-designed polyester-and-vinyl pouch from an expensive baby-wear shop, but not in a beaded back-basket featuring the dragon, the tiger or the human figure. After all, these are aristocratic designs!

BEADS AS WEALTH

"Good" beads are not only valuable, they also reveal status. Owners usually keep their beads carefully. In the past, glass and stone beads which are liable to

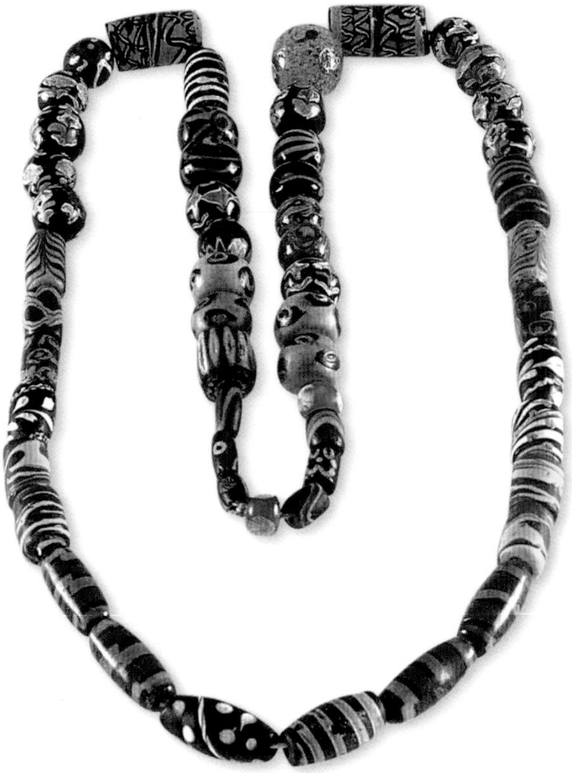

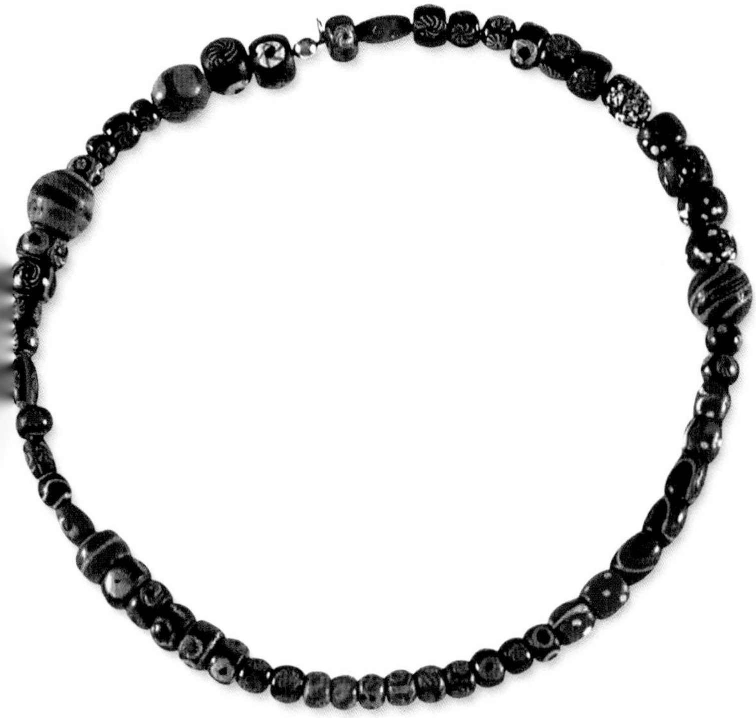

Fine examples of Orang Ulu value beads in these necklaces.

LEFT: This string includes a longish cylindrical *buah wang batang uma* ('length of a longhouse') bead at the top of each curve, a greenish-blue bubbly glass bead at the right inside corner, and polychrome beads mainly from Venice.

BELOW: Almost every bead in this valuable necklace is a *lukut*-type bead. Some of the smaller rosette ones are actually *lukut sekala*.

WAR OVER ONE BEAD

Among the indigenous societies of central and west Borneo, the value of beads, in prestige or monetary terms, can hardly be exaggerated. A high-ranking chief who owned a unique bead, so Maloh legend has it, was visiting a longhouse with which his tribe had a friendly relationship, though no immediate kinship. He and his followers were entertained for several days and the visitor proudly wore his best beads to honour the occasion. One evening, in the midst of much drinking and dancing, he was murdered at the instigation of his hostess and his bead taken, the killer more or less apologizing while he did the deed: "She made me do it!"

The story has distinct classical overtones. The longhouse chief's wife nagged her husband until he agreed to commit the crime. She drugged the drink served to her guest's entourage so none could come to his aid. But punishment, though slow, did come. When the victim's sons grew up, they avenged their father's murder most bloodily – the victors returned to their longhouse in a war boat decorated with the heads of this Dayak Macbeth and his lady. The story meanders on to other events, but the central theme – that a man may be threatened, extorted or killed for a bead – is quite plausible in the Borneo context. Not all such incidents have survived in story form, but there may well have been similar raids and skirmishes that have been forgotten.

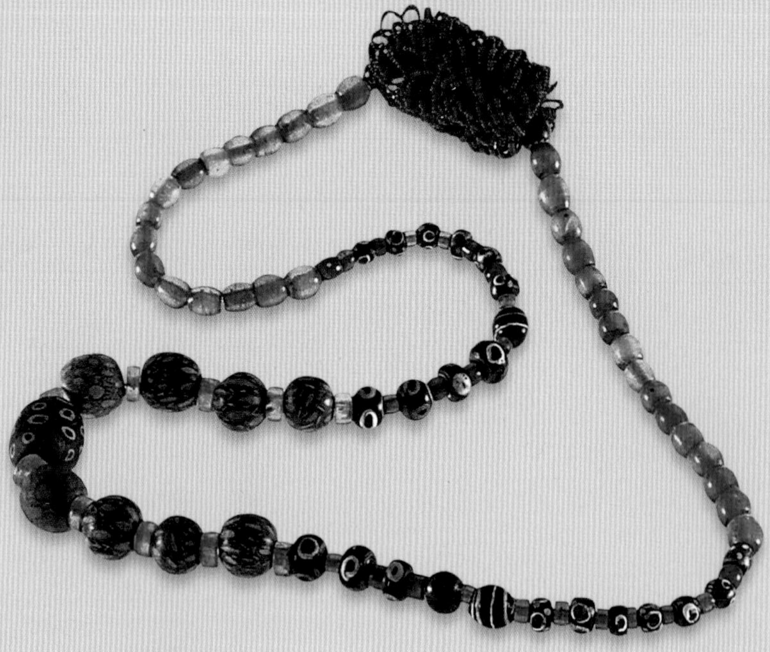

ANTI-CLOCKWISE FROM LEFT:
Orang Ulu bead string containing green-yellow and red-yellow Jatim beads, which used to be very uncommon in Borneo, a rare black-white eye bead, blue barrel beads and a red seed bead bobble; Orang Ulu bead string with the colourful, rare and highly-prized chequerboard bead in the centre; Melanau value beads; and Orang Ulu value beads.

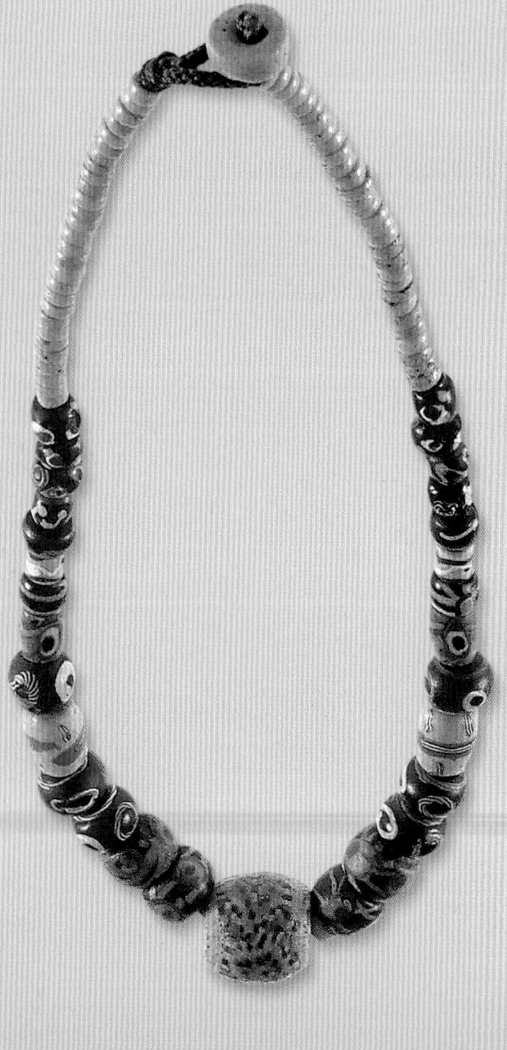

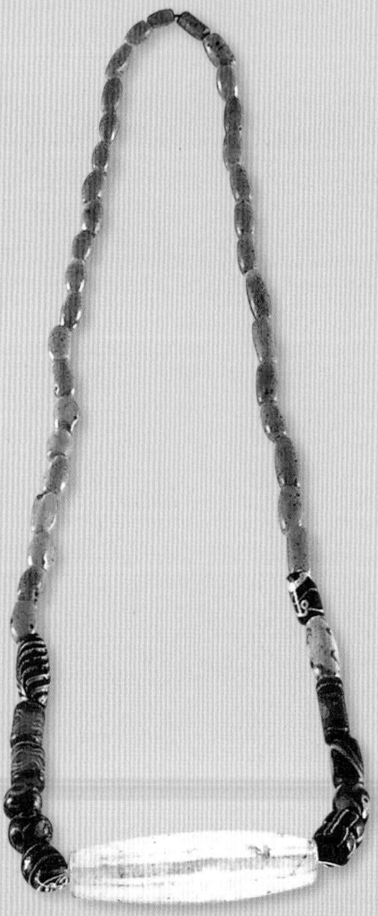

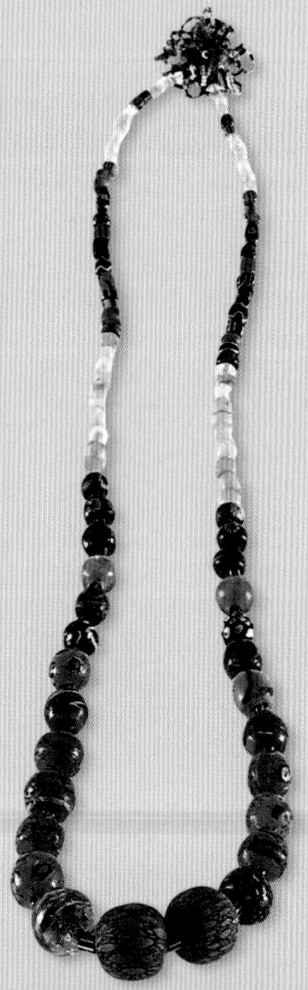

FROM LEFT: The first five beads are Orang Ulu value beads, followed by five old and new millefiori beads. Some millefiori beads are treasured by the Orang Ulu as value beads. The last four beads are *lukut sekala*-type beads, which are the top-value beads of the Orang Ulu.

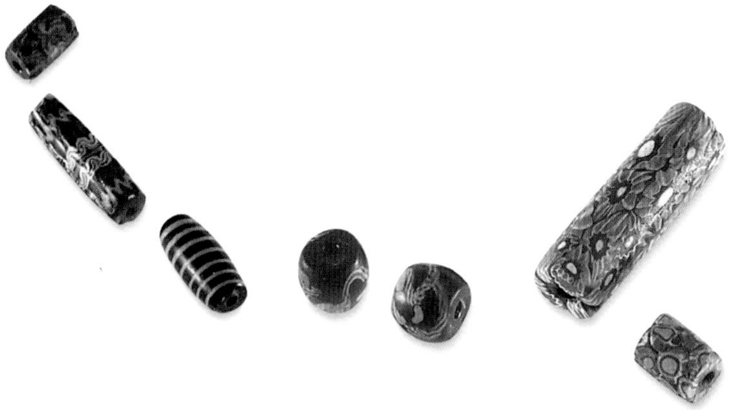

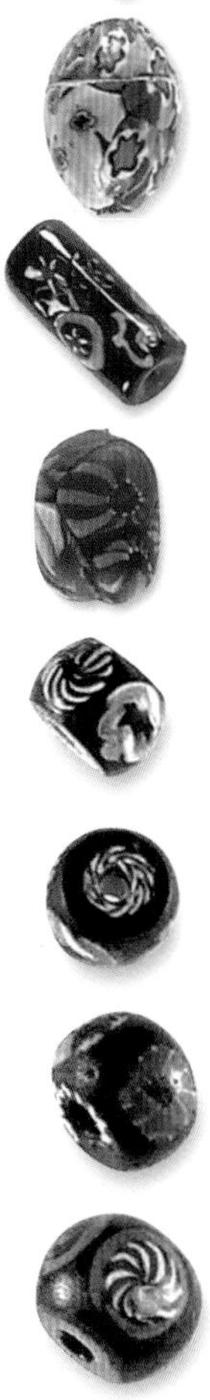

chip or crack, were carefully wrapped in pieces of cloth, which was rarer and more valuable than it is now. Many owners had a special, decorated basket for their heirlooms, some Orang Ulu women still treasure granny's bead-basket though they keep their own bead collection under lock and key. Many women, even now, take their beads with them wherever they go. When the family moves to the farm huts during the busy planting and harvesting seasons, mama takes along her beads. She is not likely to wear them while labouring under the sun, but she likes to have them in her own immediate keeping.

For travelling, from upriver down to Marudi or Miri for instance, enterprising matrons have ordered a "Baram safe" from the local tinsmith. This is a stout tin box with a hinged lid, about the size of a large shoe box, fitted with a carrying handle and padlock. This container is not meant to protect beads from thieves (the box could easily be snatched and carried off by an agile attacker), but to keep them together should there be a boating accident. The shallow longboats used in the more turbulent sections of the river do capsize occasionally. It would be easier to salvage one box, rather than grope for a few dozen strings of beads swept off between the rocks of a rapid, or so the owners reason.

Shipwreck, theft and fire also pose threats to valuable personal possessions. The worst tragedy would be a longhouse fire. Once a dry, leaf-thatched wooden structure catches fire, there can be no thought of saving anything except the inhabitants.

One Kelabit lady, whose longhouse home burned down in the 1990s, was proud of her presence of mind on that occasion. She told me that she and her husband heard the cry, "Fire! Fire!" and were just in time to save their most important belongings.

"The children were all in school, only two of us were at home," she recalled. "My husband grabbed the biscuit tin he kept all the papers in, things like the birth certificates and his diploma. I snatched up my bead basket and then we ran for our lives!" After the tragedy, the community rummaged through the smoking embers. Some found a charcoal-studded lump of multi-coloured glass – all that was left of heirloom beads and the basket or canvas bag they had been stored in.

Wealthy ladies rival each other in the possession of high-value beads. A person in severe financial difficulty may have to decide between selling beads or land. Relatives resort to litigation to recover a high-value bead lent to a cousin and not returned, or declared "lost". Such suits are usually brought before the longhouse elder and heatedly argued for hours on end. If the local chief is unable to settle it, the dispute would then be taken to a higher level. The district office records contain instances of such cases from the 19th century onwards, which sometimes dragged on for months and even years. Neither side

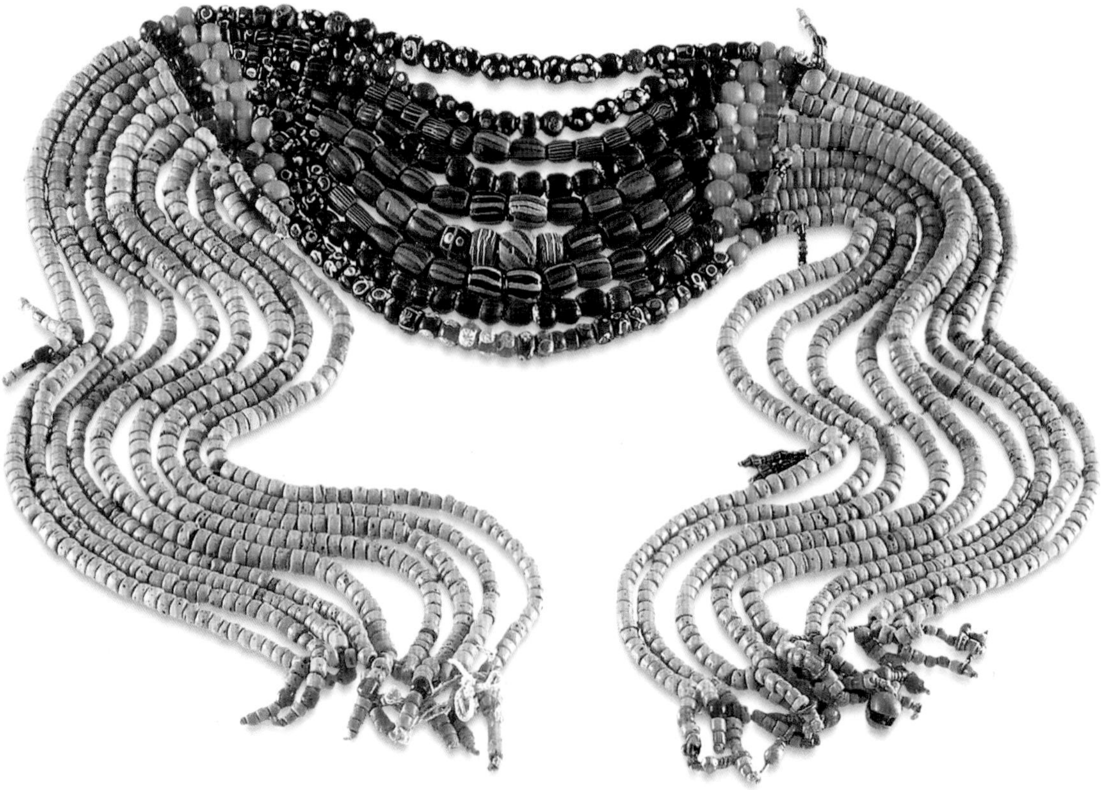

Nine-strand Orang Ulu belt of mainly top-value beads. Rows two and six on the central curve, counting from below, consist entirely of Amsterdam chevrons. The sides of the belt are made up of 'yellow doughnut' or *lavang* beads, which are of considerable ritual value.

was prepared to give in. In addition to the value of the beads in question, personal pride was also at stake. Another example of beads as wealth can be seen in obituaries in the local press, which often feature an official-looking picture of the deceased in formal attire. In such an obituary, a Kelabit matron may be depicted wearing her bead cap.

There can be quarrels over heirloom property when dividing an inheritance, especially in the absence of clearly-expressed last wishes. Beads, unlike a gong or a jar, can be divided among several claimants. Sometimes artifacts like bead caps or necklaces are undone, and shared out as individual bead lots. A bead owner may give away some or all of her beads in her lifetime, or at least allocate them to family members on her deathbed. Occasionally, a wealthy person without close relatives may order that all her beads be buried with her. Such a request is punctiliously carried out. To pre-empt any attempts at grave robbery, the bead owner may request that her beads be smashed first, and then buried. This, also, will be done by the grieving relatives.

While there are certain accepted rules about the ownership and inheritance of heirlooms, beads are in most cases considered personal property. A mother's generosity, or otherwise, is shown by the kind and number of beads she dowers her daughters with, or gives to a new daughter-in-law. She could give beads to a distant relative or to anybody at all. The family may comment on such whimsical liberality but cannot do anything about it.

A Kelabit mother, who decided to endow her daughter with beads upon the girl's marriage, did so partly from family affection, and partly to give the bride respect among her new in-laws. In a status-conscious society this was important. "And if she ever needs to buy something for herself, she can use them to raise funds!" this Kelabit matron told me.

In this sense, beads were invested property to be turned into goods or money for a purpose. In theory,

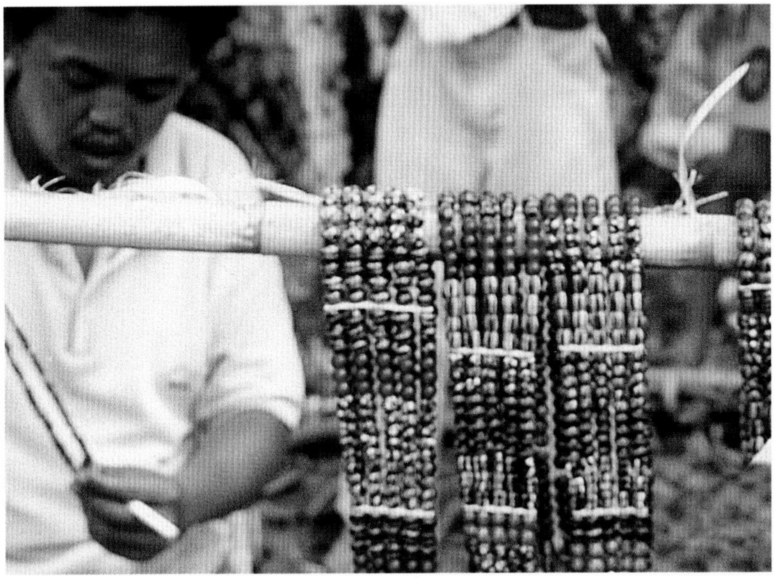

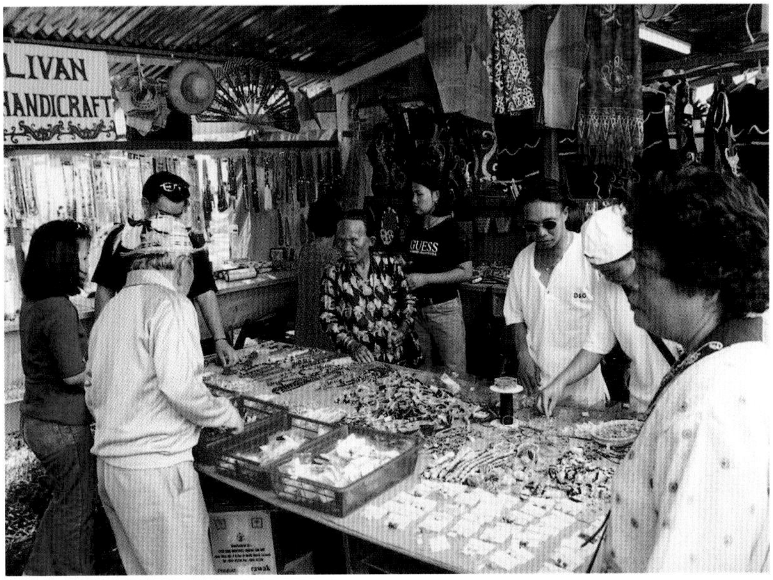

only the owner herself could dispose of her beads. In practice she might be coerced into parting with her property by her husband's wish to splurge on feasts in honour of his ancestors. The wife's dowry, now considered matrimonial property by her spouse, finally served to shore up *his* status. As one old song laments:

I was a woman who wore a cap of orange alai sia beads
Who wore, full beneath my neck, many necklaces of green beads
They are all gone now, sold by my husband
To buy rice for the feasts to honour the dead...

BEADS USED IN FINES

Beads usually formed part of the fines levied for a wide range of offences. To quote one expert, the late A. J. N. Richards, who was former district officer in various parts of Sarawak from 1938–1964 on *adat* law: "The Iban *adat* law doesn't know the apology, it only knows the fine." People are fined petty sums for petty offences such as bad manners. Mocking a little boy's genitals, or making music while another family was in mourning, are examples.

The longhouse elder as the enforcer of the traditional *adat* law levied and collected the fines. Their main purpose was not so much to make pecuniary restitution for somebody's loss, but to redress the balance in nature and society which had been disturbed by the breach of law.

TOP: An itinerant bead seller at a Kenyah longhouse festival.

ABOVE: Bead sale on an upcountry market day in Marudi, Sarawak. Some Bornean grandmothers buy large amounts of beads, which they know to be inferior, for everyday wear.

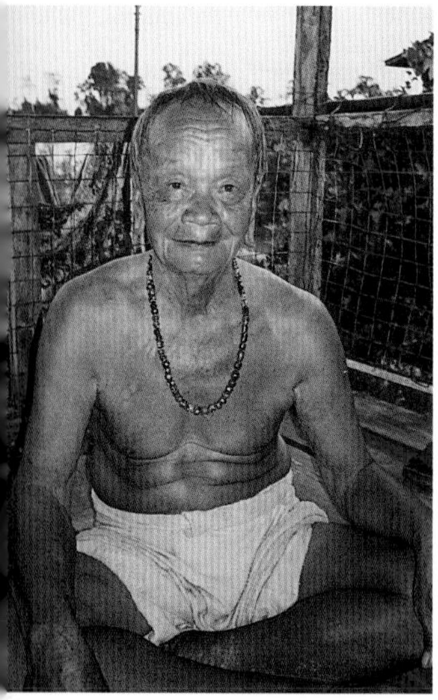

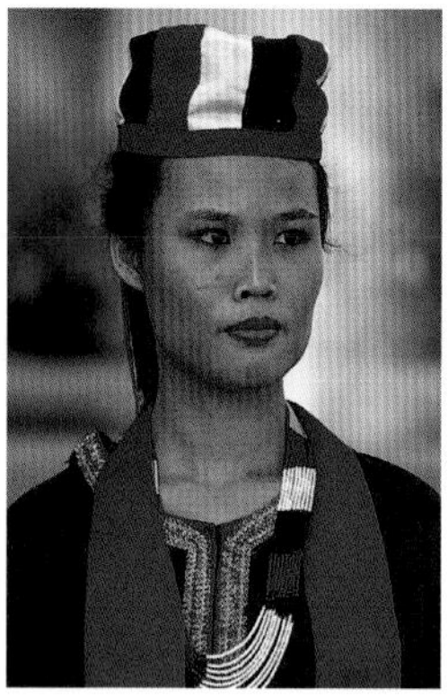

LEFT: Elderly Bahau man wearing a string of antique value beads.

RIGHT: Bidayuh woman wearing a necklace of beads strung in colour blocks of red, white and black. Bidayuh housewives still traded small amounts of household commodities, such as a cup of sugar, for one or two black beads in the 1970s.

After the mid-19th century, the White Rajah's District Officer could and did impose fines as punishments. The Rajah's government fined communities for breaches of peace not involving bloodshed; punitive expeditions were sent out to check outbreaks of headhunting, for instance. Forfeits or good-behaviour bonds typically consisted of jars, beads, brassware, buffaloes or pigs, and sometimes padi.

Government fines were meant to sting, and usually they did. One defiant early 20th-century Kelabit song suggests otherwise, however. In the song, the female singer vows to raise her little brother with care and devotion so he will soon be strong enough to carry on an old feud and go head-hunting in enemy territory, as befits a brave young man:

> *...never mind the fine of the government officers with white eyes*
> *We can pay any fine, we have plenty of valuable articles in our house*
> *So many we can throw them in a big river and the fish will be stunned...*

VALUE OF BEADS

Not everyone was prepared to stun the fish in the river with their antique ceramics and beads, then or now. Women know the worth of beads in buffaloes, padi or money. In 1950s Bario, one lady's cap of good pedigree was worth one buffalo, so were 30 yellow peanut (*let alai*) beads. One such bead bought four baskets of husked rice. One ordinary orange drinking straw (*ba'o rawir*) was exchanged for a basket of rice, an old specimen of the same kind was worth double. Twenty years later, three *gantang* (approximately 3 gallons or 0.014 cubic metres) of rice could be bought for one long carnelian bead.

At the end of the 20th century, such values were more commonly expressed in monetary terms. One yellow peanut bead was worth RM250 to RM300, one deep-blue *let bayong* RM150. A bead cap made of the old, heavy beads, which were no longer fashionable and were becoming rare, would be worth one storehouse full of husked rice if anyone was prepared to sell it, while a cap of the lighter drinking straw beads could change hands at RM30,000. Kelabit matrons agree among themselves that this price could rise: If a very rich lady really wanted a particular cap, well known for its quality and antiquity, she would pay whatever the seller demanded.

The barter trade system is still used in some cases. In the 1990s, an Indonesian who had crossed the border on foot and wanted to travel downriver from the middle Baram bought a second-hand outboard engine for one *lukut sekala* rosette bead. This kind of deal is no longer common. The villagers who had witnessed the negotiations remember it quite well. They told me that "the bead was a little damaged, or it would have been worth a new

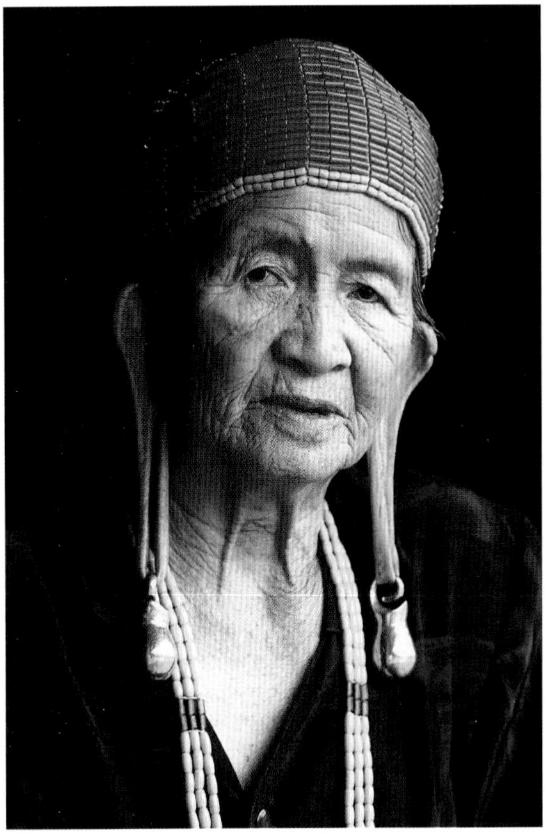

A Kelabit elder wearing her bead cap or *pata* of orange 'drinking straw' beads and 'yellow peanut' beads. In 1950s Bario, the main Kelabit settlement, one lady's cap of good pedigree was worth one buffalo.

engine". Another reason for this barter transaction may have been that the trader had no Malaysian ringgit on him, and the seller did not want to deal in rupiah. Beads were also exchanged for household commodities. Instead of lending a cup of sugar and expecting the sugar to be paid back later, a *Bidayuh* housewife in the 1970s was prepared to accept two black, pea-sized beads as payment.

Wealth commands respect. Traditional Kelabit songs are not above praising people who are rich enough to carelessly waste valuable things:

...then she strings bright aki beads
and round let pudun beads
with holes straight in the centre
those beads with holes not perfectly straight
she throws through the floorboards
and they fall onto the backs of the pigs
and roll off for the chickens to peck at...

Beads are subject to inflation too. In some communities their value is practically nil today: Children are allowed to play with granny's beads, and if these drop through cracks in the longhouse floor, nobody says a word or tries to retrieve them from the mud under the house.

In other communities, bead value has increased exponentially. The recent appearance of acceptable-looking new beads, which are replicas of the old, adds some confusion to a situation in which the beads a person possesses indicate his or her social status.

Kelabit grandmothers grumble that during the Japanese Occupation, perhaps one family in five owned a really good bead cap. You could tell at a glance who was of "good" standing and who was not, one of them remarked, adding that now, everybody has a cap or two – standards are slipping!

This situation, however, does not stop granny and all her friends from buying large amounts of new beads. They are well known to be inferior, but they would do fine for everyday wear, they reckon. The smart thing to do, so distaff opinion in the longhouses has it, is to buy beads, wear them, and keep them for children and grandchildren. "When my grandmother bought this string," one Kayan matron explained to me, lovingly fingering the fine ornament around her neck, "the beads were all new." The lady was in her

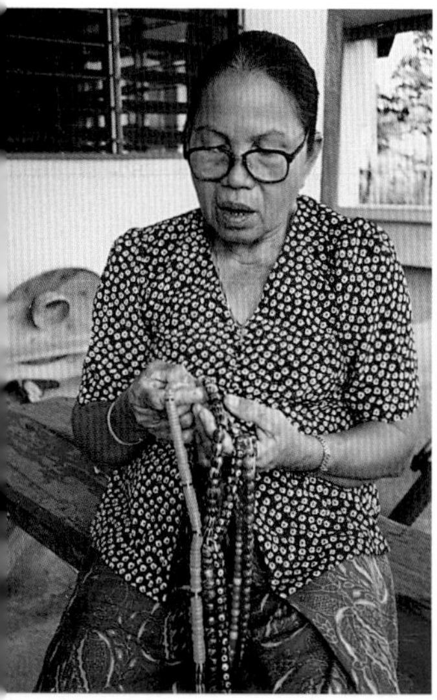

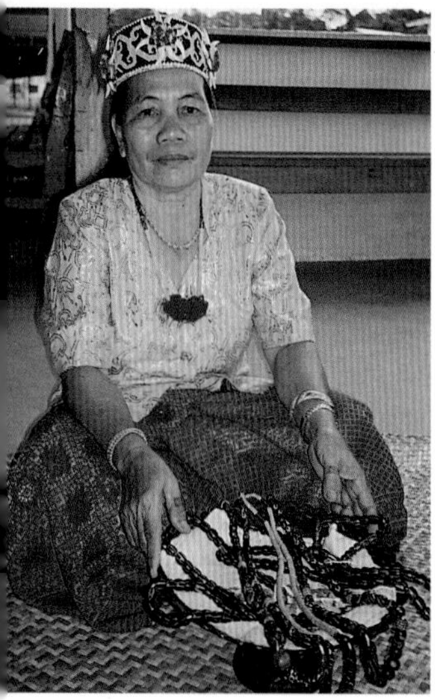

TOP: Madam Unyang Wan singing a bead song for the author on the Baram.

ABOVE: Madam Hinan Tijan, a Kayan chief's wife, displaying her beads. Madam Unyang Wan referred to Madam Hinan Tijan and her beads in the song.

80s, so the beads she wore must have been at the very least 120 years old.

TELL A TALE OF BEADS

Early travellers to Borneo occasionally noted that a group of longhouse ladies could while away an evening "telling their beads", and this did not mean praying using a rosary. A group of women would discreetly display and compare their treasures: The beads are named one by one, with the occasional discussion about their finer points. The older women generally take the lead as the younger ones learn to recognise the slight differences that distinguish two or three visually almost-identical beads.

In the Kayan community, one gifted singer may actually sing a tale of beads. Such songs are improvised on the spur of the moment, often to entertain (and impress) visitors. After all, the bead stock of a family is an indicator of wealth and status. When a bead song is sung to welcome a visitor, it serves to inform him or, more usually, her, that she is visiting the home of a rich, important family.

In a bead song performed for me on the Baram, the singer ceremonially addressed me as "lady from the rivermouth", but she made much reference to her longhouse chief's wife:

These beads belong to the mother
The beautiful one.
There is a lukut sekala that belongs to her
The shining one...
She owns precious heirloom beads
In great abundance...
Here are beautiful lukut tavei
Hinan Tijan has lots of them...
Which she showed to you
Lady from the rivermouth...

LUKUT SEKALA, THE PEERLESS BEAD

As far as the people of Central Borneo are concerned, the *lukut sekala* or rosette bead (see Chapter 7) is the King of Beads, or else the Queen. *Lukut sekala*, like many top-value beads, have gender. An expert distinguishes between a male and a female *lukut sekala* based on size and shape – the male ones tend to be slightly longer than wide – the exact details of the colouring, and often the individual bead's history.

It is said that a *lukut sekala* is "worth one life". Re-tellers of old tales, especially those involved in writing tourism literature, have interpreted this to mean "you could buy one slave for a *lukut sekala*". However, none of my informants agree with this simplified interpretation. For one thing, a *lukut* is worth a lot more than any slave, and for another, the people of Borneo's interior did not capture, sell and buy slaves the way the seafaring coastal people did.

In the old days of inter-tribal warfare, however, a *lukut sekala* could be used to ransom a high-ranking

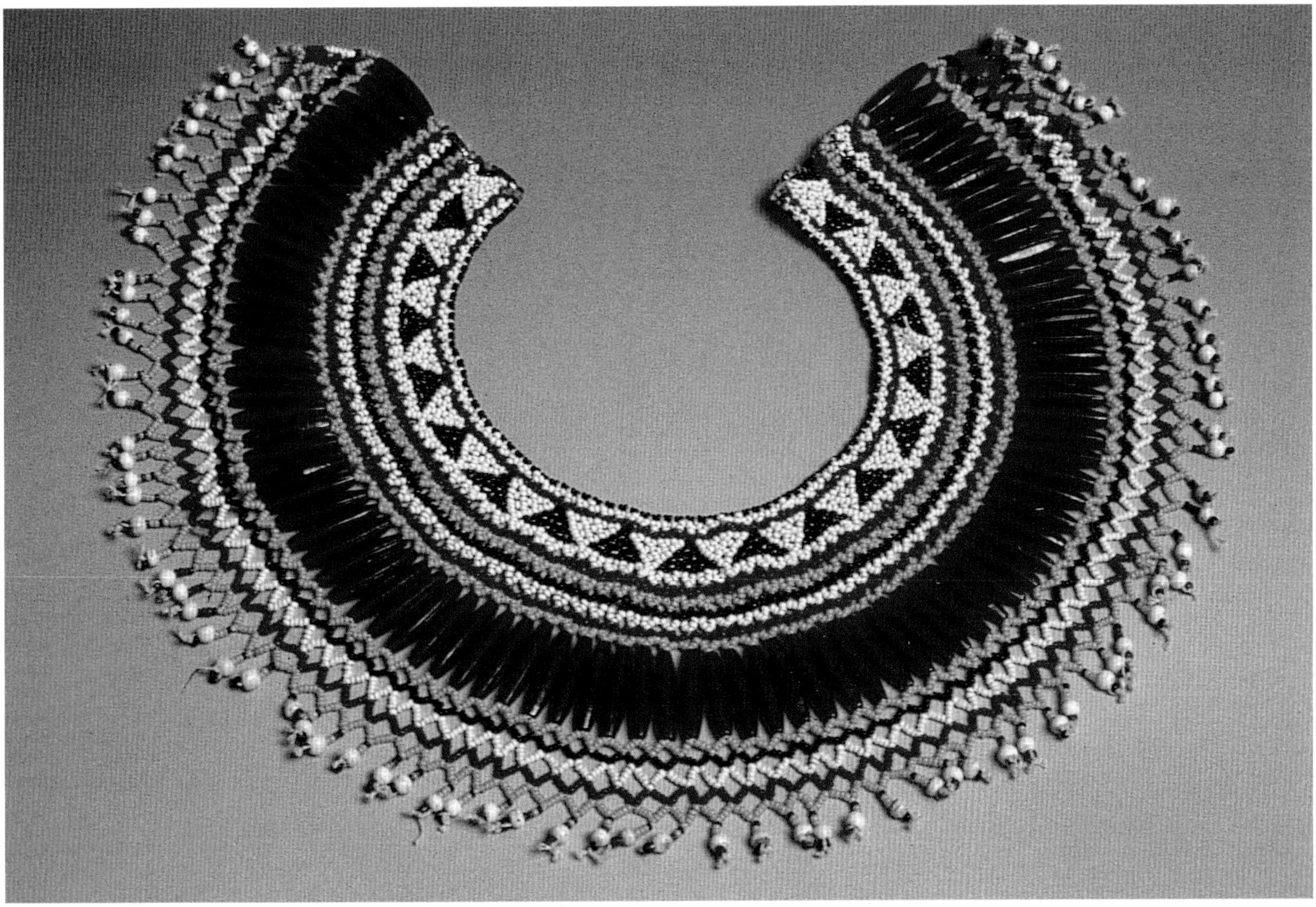

captive. A longhouse surrounded by an overwhelmingly stronger enemy force might manage to buy the attackers off with a payment of valuable beads. The *lukut sekala* had to be presented as part of a child adoption ceremony or in the manumission of a slave. Today, it is still required as part of the engagement gifts for an aristocratic bride.

This bead's value lies in its rarity. Knowledgeable Orang Ulu women reckon there are perhaps only 40 or 50 genuine pieces in Sarawak, and a few dozens more in Kalimantan. The origin of the *lukut ṣekala* is shrouded in mystery. The assertion that it is Egyptian has not been properly documented. Researchers consider the Venetian-made *lukut sekala* of the 18th and 19th centuries to be an imitation of a much older bead, which has not yet been satisfactorily identified.

AGE OF BEADS

Those Dayak who value their beads as investments and status symbols are highly conscious of the age, as determined by family history, of each artifact. Other indicators of age are more tentative: A bead may look old because it is worn-out or pitted. According to one Melanau shaman, beads with large perforations are old. He was referring particularly to the translucent blue "wedding beads" highly prized by his people.

Towards the end of the 20th century, the Kelabit ladies of Bario, eastern Sarawak, started to seriously think about registering their old beads in order to

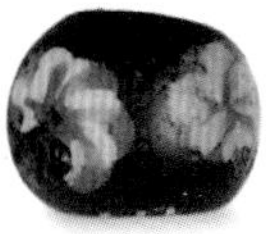

TOP: An Iban *marik empang* or bead collar with a row of spindle-shaped glass imitations of carnelian beads.

ABOVE: One type of *lukut sekala*, the top value bead of the Orang Ulu. It is believed that there are only 40 or 50 genuine *lukut sekala* in Sarawak, and a few dozens more in Kalimantan.

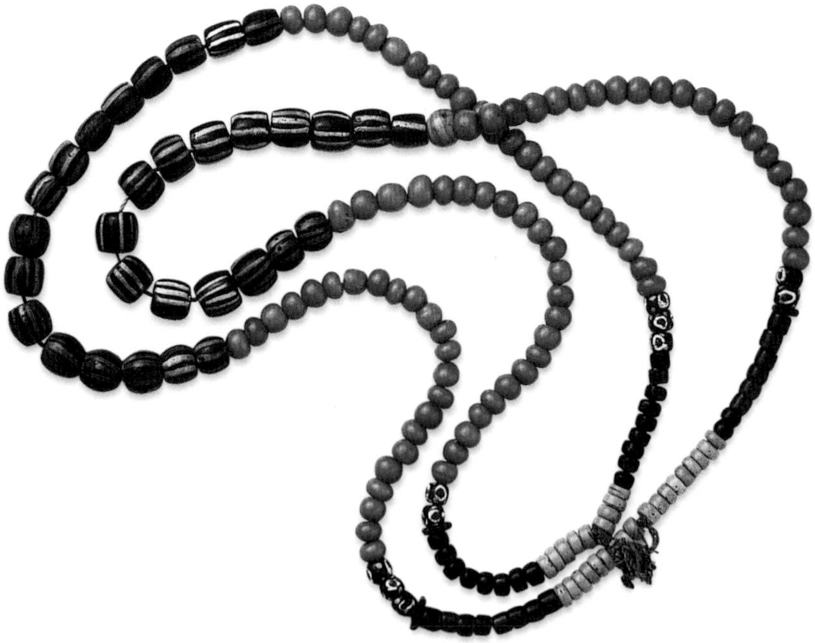

TOP: Orang Ulu beads which include pyjama, *lavang*, and turquoise beads. Dayak who see their beads as investments and status symbols are very conscious of the age of their artifacts.

BELOW: Kelabit ladies of Bario, eastern Sarawak. Towards the end of the 20th century, they started seriously thinking about registering their old beads so as to guarantee their authenticity.

guarantee their authenticity. The advantages to the present owners of antiques are obvious. Unfortunately, so are the drawbacks. As population mobility increases, it becomes extremely difficult to keep tabs on personal belongings such as bead ornaments. What if an unscrupulous owner of three old strings decided to take them downriver, buy identical-looking new beads, and re-string a mixture of old and new into 10 new necklaces?

Where beads are used for ritual purposes, however, age does not usually appear to be a determining factor. The very well-known spindle-shaped carnelian has been duplicated in stone and imitated in

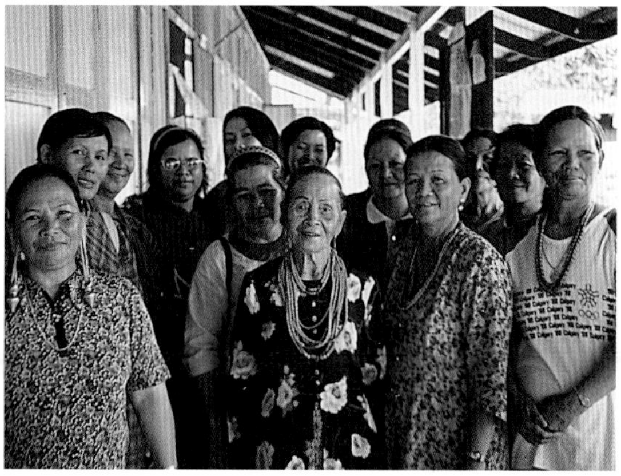

glass from the late 18th century onwards in Gablonz, specially for the East Indies market. Eventually the Bohemian manufacturers went overboard.

The Rungus of Sabah own octagonally-faceted beads which are 15 to 20 cm (6 to 8 inches) long. Instead of only imitating the red-brown colour of carnelian, they were made in green (possibly to imitate jade), opaque white, blue, wine-red and amber. Nobody seems to have rejected these obvious "fakes" then or later.

An Iban healer may have both stone and glass "carnelians" in his medicine box, and Melanau wedding beads may be of banded agate or very obviously of brown and white glass. The fact that the bead looks acceptable, and was passed to the present owner by an older relative, seems sufficient guarantee of its efficacy.

A HISTORICAL PERSPECTIVE

Earlier researchers were fond of tossing terms like "Roman", "Coptic" and "Egyptian" into their descriptions of the more colourful beads found in Malaysian contexts, judgements which were based purely on visual examination.

The "Gardner Collection" of beads from Johor

Lama in West Malaysia is a case in point. The delighted finder concluded that he had stumbled upon a hoard of Roman, Egyptian and Hittite beads. They are in fact of much later, possibly of Mediterranean, origin.

The famous post-war Curator of Sarawak Museum, Tom Harrisson, published his opinion that the deep blue barrel beads worn by the Kelabit in Sarawak were "apparently parallel to ... beads 3,000 years old, from excavation sites thousands of miles away."

Harrisson corrected this statement after spectrographical analysis showed that the beads in question could not have been from Ur of the Chaldees, but this has not stopped every antique-seller between Kuching and Kota Kinabalu from gleefully making such a claim ever since to enhance the value of their wares.

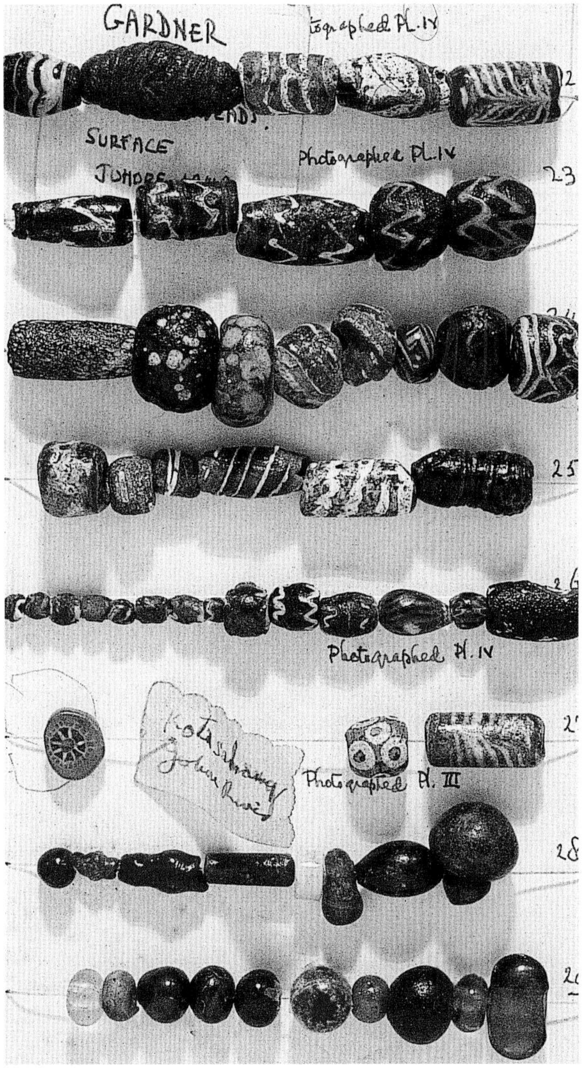

The Gardner Collection of beads from Johor Lama, West Malaysia. Most of these types are still known, and worn, in Borneo.

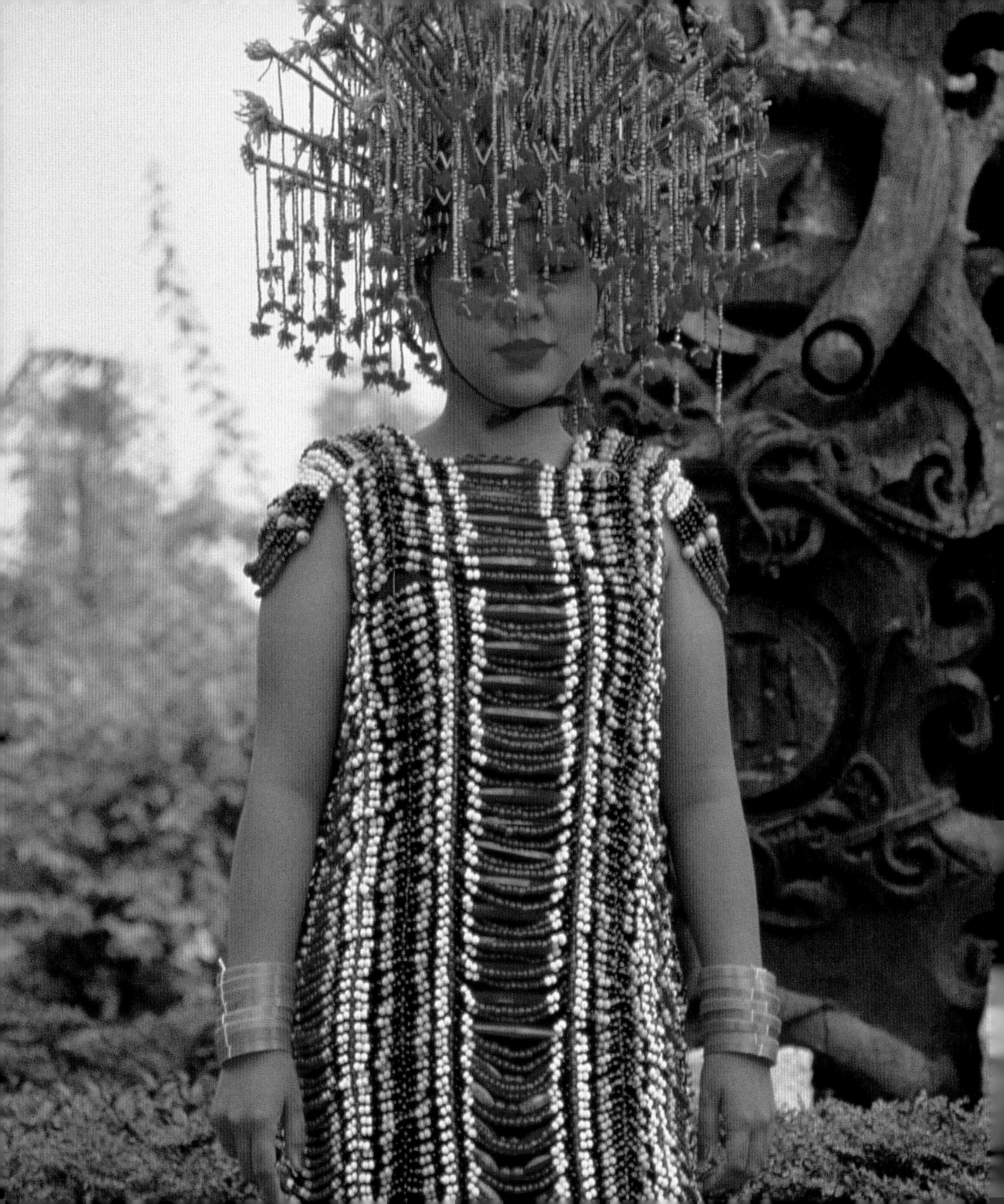

[CHAPTER 5]

BEADS OF BEAUTY

A look at how beads, esteemed for their colour and beauty, are used to decorate clothing.

FACING PREVIOUS PAGE: An Iban bride wearing the *ulu* Rajang wedding outfit. This outfit comprises a colourful bead dress and an elaborate hat. The latter's centrepiece is a mast with horizontal yardarms, held in place by a well-fitting rattan cap. Strings of seed beads dangle from this framework, almost covering the wearer's head.

TRADITIONAL COSTUME

In most Borneo societies today, beads are no longer believed to have any ritual or magical power. However, this does not mean that people have abandoned their old predilections. Beads are still esteemed and worn for their colour and beauty, and are commonly used to embellish traditional costumes. In many cases, more beads are used today than the older generations ever owned or dreamed of.

"Traditional costume" means different things to different people in Borneo. The tropical climate does not require much covering for creature comfort. Most indigenous people wore the necessary clothing to preserve decency: The men in their loincloths and the women in their short skirts may have looked "half-naked" to the outsider, but they were most particular about maintaining their own standards of modesty.

Information on the traditional clothing of Borneo's indigenous people dates back no more than 200 years, when foreign explorers and administrators described or sketched the "barbaric finery" of the natives they encountered on their travels. However, only a few of them, Carl Bock and A. W. Nieuwenhuis in particular, took the trouble to observe carefully, and interpret objectively. Both these writers noted and illustrated textile and bead fashions.

What about earlier periods? Glass and stone beads were imported into Borneo, as documented by archaeological evidence at the consumer end of the trade. There is evidence from the seller's side too: Beads are specifically mentioned as trade goods in the Chinese Inspector of Maritime Trade Chau Ju Kua's 13th-century handbook for mariners, *A Record of Barbarian Nations*. Vessels bound for Borneo, most likely the port of Brunei, were advised to have a good cook onboard to prepare a feast for the ruler upon arrival, after which the crew would get permission to dispose of a cargo of textiles, trade-gold and trade-silver, green porcelain, glass bottles and glass beads.

Another Chinese work is quite specific on the costume worn by the "southern barbarians", as the Chinese called them, of the Malay Peninsula. It states that the common people of Pahang and Kelantan "keep their hair in order with bead rings of five colours". How did this headgear look? Did these bead rings circle the head like the rattan and bead bands worn in Borneo today, or did they hold together a topknot of hair? Were they made of small "seed beads" or larger, possibly ornamented pieces? Both kinds of beads have been recovered from archaeological sites of West Malaysia and southern Thailand.

Undisturbed burial sites may reveal beads near the head, chest and waist of the skeletal remains, suggesting headbands, necklaces and belts, but the stringing or textile backings have long since crumbled. The earliest information we have of costume details are from the 18th century.

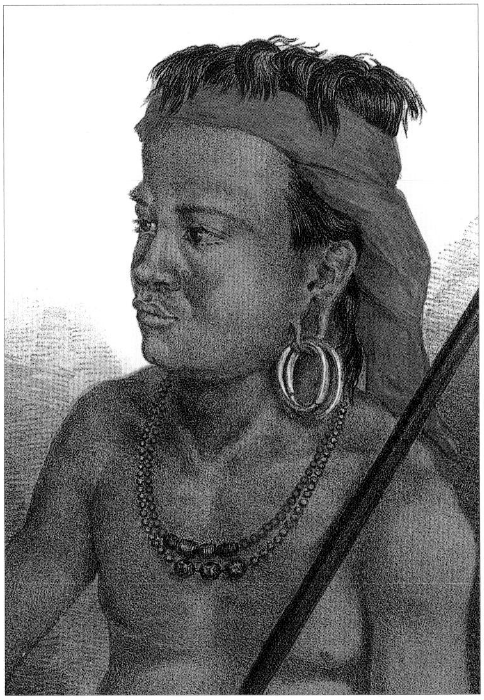

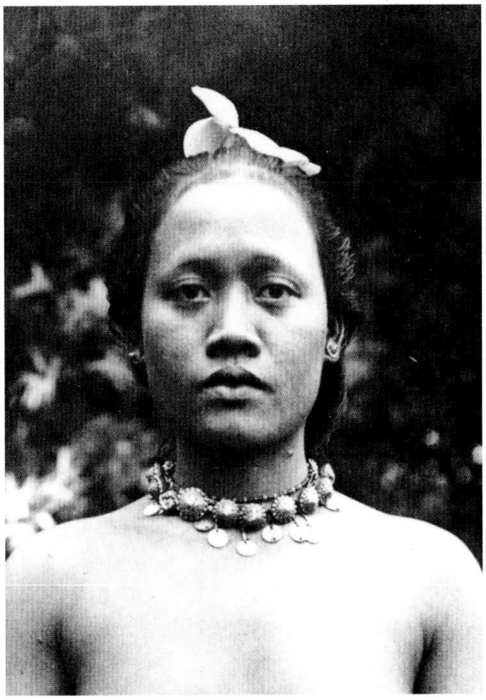

For most of Borneo's indigenous people, the tropical climate did not require much clothing for creature comfort as these photographs and drawings illustrate.
CLOCKWISE FROM TOP LEFT: 19th-century drawing by Norwegian natural scientist Carl Bock entitled 'Hetdung, My Favorite Dyak Boy'; 19th-century Iban woman wearing silver button beads; 19th-century drawing by Carl Bock entitled 'Dyak Boy at Home'; and early 20th century photo of Baukan Sook man from west Sabah wearing beads and loincloth.

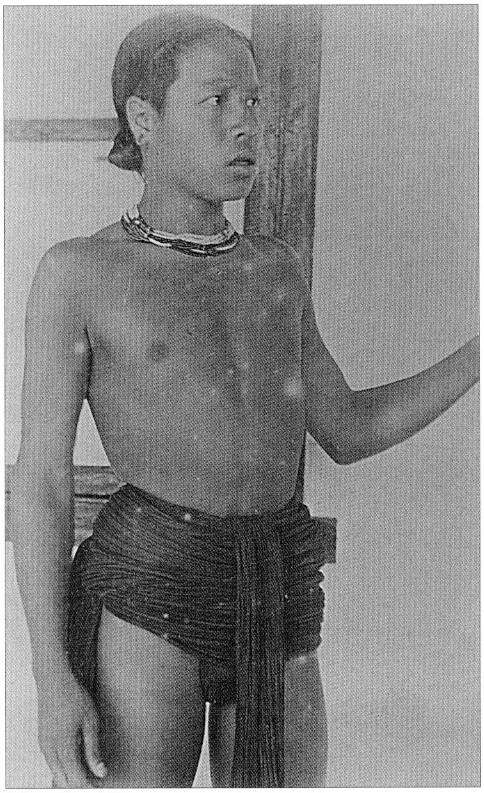

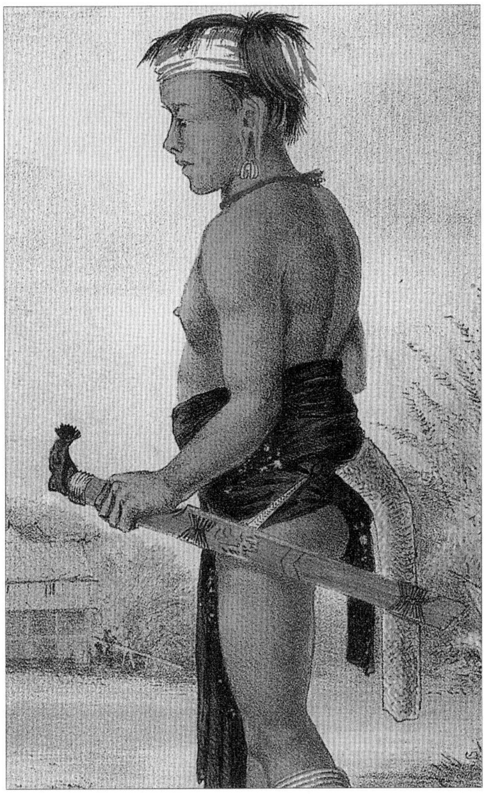

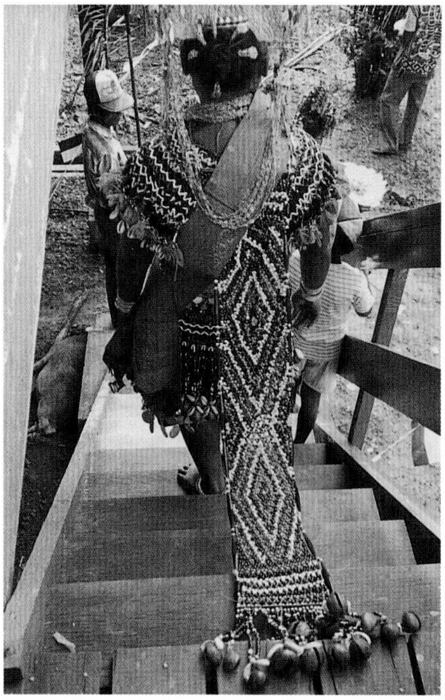

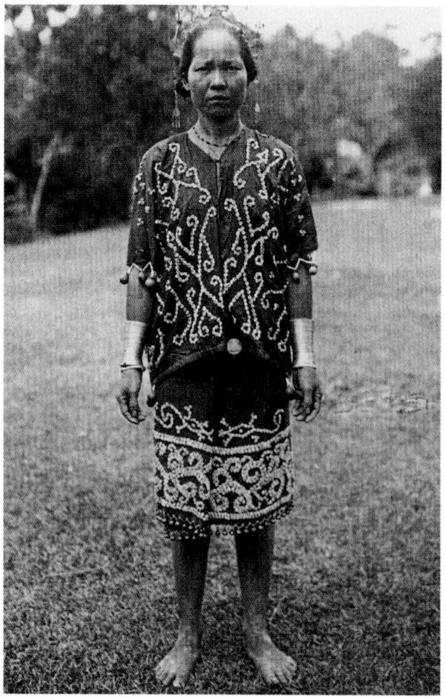

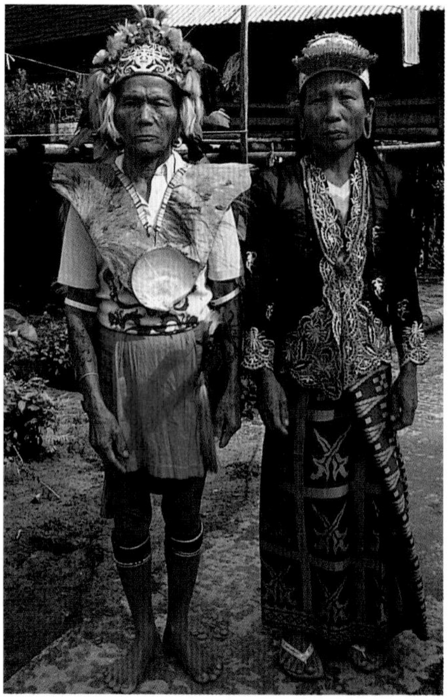

TOP LEFT: Iban girl from the *ulu* Ai area in Sarawak wearing a bead collar and train with 'frog head bells' at the end. Photo taken in the mid-1960s.

CENTRE: Nineteenth-century Iban lady wearing a shell-embroidered jacket and skirt.

RIGHT: Orang Ulu from Kalimantan dressed up for a festival or ceremony.

BEAD FASHIONS

Eighteenth and 19th-century sources describe clothing made of bark and handwoven cloth, embellished by painting, fancy weaving, stitching and beadwork. In the 20th century, these homely garments gave way to shop-bought textiles and ready-made clothing. Frequent contact with strangers who ogled their breasts moved the womenfolk to cover up with stout cotton bras and blouses. Skirts became longer, the "double apron" of the Orang Ulu, two overlapping pieces of cloth tied on the hips, disappeared. Some Dayak women adopted the costume of batik sarong and muslin blouse pinned shut with a set of gold brooches worn by the *nonya* – Chinese women born in the archipelago who had adopted traditional Malay dress. "Traditional" styles are changing all the time. People embrace new fads, copy their neighbour's design, and quite literally cut their coats according to the available cloth. There is no reason to believe sartorial fashion was ever static.

The pendulum swings. After decades of comparative neglect, the various indigenous Borneo people see new value in their traditional customs and costumes. Social and political developments after World War II promoted the hitherto unheard-of concept of the nation-state. Democracy, material progress, universal education were seen as much more important than narrow tribal affiliation and with it the long history of internecine warfare; party politics provide a comparatively harmless outlet for the old warrior traditions. The majority cultures of Indonesia and Malaysia respectively washed over Borneo like a huge wave. Propagation and use of the respective National Languages was aggressively promoted.

Today, in the early 21st century, there is a new interest in the many languages and cultures of Borneo. Music, dance, costume, material culture and traditional arts are fostered in a renaissance of ethnic consciousness and as valuable adjuncts to the tourism industry. There are special celebrations like Gawai

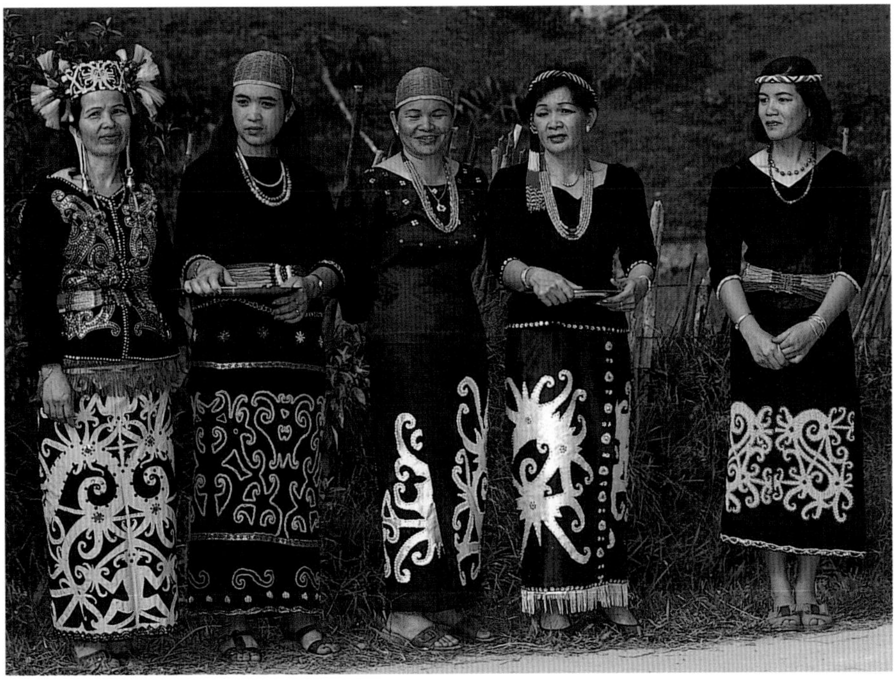

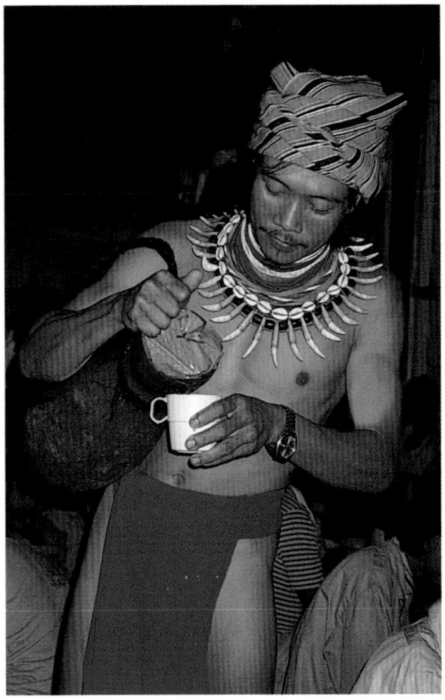

Dayak in Sarawak, Harvest Festival in Sabah and the Erau and Mamat festivities in Kalimantan, in which parties and processions highlight tradition, including costume. Hotels and entertainment outlets have begun to feature cultural shows, mainly for the entertainment of tourists, presenting traditional music, dance and very glittery outfits. The latest in "ethnic chic" are weddings, usually urban ones, in "modern traditional" costumes.

The "modern traditional" styles make allowances for the wearer's modesty, his or her wish to appear well-dressed and graceful, and prevailing fashion trends. Blouses, jackets or sashes are worn by all women. Going topless is seen as old-fashioned, even indecent. Politically-correct editors, who use old illustrations in various publications camouflage, air-brush or simply ink out any exposed female breasts.

The Iban and Bidayuh of Sarawak and a few related groups on the middle Kapuas have retained their short skirts, but almost all Orang Ulu, Lun Bawang, Kelabit, Murut and Kadazandusun ladies now cover their legs. There is a trend towards the *kebaya* suit, which can be bought ready-made from Kalimantan. This is an ankle-length tailored sarong with a frontal pleat or overlap, teamed with a well-fitting long-sleeved jacket of bright blue, maroon or black plush, thickly encrusted with traditional motifs in gold braid, glittery sequins and embroidery beads.

When traditional costume is called for, some men, particularly in Sabah and east Sarawak, opt for long black trousers with matching gold-braided jackets or tunics. In other areas, the undoubtedly traditional loincloth has become something of a touchstone – does he, or doesn't he, dare to wear it? If he does, will he wear it over a pair of (very visible) shorts, or over bikini briefs? Many men feel more comfortable in jeans or slacks, topped off by a colourful waistcoat of bark or hand-woven cloth and the traditional hat of their own group.

Being too conscientiously traditional can be an embarrassing thing. Male dancers at the Sarawak Cultural Village complain that they are frequently

TOP LEFT: Ladies dressed for an important occasion in 'modern traditional' costumes. The second and third from the left wear Kelabit costumes while the rest are in Orang Ulu ones.

TOP RIGHT: Bidayuh man wearing a traditional loincloth and his grand-father's warrior beads. He is pouring *tuak* rice wine from a gourd.

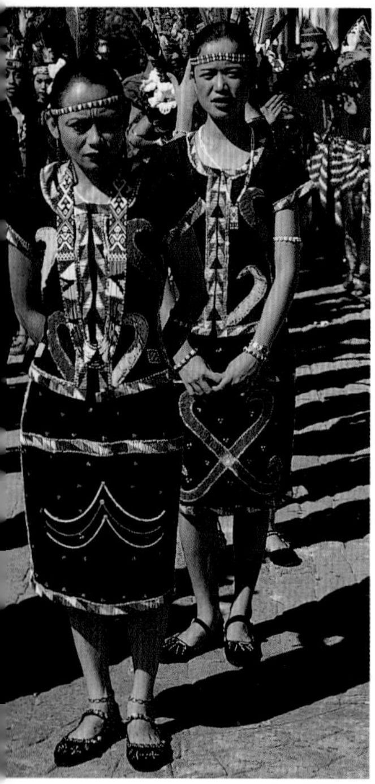

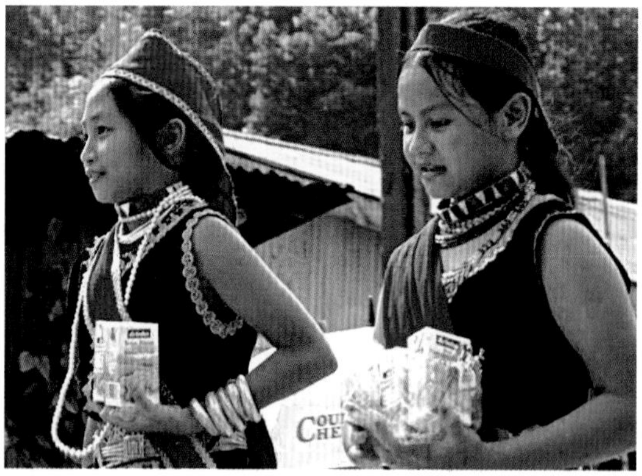

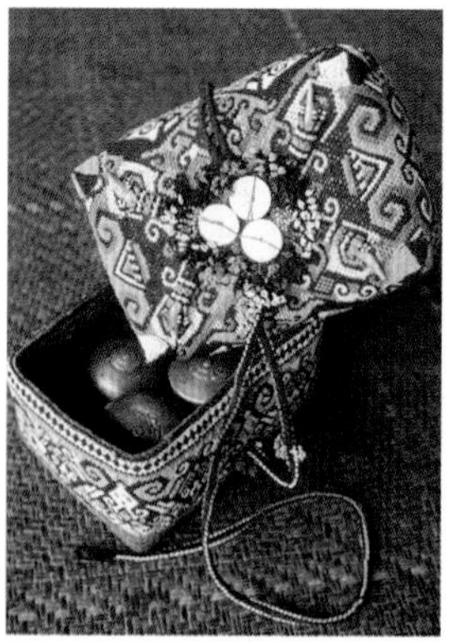

ABOVE: Murut girls from west Sabah dressed in 'modern traditional' finery.

CENTRE: Bidayuh girls dressed for a festival and wearing finely-worked seed-bead chokers.

RIGHT: Orang Ulu betelnut basket from the Ulu Mahakam, covered in beadwork.

annoyed by tourists asking them the Scottish Question: "Anything worn underneath?" One Kalimantan compromise consists of slacks or jeans with a loincloth front and tail tucked into the belt like an apron so it hangs down fore and aft.

Beads, too, are affected by fashion changes. For one thing, the rules regarding the use of beads have become very liberal. What used to be "restricted" beads, to be worn by priests and priestesses, are now part of traditional costume. New beads are happily worn instead of the valuable old ones. Seed beads in every colour of the rainbow are fashioned into the hats, necklaces, shoulder yokes and garments that were formerly restricted both by ritual considerations and by the scarcity of the material.

BEADWORK

Small opaque glass beads of varying sizes, from peppercorn to mustard seed, have been used in Borneo since the earliest days of maritime trade. They are still very popular. A traveller who crossed Borneo on foot in the late 20th century took along several kilogrammes of seed beads to pay guides and helpers at the rate of one tablespoon per day. Within the last two centuries, seed beads sold in the trading radius of Singapore originated mostly from Italy, Bohemia, France and England. Japan and South Korea have joined the ranks of seed bead exporters since World War II.

The most common colours of old beadwork artifacts are red/russet, white, yellow and black, the hues of the majestic hornbill's huge beak. Muted blues and greens were added to the palette in the late 19th century. Whether this choice of colours reflected the craftswomen's preference or the availability of the materials, it is now impossible to say.

In most communities, seed beads are used to embellish clothing, fashion personal ornaments and make or decorate items for daily use. If the whole item is made, actually strung, of seed beads, it is called "beadwork", as distinct from "bead embroidery", which is stitched onto a backing cloth.

One fairly localised technique found in Ulu Bahau in north-west East Kalimantan and adjacent areas is to cover a bark cloth jacket with stitched-on bead strings, fixed to the backing at intervals of about 10 cm. The overall effect is that of a beaded chequerboard.

Unlike protective or healing beads worn on a string, beaded garments were long considered a luxury. Most people owned a few beaded garments for festival wear. Many of their tobacco-and-*sireh* (betelnut) pouches or boxes were decorated in some way with beads or bead tassels. Only the upper classes would have worn beaded headbands, skirts, loincloths and jackets every day.

The singer of an old Kelabit song mocks another woman, possibly a rival in love, in these terms:

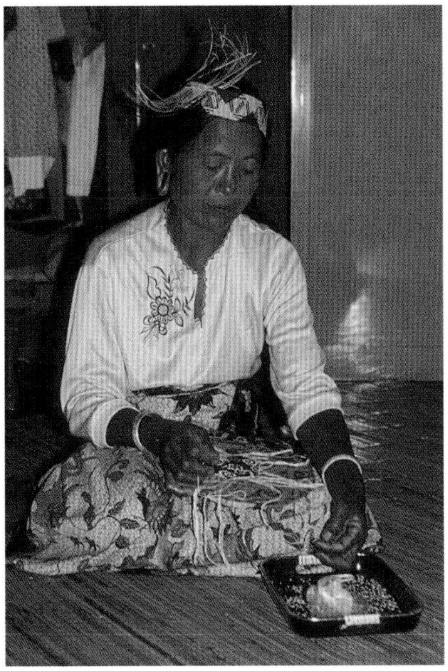

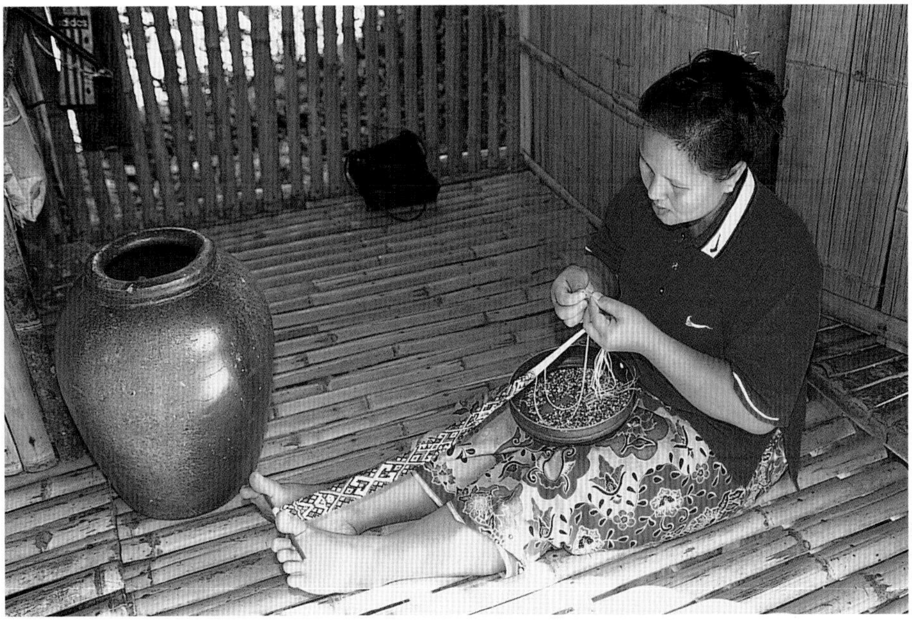

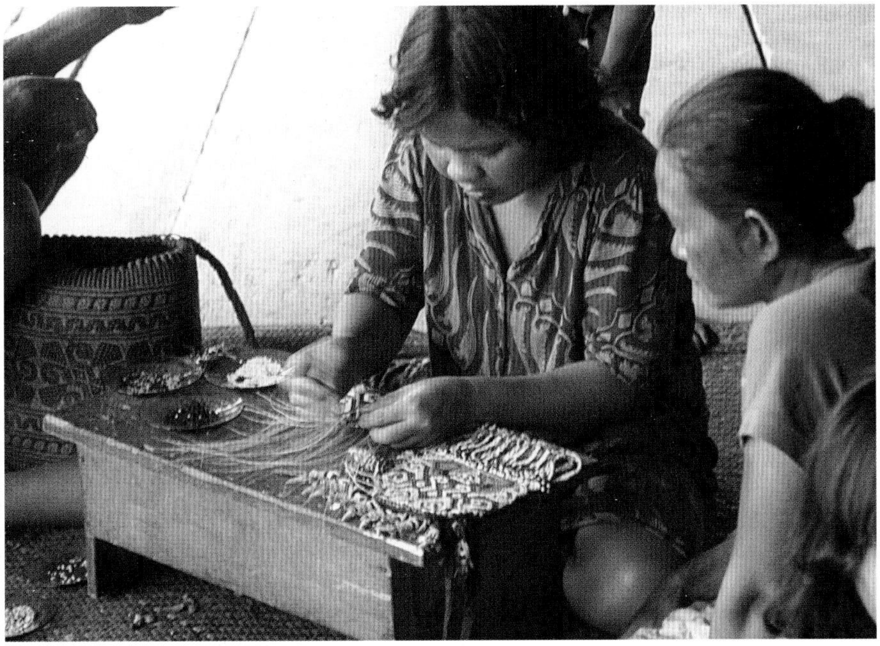

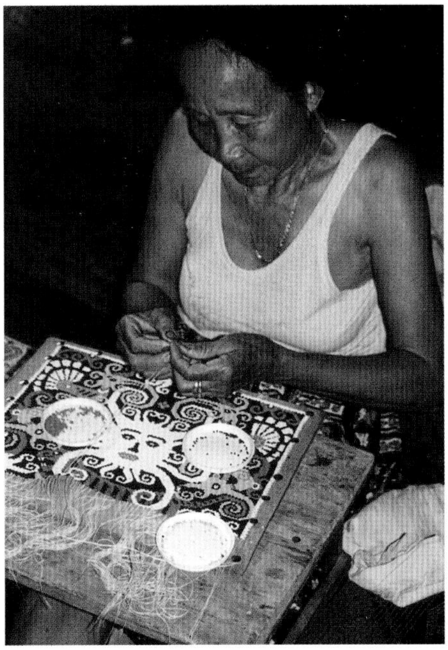

Ladies doing beadwork.
CLOCKWISE FROM TOP LEFT:
Punan Bah lady (Orang Ulu), wearing finely-worked rattan fillet headband; Rungus lady making beadwork bandolier; Orang Ulu elder; and Aoheng ladies.

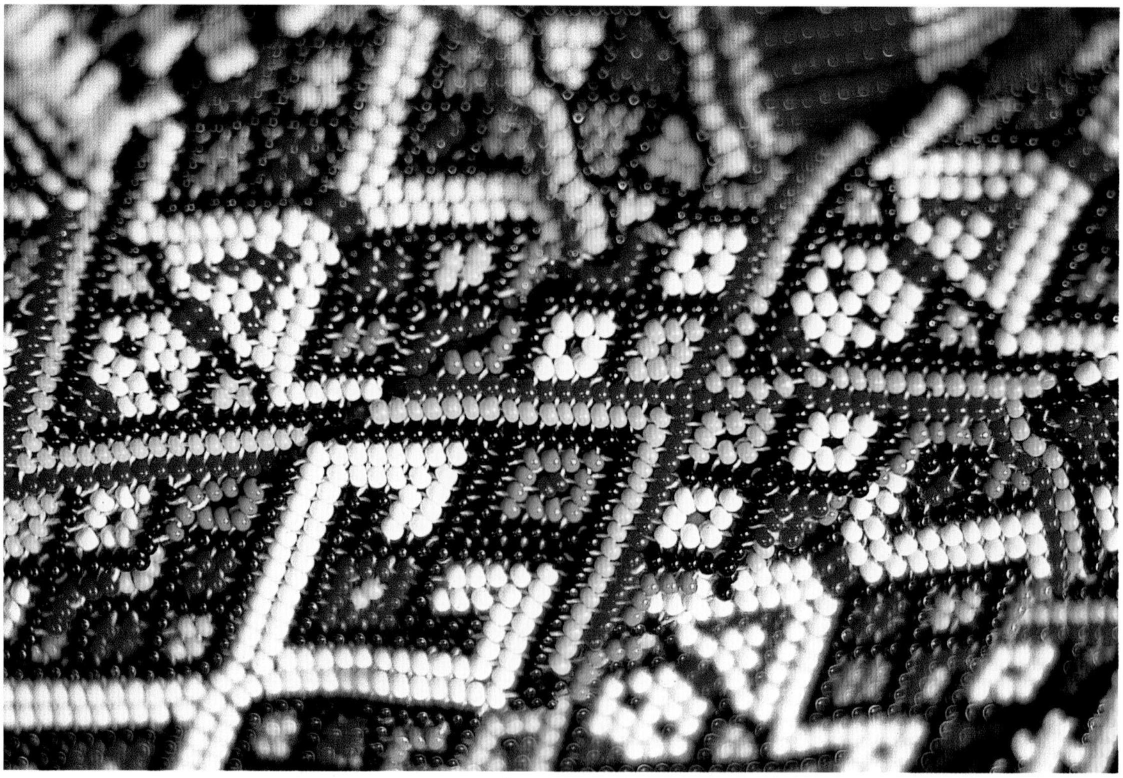

Rungus bandoliers made of colourful beadwork, which are becoming a Sabah icon on the Malaysian cultural scene.

Everybody has heard about how many clothes you have covering the floor so that you fall into piles of them piles of garments sewn with fine beads...

BEADWORK TECHNIQUE

To make the typical Borneo beadwork, seed beads of about 2–4 mm diameter are threaded on descending strands of fine thread. This is done without the use of needles. The thread ends are waxed to make them stiff enough to handle. The Orang Ulu insert one row of free beads – beads with only one thread through them – between the rows in which two strands are fed through each bead alternatively. The selection of variously coloured beads produces the pattern.

There are slight variations in technique. The Rungus of Sabah produce a denser fabric than most Orang Ulu by omitting the row of free beads. The Iban of Sarawak make shoulder yokes of bead net, each "mesh" five or more beads long, with a pompon edging. Most craftswomen use a wooden board as a working surface, often with the pattern carved on it or, more commonly now, a paper pattern pinned to it. In the case of the Orang Ulu, these patterns are usually designed by the men, though beadworking itself is done by girls and women.

Beadworking is common to all Borneo peoples, but the Orang Ulu of the high plateau in Indonesia and Kalimantan, and the Maloh in the upper Kapuas, may be considered the most prolific craftswomen in this field. Bead weaving on a dedicated loom is unknown in Borneo.

BEAD EMBROIDERY

Beadwork is done with either a stiff thread like pineapple fibre, or cotton thread stiffened by the application of wax. Bead embroidery can only be practised if fine needles and very fine thread are available. The Kadazandusun people of Sabah have a long

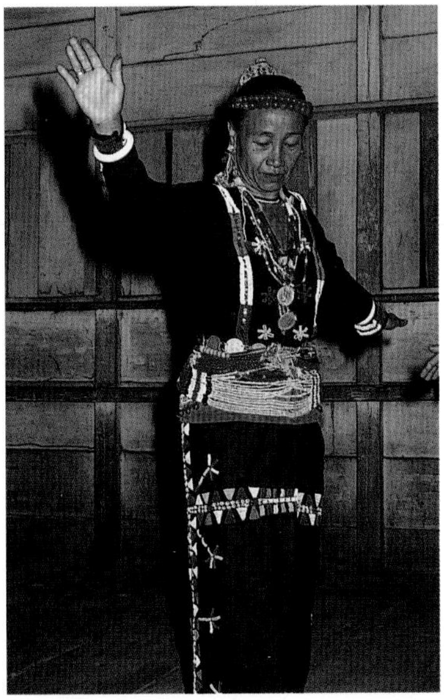

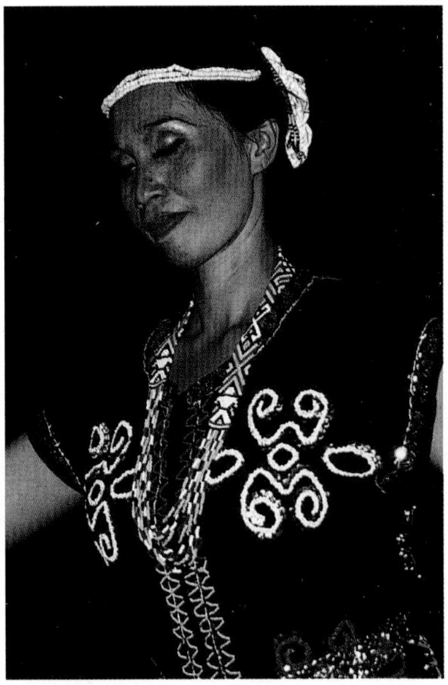

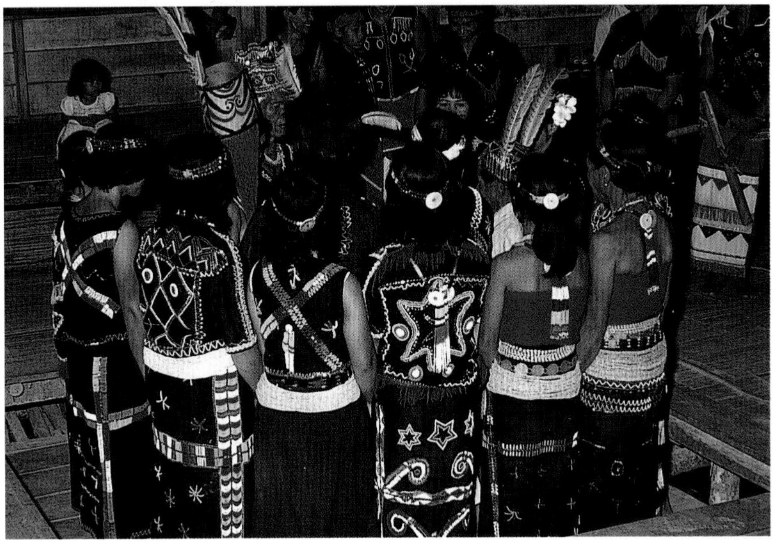

CLOCKWISE FROM TOP LEFT: Tagal dancer wearing bead-embroidered garments, carnelian headband, bead necklaces and ear dangles; lady in a modern adaptation of the Sabah traditional costume with strings of shell discs on her head and on the dress embroidery; Murut dancers wearing bead-embroidered garments.

tradition of embroidering women's skirts and hoods with shell beads, either filed-off cowries, or shell discs. Shell embroidery is also seen inland, both on clothing and on hats. Tradition credits this material with "cooling" properties, so individual shell beads or discs were kept for medicinal purposes too.

A modern development is the addition of sequins and spangles, sometimes in over-generous amounts, to "modern traditional" costumes, especially if they are used for stage performances. Under the bright lights, strong colours and decorations look better than the more muted materials and hues of traditional clothing.

There is a new fashion, introduced from central Borneo and Sabah, of embroidering garments with seed bead strings. Unlike traditional Chinese bead-embroidery, however, the beads are not stitched down individually, but in strung lengths of 3–6 cm. This technique was first used for ladies' tunics and sarongs, but it is easily adapted to decorate loincloths, hats, containers and even cushions, book covers and other similar souvenir items.

HEADGEAR

The men of Borneo frequently wear headgear of some sort, even if it is a cricket cap. In the bad old days of headhunting, hats acted somewhat like passports – a stranger coming down the forest path could

Drawing by the natural historian Carl Bock titled 'The Belle of Long-Wai'. The woman in the picture wears a tall, slightly tapered bead hat.

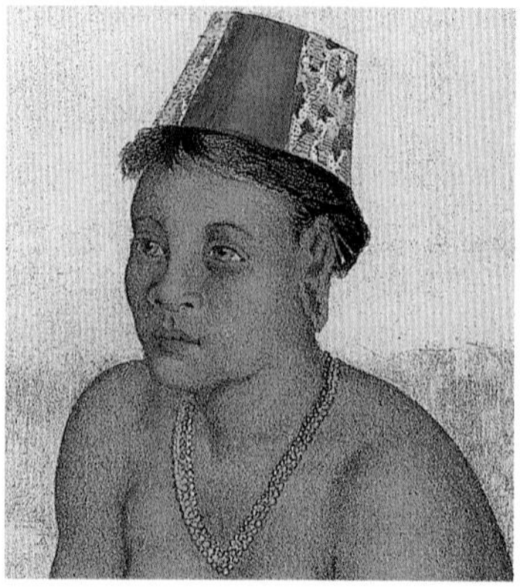

be identified as friend or foe at a glance. Even today, at Pan-Borneo Dayak gatherings, the many colourful hats worn identify their wearers.

Until quite recently, women wore their hair long, even if this style tends to hamper a busy housewife and farmer. The problem may be dealt with in two ways – hair is coiled into a chignon at the back of the head or restrained with headbands. A headband can be very plain – a piece of twisted cloth will serve the purpose. It is worn over the forehead and the hair brushed behind the ears or folded and tucked up inside the back of the band.

The older Orang Ulu ladies sometimes wear finely-plaited fillets of rattan; this is considered "plain" as opposed to the colourful bead items. Bead headbands and hats are worn on semi-formal or festive occasions to show the owner's status and wealth. Each group has its own distinctive style.

The headband of the Kenyah people in Apo Kayan and adjacent areas in Sarawak is about 7.6 cm (3 inches) wide, usually mounted on a plaited backing of palm leaf. It is worked of seed beads in the traditional patterns, which in the old days would have been restricted according to the wearer's social status. Today, anybody who has enough beads can make and wear a fancy headband or produce them for sale. Kenyah beadworkers like to add a decorative tassel at the back. This may be further ornamented with plastic flowers or metallic fringe.

Headbands for gala wear tend to be wider. They are not pushed down over the forehead, but worn like a crown, and comprise elaborate affairs of beadwork, tufts of white and red goat hair and little mirrors or gold fringe. These fancy confections are worn by dancers and lead singers at longhouse festivals. If a guest is invited to do a solo dance, a beaded hat or headband is quickly pressed on his head while he is pulled up from the floor and into the lamp-lit performing space.

An almost obsolete fashion among Kayan ladies is a tall, slightly tapering bead hat, mounted on a frame-work of rattan, lined with bark cloth. In East Kalimantan, many Orang Ulu have moved from the *ulu* highlands and live on the coastal plains, but they have carried their culture with them. Their hats, worn by men and women, are usually open at the top, concave like car tyres. The Pnihing style is distinguished by cylindrical knobs, also beaded, at the side or back. Beaded-over *kopje* (flat-topped velvet cap worn mostly by Muslim men) are occasionally seen in the markets of East Kalimantan, together with other beaded souvenir items.

The hat of the Bahau people is also worn by "downriver migrants" in coastal areas well beyond the catchment of the Bahau River. Occasionally found in the curio shops on the coast, it is a popular, if somewhat pricey, souvenir. This brimless hat of black or red cloth is strengthened by a rattan frame.

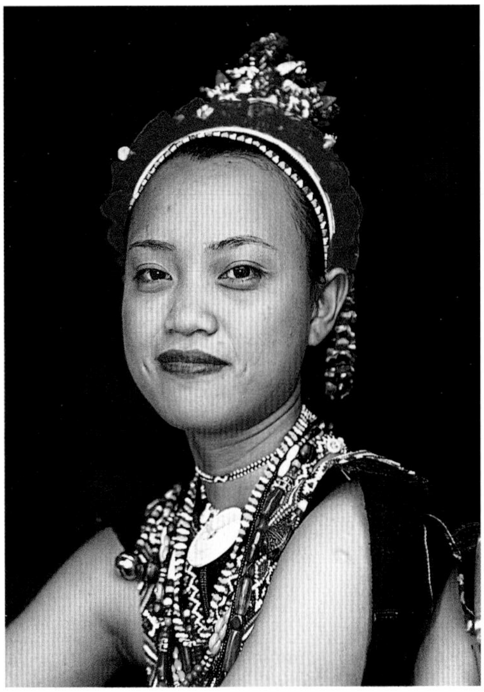

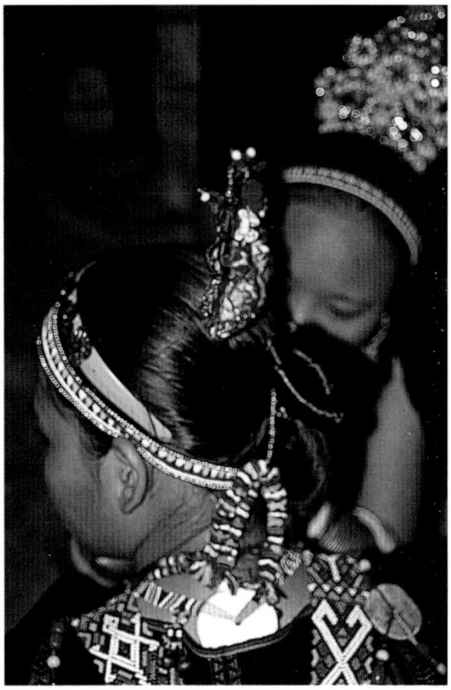

RIGHT AND EXTREME RIGHT: Front and back of the Rungus headdress. The headband is worn tightly around the hairline and fastened at the nape of the neck.

About 15 cm (6 inches) high and slightly tapering towards the top, it is embellished with blazes or panels of beadwork, trimmed with leopard teeth (genuine in old hats, fibreglass imitations in new ones) or bear claws pointing downwards and sometimes topped off with hornbill feathers.

The Tagal in west Sabah wear headbands of two or three strands of very chunky round carnelians, up to 3 cm (1.2 inches) in diameter. Semi-precious stone beads must have been available in the highlands at one time.

Not all headbands are needed to keep the hair out of the wearer's eyes. The Maloh of the upper Kapuas, the Rungus of north Sabah and the Lotud of Tuaran, Sabah generally dress their hair in chignons. They wear narrow beaded headbands to cover the hairline, fastened at the nape of the neck. This band is decorative, but it also serves a purpose: It holds decorative plumes, ranging from bunches of feathers to quite elaborate wooden "masts", which in turn hold bead and cloth tassels or feathers. Dancers in cultural shows tend to eschew the plumes, which may hold some ritual connotation, and stud their headbands with fresh or artificial flowers instead.

BEAD CAPS

The Kelabit, Saba'an and Lun Bawang ladies of east Sarawak, west Sabah and the adjacent parts of East Kalimantan share a unique bead fashion – the bead cap. This is either a very wide, fashioned headband with a hole at the top, or a hemispherical cap, entirely made of small and medium-sized value beads, but without any framework or stiffening.

This cap or *pata* illustrates the change in bead fashions. An older version of the Kelabit *pata* was made of long, heavy carnelian beads at the front, equally heavy shell beads at the sides, and cherry-sized glass beads at the back.

The "modern" Kelabit *pata* is of the same head-fitting shape, but the beads have changed. Long thin reddish-brown glass beads, locally known as *ba'o*

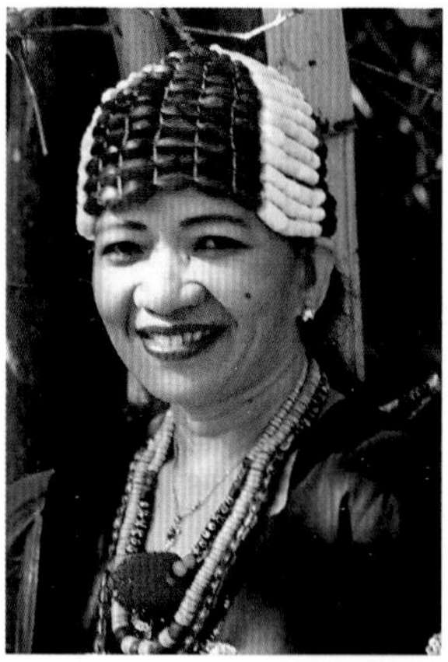
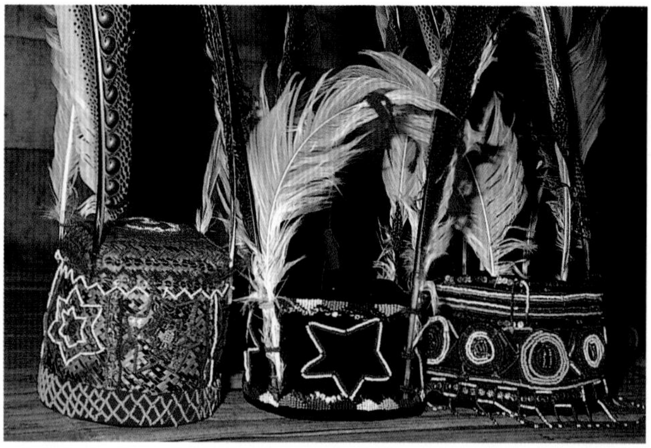
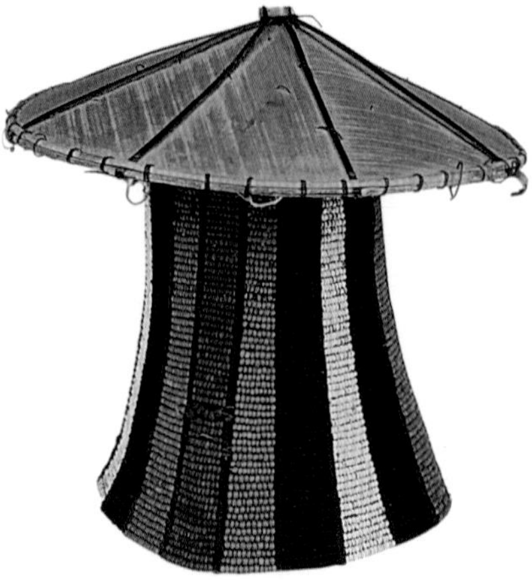

FROM TOP LEFT: Kelabit lady wearing bead cap with carnelian beads in the front; Murut men's plaited rattan hats with beadwork, bead embroidery and feathers; and Bidayuh priestess' bead hat from West Sarawak with glass beads strung on split rattan, a rattan frame and a palm-leaf hat top.

rawir, make up the front portion. The sides and back are of smaller turquoise, red or white beads, often with one row of home-made lead beads. The whole item is lighter than the old model if no cheaper – one genuine, old *ba'o rawir* bead can cost up to RM30 – and it takes at least 60 to 70 to make the front part of a *pata*!

The Saba'an ladies just across the border from the Kelabit highlands favour the same style, with the *pata* sometimes made of turquoise-coloured small beads. The Lun Bawang *pata* is made of opaque yellow glass beads, with contrasting side panels of long carnelians or their glass imitations. Unlike the Kelabit version, it is open at the top. Both types of *pata* were used to demonstrate status and wealth, and to hold the wearer's hair in place. The lady wraps her long hair around one hand, holds it against the back of her head, and tilts the cap over it.

Two distinctive kinds of beaded headgear were worn by the Iban ladies. One of these has disappeared, while the other is still used for special occasions in the area of the upper Rajang.

The first, obsolete one is described by a 19th-century traveller in this manner:

> Upon their heads was placed a piece of bead-embroidered cloth, in which were arranged thin skewers of painted wood about five inches long. There were about twenty of these bits of wood disposed about their heads, and each was attached to the other by strings of brilliant glass beads. Five or six of these many-coloured loops hung from each skewer, and they were intertwined into a graceful network.

This rather fragile arrangement had to be constructed each time a girl wanted to wear her finery. A few families still keep incomplete sets, with scraps of bead strings and cloth streamers linking some of the skewers. Elderly informants remember dimly that the skewers fitted into the perforations in a flat piece of wood that had to be strapped to the wearer's head, but only a few of them can recall ever having seen it worn.

The "*ulu* Rajang wedding hat" is slightly more stable, which may explain why it has stayed in use. Its centrepiece is a mast with horizontal yardarms, held in place by a well-fitting rattan cap. Long strings of seed beads dangle from this framework, almost covering the wearer's head. The ornament is cumbersome in the extreme, and forces the lady to move and walk very slowly. Sometimes she needs assistance as the bead strings obstruct her vision.

BEAD HATS

The distinctive Orang Ulu hats, hemispherical reedwork with quarter-brims fore and aft, are

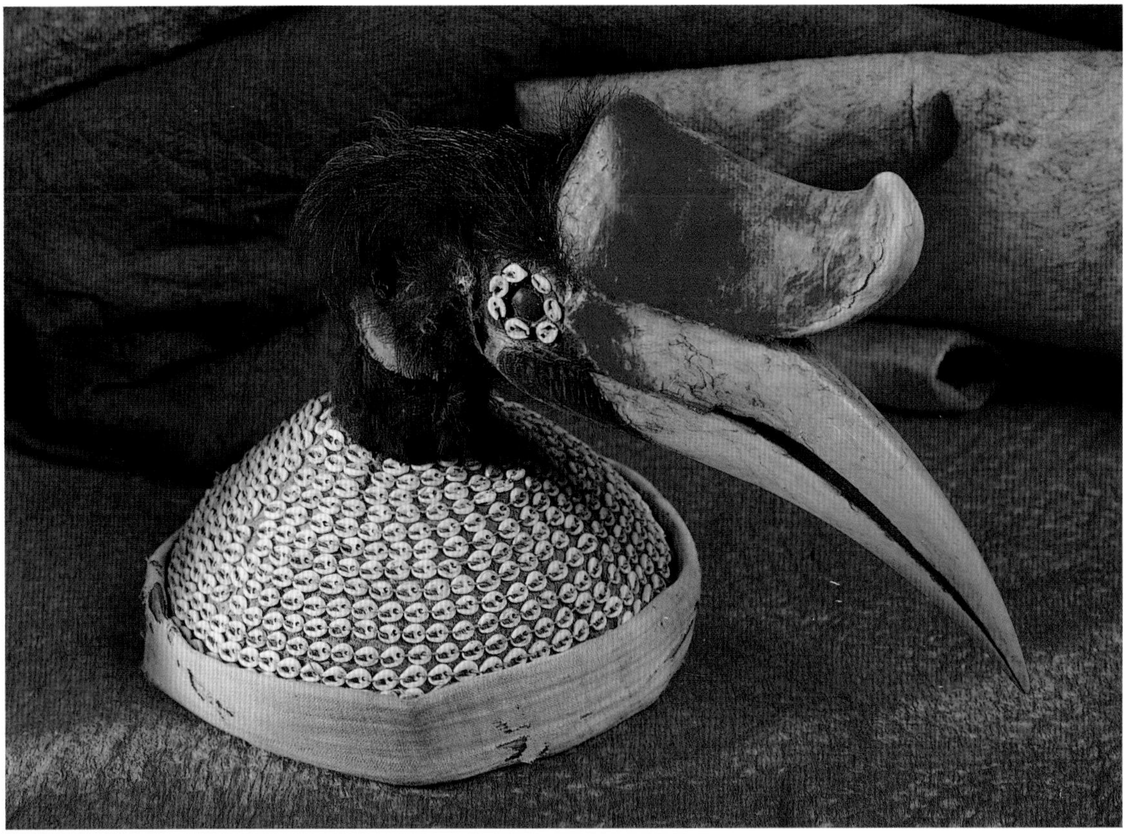

A rhinoceros hornbill's head decorates a Kenyah chieftain's skullcap, which is embellished with cowrie shell beads.

occasionally decorated with some beadwork at the front. The Kayan "war bonnet" is based on this hat. It is decorated with a frontal blaze of beadwork, and a rich complement of tufts of goat hair, beads or small mirrors. A set of spikes at the back may be studded with the feathers of the protected hornbill. The hat may have been used by warriors in the past. Today it is worn by both men and women at festivals, especially traditional weddings.

A common type of Iban man's hat is plaited of finely-split rattan. The hat's unique feature lies in its many-peaked shape. Other than this, the hat is not usually decorated except with argus pheasant feathers. There is, however, one fully-beaded specimen in the Sarawak Museum collection. The Murut of Sabah have taken to covering plaited rattan hats with beadwork and surrounding the lower edge with bead fringe. This seems to be a fairly modern development.

There are two well-known types of Melanau sun hat: One is made of broad panels of red, black and buff palm leaf, the other is plaited of bamboo skin strips. The palm leaf hat is worn by farmers and fishermen in their daily work. The more delicately worked, slightly smaller *terindak* Matu or *terindak* Sambas sports decorative plaiting and often decorative beading as well. It is a much sought-after souvenir item for collectors who want something more than the "common" shade hat. At festival times, the sun hat is sometimes surrounded by a bead fringe, but this is no longer common.

The spectacularly tall hats worn by the Bidayuh priestesses have already been described earlier. While the ritual specialists still don their distinctive

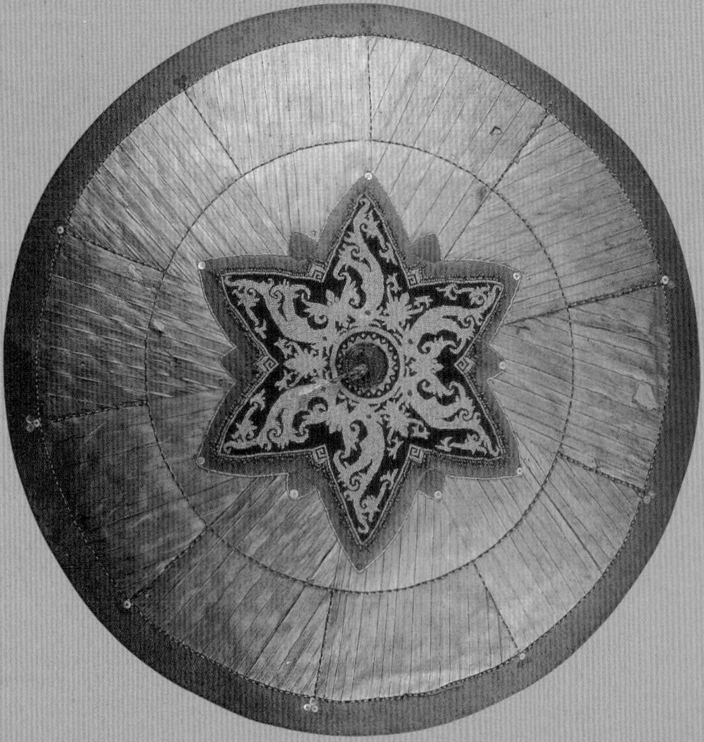

Sun hats of Borneo with beadwork. The base of the hats is made of palm leaves stretched over a circular rattan frame.

LEFT: Orang Ulu sun hat from Sarawak.

SECOND ROW: Kenyah sun hats of different patterns.

BOTTOM ROW, FROM LEFT: Kenyah hat tops with four 'faces', dragon and two 'faces' motifs.

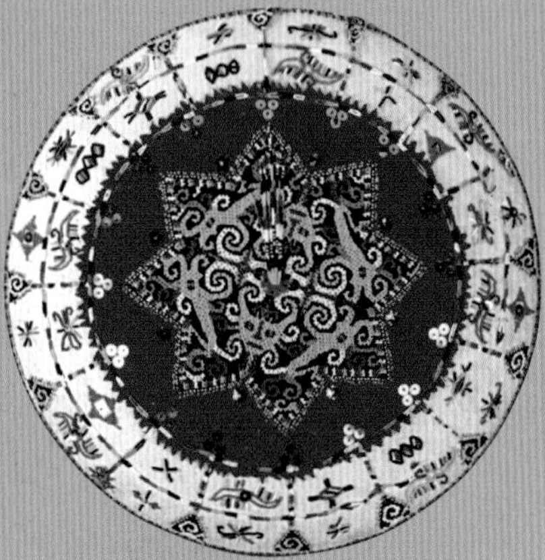

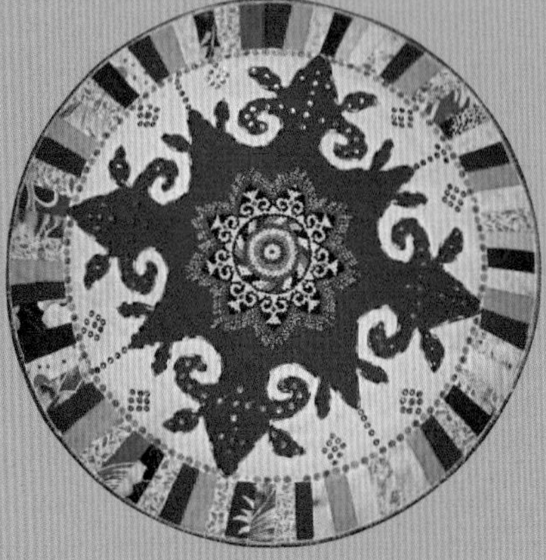

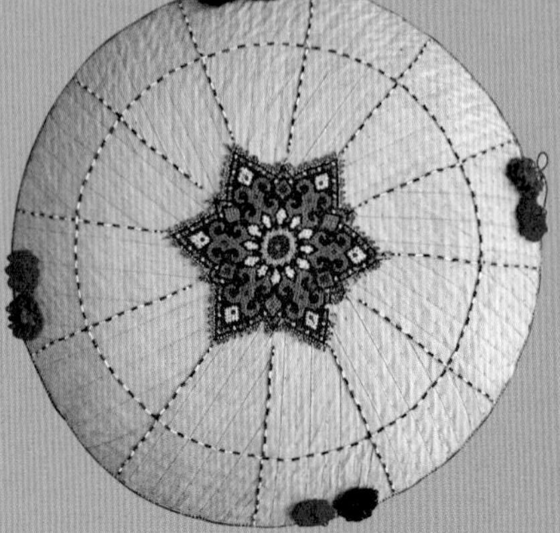

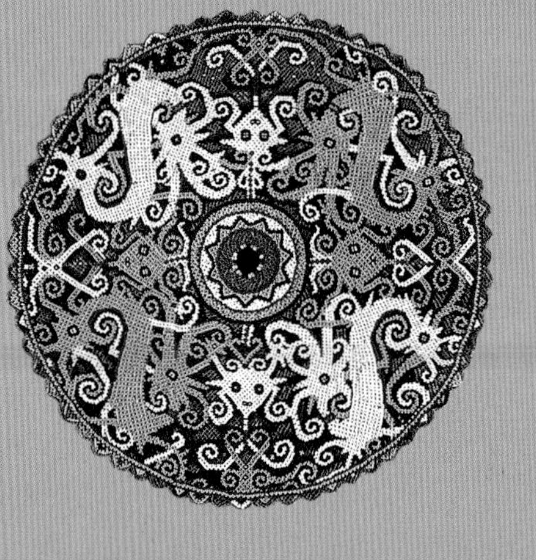

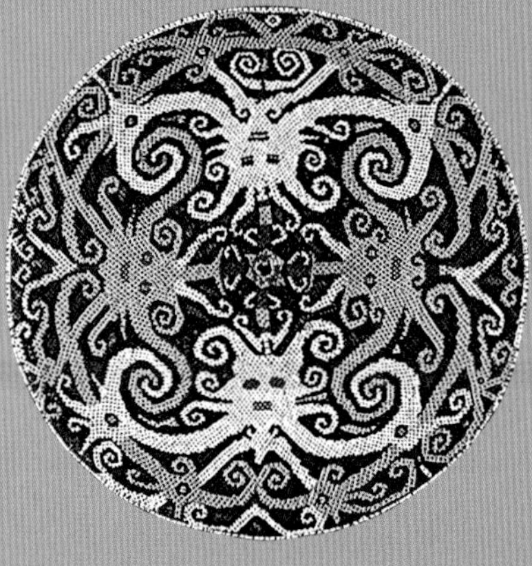

RIGHT: Kenyah hat top featuring old beads.

SECOND ROW, FROM LEFT: Kayan sun hat from Long Laput, Sarawak; the Melanau *terindak* Matu sun hat, which is plaited of finely split and dyed bamboo strips; and the Lun Bawang hat, which is coiled of root fibre.

BOTTOM ROW, FROM LEFT: Detail of Kenyah bead hat; and detail of late 19th century Kayan man's bead cap from the Ulu Mahakam.

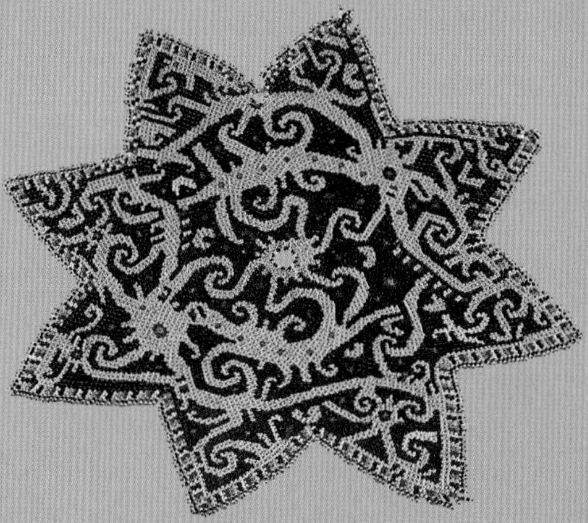

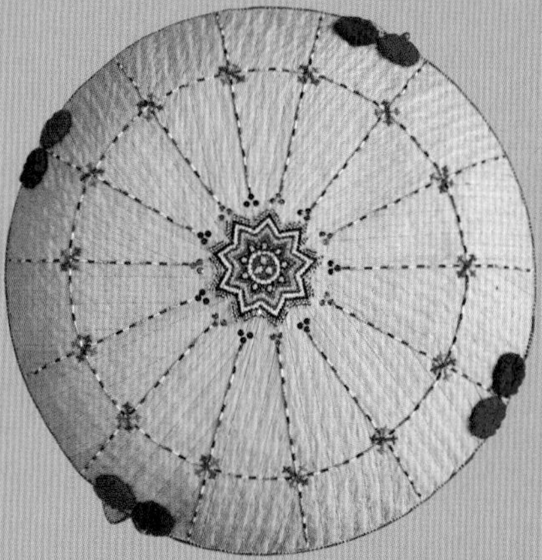

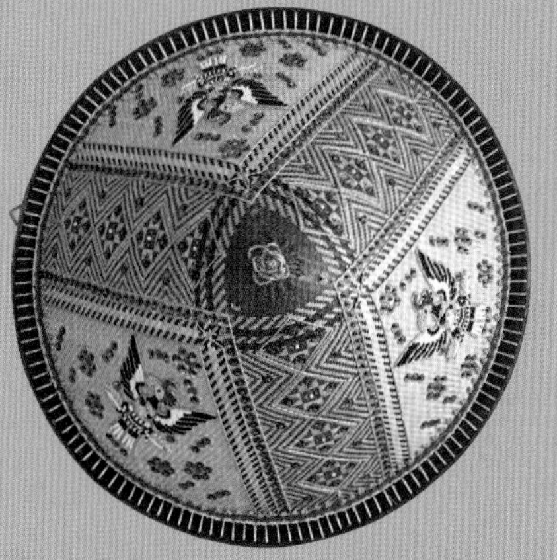

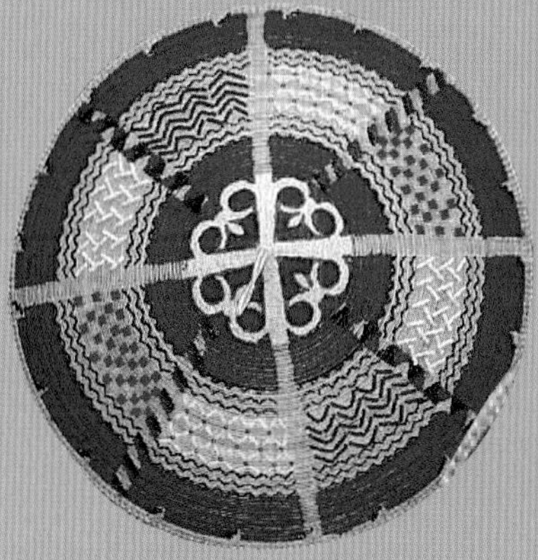

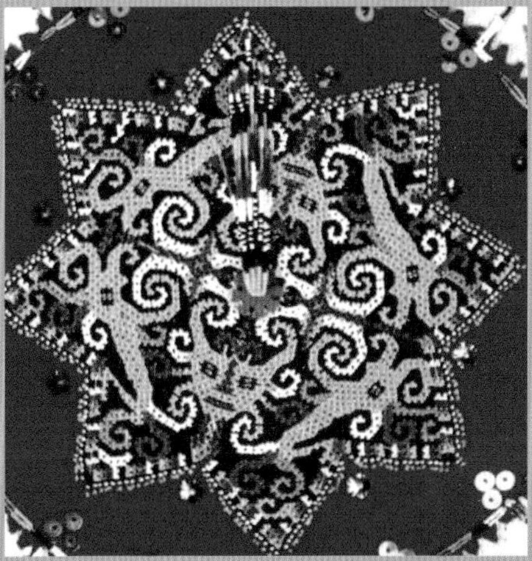

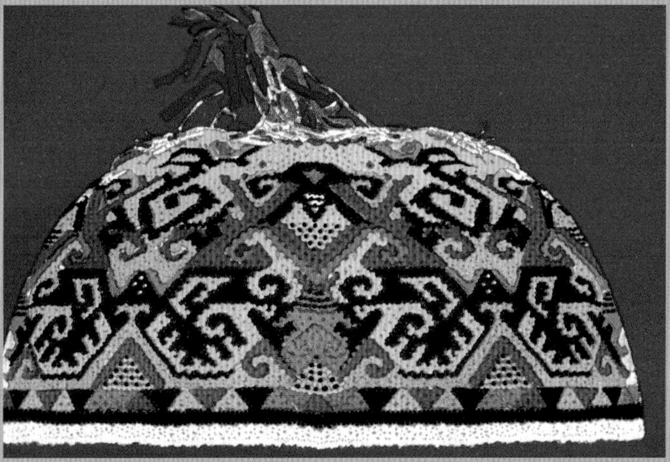

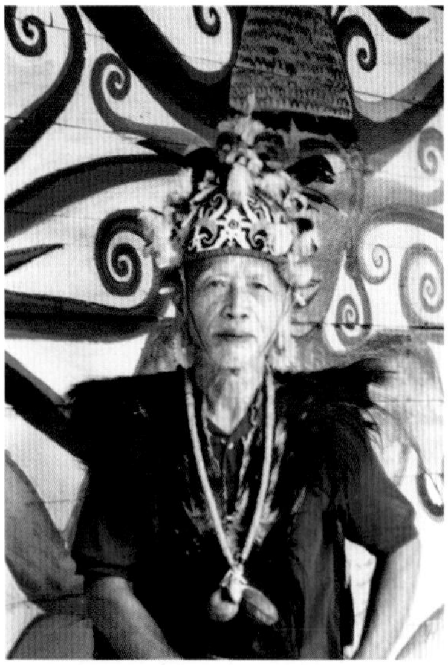
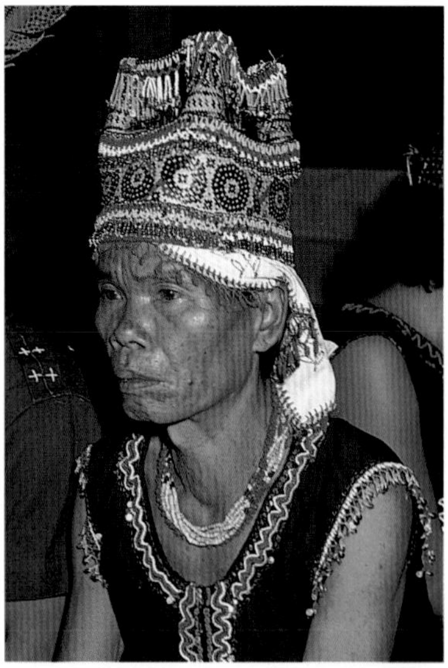
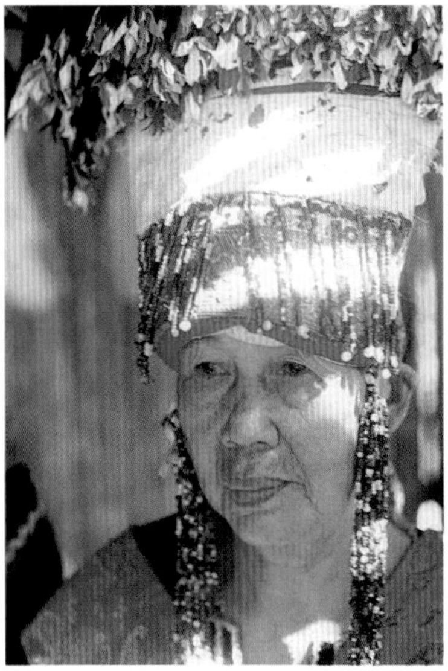
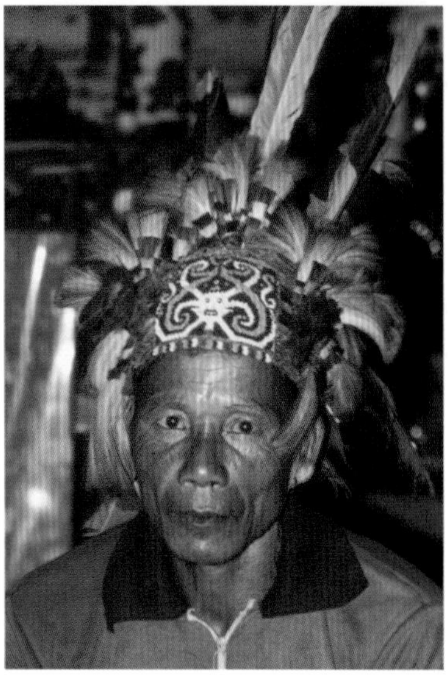

CLOCKWISE FROM TOP LEFT: Kenyah man wearing war/dance cap; Murut man wearing lavishly-beaded hat and vest; Aoheng man from the Ulu Mahakam, East Kalimantan, wearing war/dance cap; and a Kadazandusun priestess of Penampang, Sabah wearing her ceremonial half-hat.

headgear for ceremonies, young people are no longer afraid of making replicas of them for use in costume parades, cultural shows and the like. These new artifacts tend to be more colourful than the old ones, with the traditional red-black-yellow palette augmented with every hue of the rainbow and enhanced with sequins, bugles and gold beads.

The same fate has befallen the towering half-hat of the Kadazandusun priestess of Penampang, Sabah. There are scattered records of brides wearing the feathered headdress, but today it is either a fairly old specimen worn at harvest ceremonies by authorized ritual experts, or a new one, made-to-order for a cultural show.

Some observers deplore this "secularisation" of formerly restricted clothing and ornaments. But not everyone agrees. The old tribal religions are disappearing fast, but with this newly-adapted use of the associated costumes and artifacts, at least one part of the material culture has been salvaged and carried over into the 21st century.

EAR DANGLES

Most Dayak men used to wear ear ornaments of some kind. The "ear weights" of lead or brass, which stretch the ear lobes right down to the shoulders in some cases, were common to both sexes among the Orang Ulu. Men also used to perforate the upper lobe of the ear, and wear a set of leopard teeth in the holes.

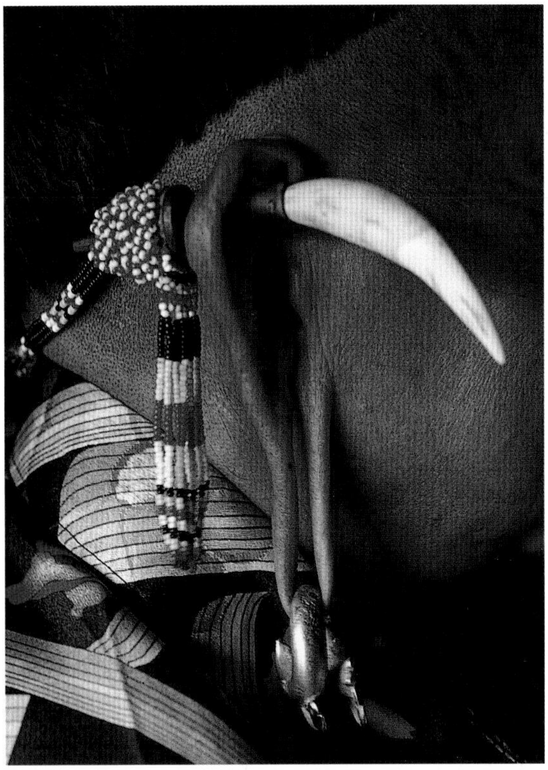

Kelabit man from the Bario highland in Sarawak wearing a leopard tooth in his ear as an ornament.

To secure these very valuable ornaments (if genuine), they were linked with strings of seed beads which passed behind the wearer's head from ear to ear. The teeth could be secured with bead tassels, which acted as counterweights, too. Occasionally, bell-shaped bead dangles were worn from the ear lobe.

Elaborate ear dangles were a young man's fancy. Middle-aged men might wear a set of animal teeth as signs of status and physical prowess, but not much colourful beady stuff. The weight of ostentatious ornaments tended to damage the ear lobe and the outer, cartilaginous ear top; deformed ears are not uncommon among the older generation.

NECKPIECES

The most obvious way of wearing beads is around the neck – either one very special bead on a string, a necklace, or a many-stranded neckpiece. Ritual beads included all and any of these styles. They have been reproduced for "modern traditional" wear, and for sale.

Designers and artists base their creations on ethnic designs. The rigid, claw-studded Biatah bead collar of west Sarawak is one such example. Bead bandoliers were worn by the Jagoi of Sarawak and the Rungus of north Sabah; both styles are now reproduced without fear of ritual prohibitions.

The Rungus favoured two distinct versions – one, a string of long carnelian (or glass imitations) and other assorted beads centred on a large shell disc, and the other made of colourful beadwork. The latter is becoming a Sabah icon on the Malaysian cultural scene. Young ladies in south-west Sabah wear the Lotud necklace without fear of taboos, and silversmiths have begun to replicate the decorative silver "cones" that typify this ornament.

Seed bead necklaces are a modern development and are hugely popular. They come plain and fancy, with frontal tassels, bobbles, "bells" and knots, multi-stranded or intertwined. A beaded "rope" neckpiece has been recorded from the mid-19th century. The technique of working seed beads as a hollow tube has been adapted to many uses other than personal ornamentation.

A very interesting case of adaptation is the beadwork yoke, strictly speaking a circular bead net edged with coloured wool pompons that has become almost a uniform with the Iban costume. F. Boyle, a traveller who attended a festival in Rumah Gasing,

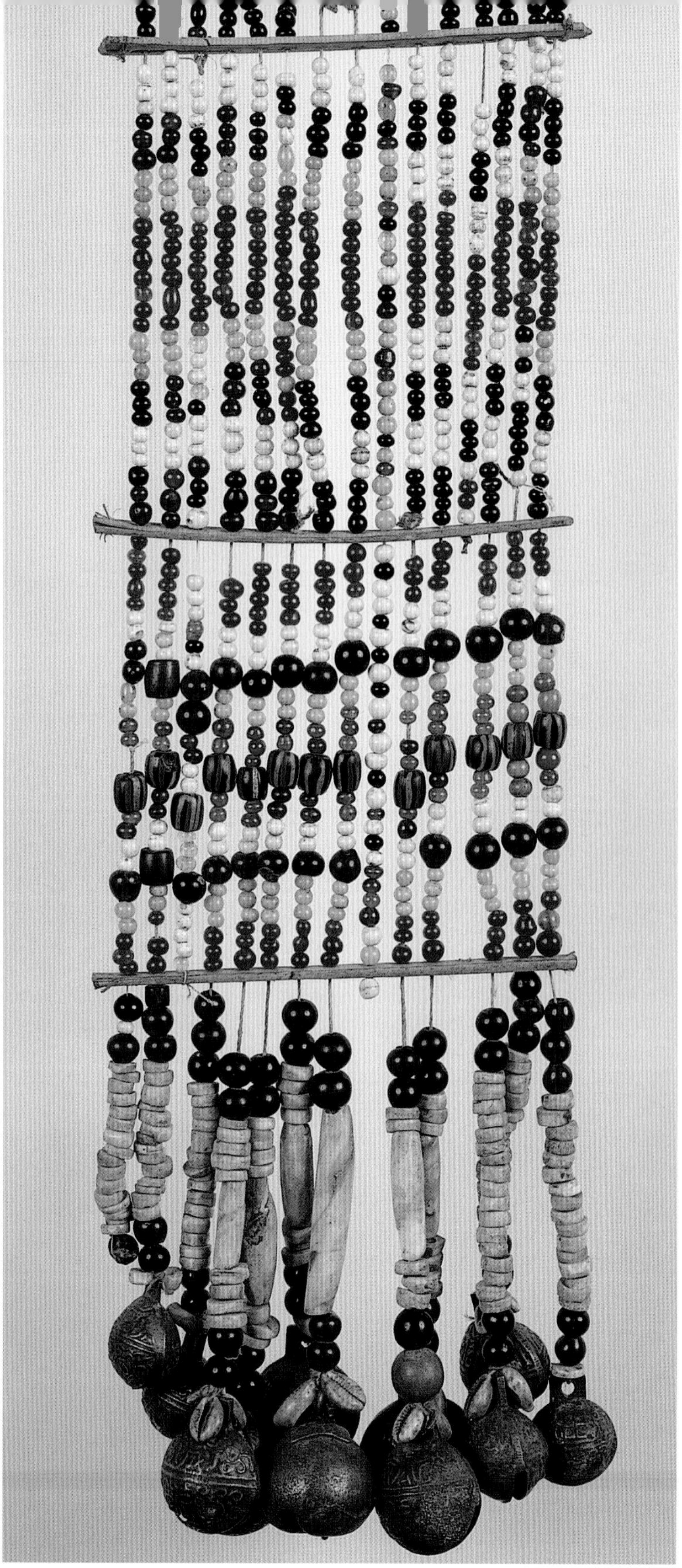

A 'bead tail' worn either separately or as part of a beaded collar by Iban women during festivals. It hangs from the wearer's shoulders down the back, and if it is long enough, the 'frog-head' bells trail and tinkle on the ground.

Sarawak, noted that the ladies "from the neck to the hips were covered over with large agate beads; string of them was heaped on string, till many of the women were cuirassed an inch thick in solid stone before and behind..."

This was in the 19th century on the river Skrang. On the upper Rajang in central Sarawak, an elongated version of the same fashion still exists. An over-dress is constructed entirely of carnelian and pea-sized monochrome beads. The bead strings are vertically connected to keep them from tangling and to give some stability to the garment which can weigh up to 15 kg (33 lbs)!

The ladies of the Skrang and Saribas areas, however, either got tired of carrying such loads even in the cause of beauty, or they had easier access to colourful new seed beads. A bead yoke, similar in shape to that described by Boyle, was constructed of light, colourful bead strings. To keep the artifact from unravelling, the end of each descending string was stopped by tying on a bunch of loom cut-offs. In the days when every woman was a weaver, this was an obvious source of spare thread.

By the mid-20th century, weaving was no longer common, but coloured wool could be bought in the main townships, and the arts of crocheting and pompon-making spread through needlework classes in school or the handicraft efforts of the Women's Institute.

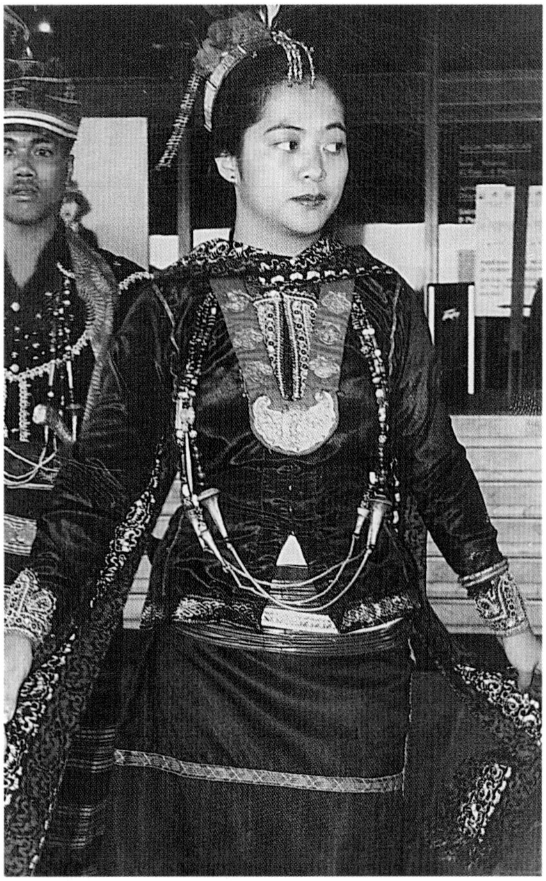

Woman wearing Kadazandusun Lotud necklaces with silver cones. Photo taken in the late 20th century.

ARMLETS

Beads were and are tied to people's wrists, but this tends to be for ritual purposes. The current knotted and beaded "friendship bracelets" exchanged by school girls are a modern craze imported from youth magazines and, of course, the Internet. Of such fads are "modern traditional" styles born! The Lun Bawang used to make sets of bracelets, carefully fashioned to fit a lady's forearm from wrist to elbow, but these are rarely seen.

BELTS

When bark cloth was generally worn, some kind of belt was needed to hold a woman's skirt up – bark cloth does not tuck and fold the way woven fabrics do. Those Orang Ulu, Lun Bawang and Murut who could afford such luxury wore heavy, many-stranded belts of precious beads. The lower classes, however, might have to make do with one or two strands, augmented by rattan hoops.

At longhouses today, bead sellers do a roaring trade with ready-strung belts of "new old" beads, i.e. replicas of old beads. Cultural associations also buy such items by the dozen to equip their dancing troupes.

One type of bead belt was made of hundreds of small shell beads, which were considered more valuable in the mountain regions, far from the sea. A district officer in coastal Sabah noted a visit by some Dayak traders from Sarawak in the 1920s, who had come to buy shell beads. Some of these probably ended up as belts while others were stitched onto black cloth skirts or hat tops.

Besides belts there are girdles described as "hip-lace", attached to the silver-ring corset of the Iban ladies, or worn from hip to thigh by the Rungus of north Sabah. They are strung of beads, but may also be hung around with silver coins, brass wire, hawks' bells or feathers.

GARMENTS AND GARMENT ADDITIONS

The Maloh of the upper Kapuas have a long tradition of making not just bead ornaments, but whole skirts, tunics and jackets entirely of beadwork. This requires great skill and access to

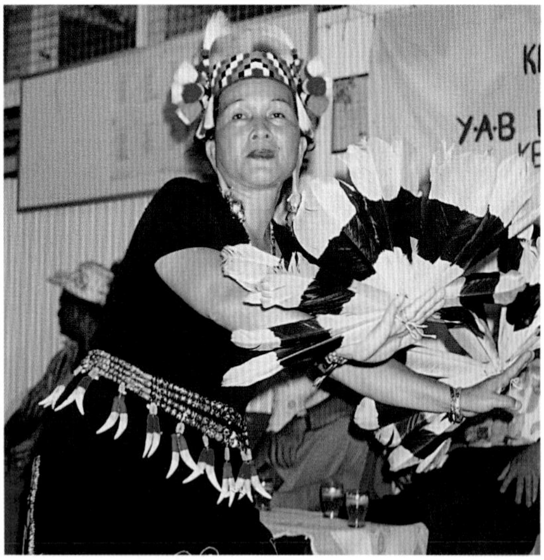

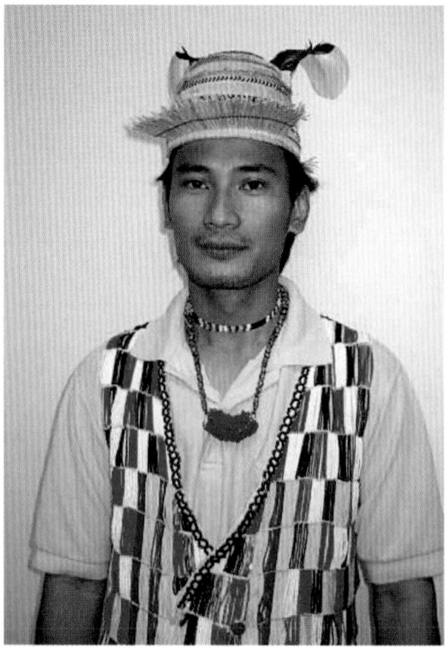

ABOVE, LEFT: A Kenyah dancer wearing a belt of 'new old' beads, i.e. replicas of old beads. At longhouses today, bead sellers do a roaring trade with ready-strung belts of such beads.

ABOVE, RIGHT: Kelabit man wearing a new 'chequerwork' bead jacket.

ample supplies. Even when tough pineapple fibre was used, the wear and tear of such cloth-backed beadwork garments was considerable. Once a piece of bead fabric is worn or damaged it cannot be patched like cloth. Usually it is unravelled, and the beads used to make a new item or smaller articles such as necklaces.

The beadwork garments currently owned by the Maloh community are used only on special, festive occasions. They are made mostly of new (less than 50 years old), brightly-coloured seed beads, though these may be mixed with older ones of more muted hues. The ornamental designs, however, are as intricate as ever. A Maloh or Taman skirt, even though it is quite new, is nevertheless still considered a collector's item!

Maloh skirts and jackets have been items of trade long before foreign tourists and collectors got into the picture. A fully-beaded skirt in a museum collection may be labelled "Iban", "Kantuq" or "Mualang" to indicate where it was obtained, but this does not necessarily mean it was Iban or Mualang work.

The Maloh's neighbours in the upper Kapuas region and the adjacent parts of Sarawak made skirts of handwoven cotton or black calico bought from traders, and embellished these with inset strips of beadwork. Such garments are still worn and made partly for festival use and partly for sale. They are easier to produce and more lasting in use than one made entirely of beadwork.

Some coastal people, including the Melanau and Bisaya of Sarawak, decorate women's tunics with beadwork insertions at the shoulder end of the sleeve. These strips are not more than 2 or 3 cm wide, adding colour to the sombre black or dark blue garments.

The loincloth, when worn for everyday use, is complemented by a stout reedwork "seat mat" which hangs down behind; it protects the wearer's posterior if he has to sit on damp or rough ground. For festival wear, this mat is lavishly decorated with beadwork, fringe, bugles and bells. According to one 19th-century traveller, a well-dressed young Iban man's outfit "jingled musically whenever he moved". The front and rear ends of a gala loincloth are often decorated either with needle-weaving or beadwork.

The Kelabit have a bead fashion which they may have borrowed from their neighbours and preserved

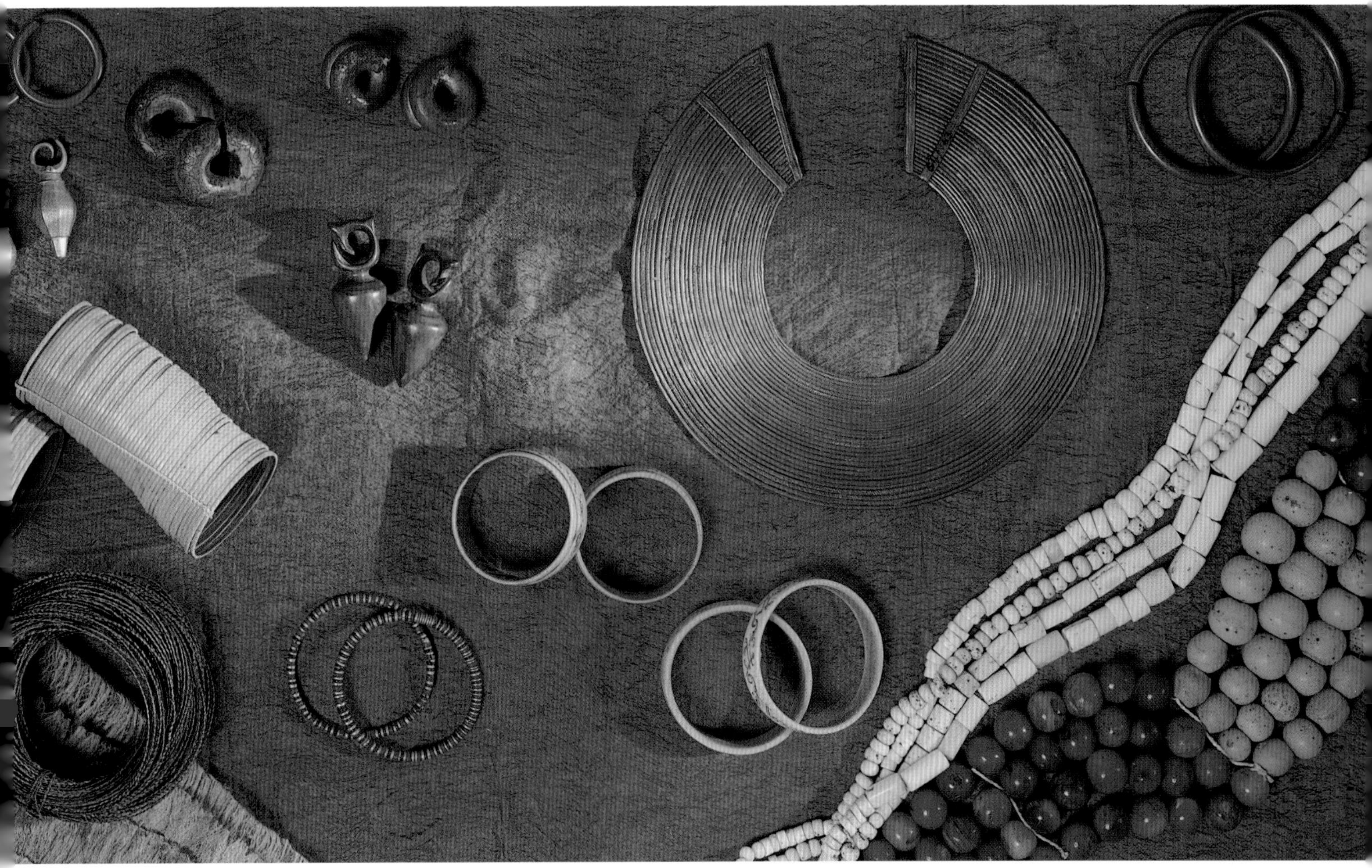

after the more fashion-conscious downriver people had abandoned it. The following is a traveller's commentary in the early 20th century:

> ...there is sometimes worn by the [Kelabit] women a chequered bead coat with bells around the fringe, being largely used on occasions of seeking good omens for crops. There is much evidence that Kenyahs at least formerly had such coats but have split them up to supply bead necklaces for everybody, as the Kelabit does with her 'Batta' head-dress...

This observation still holds true. Beadwork articles which are damaged or simply old-fashioned are often broken up and the beads shared out among those who have a claim to them, or they are re-worked into a new artifact. A few new bead coats of this kind have been made by enterprising Kelabit ladies, mostly to be worn by young men at festival times.

Borneo jewellery featuring ear rings and ear weights (top left), brass wire coils for arms and legs (centre left), fine creeper armlets (bottom left), polished shell bangles (bottom centre), brass wire collar (slightly right of centre); shell beads, and opaque white and red glass beads strung with spacers (bottom right).

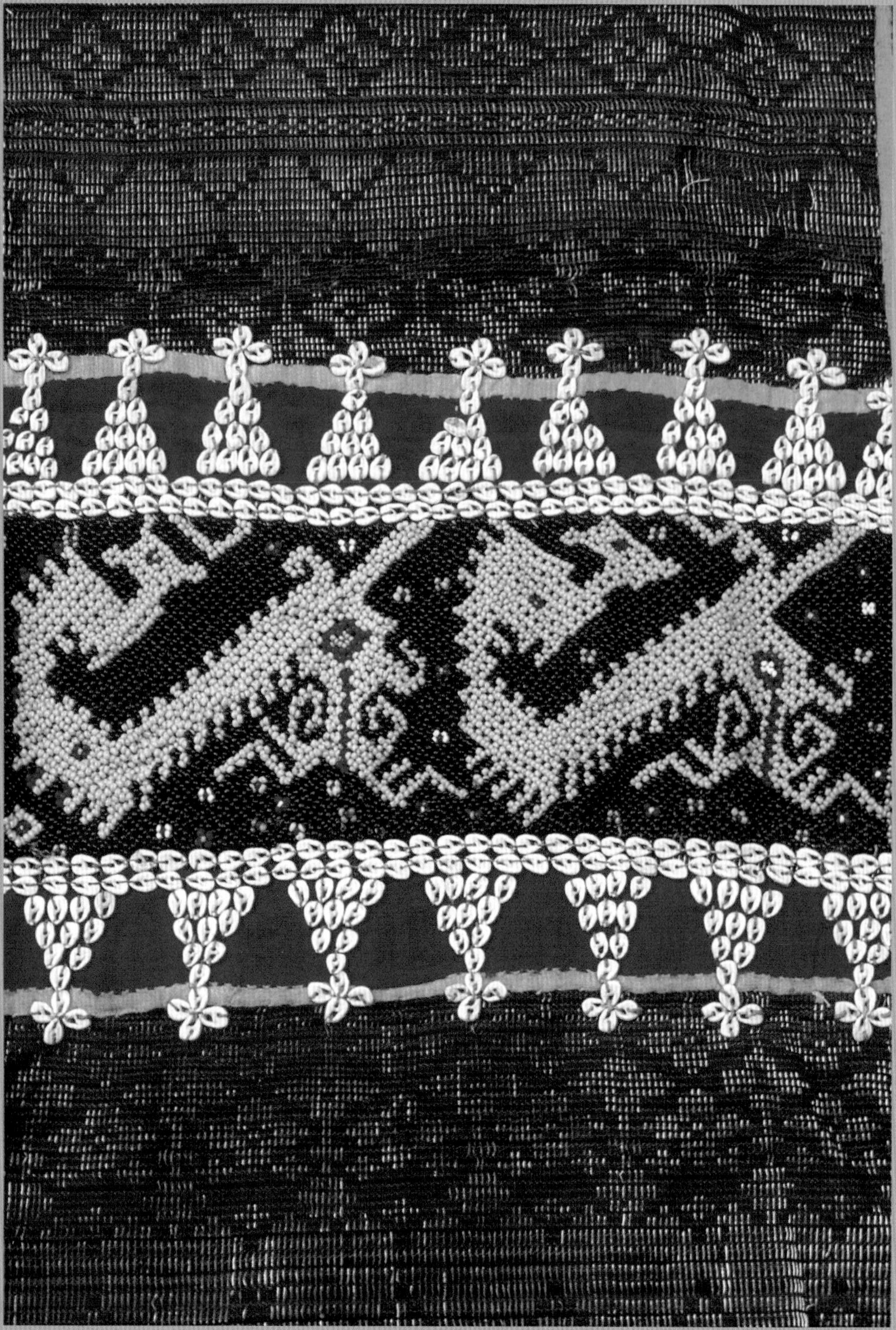

The Maloh of the upper Kapuas have a long tradition of making entire skirts, tunics and jackets entirely of beadwork.

LEFT: Maloh beaded skirt panel.

BELOW: Maloh beadwork skirt fringed with hawk bells.

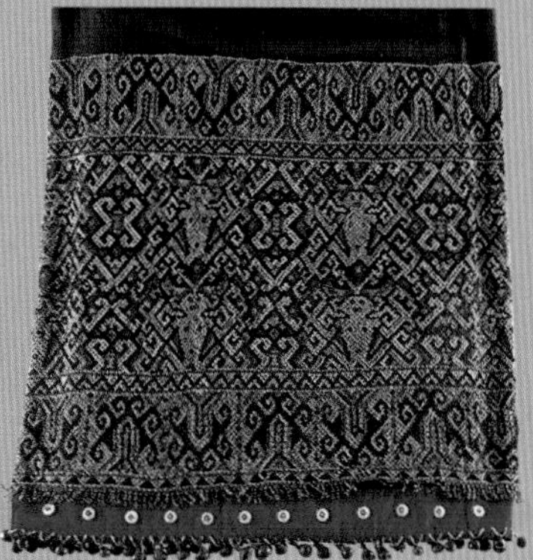

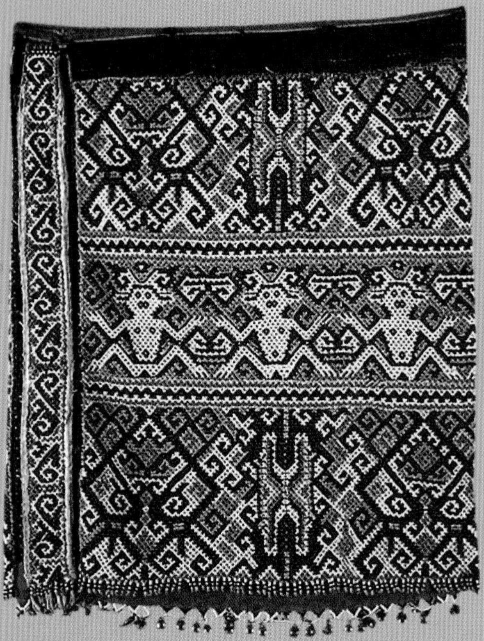

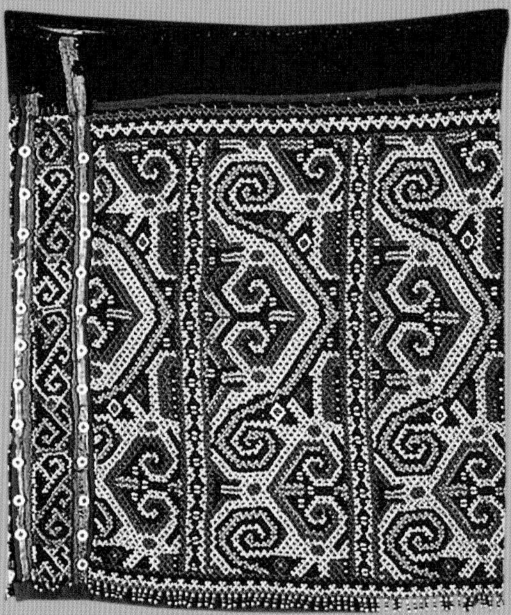

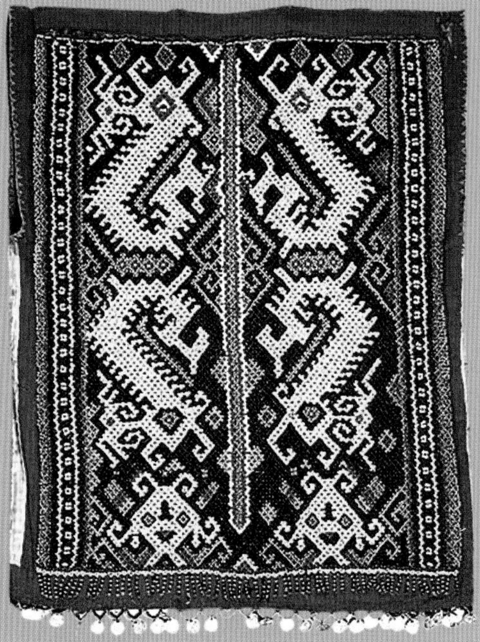

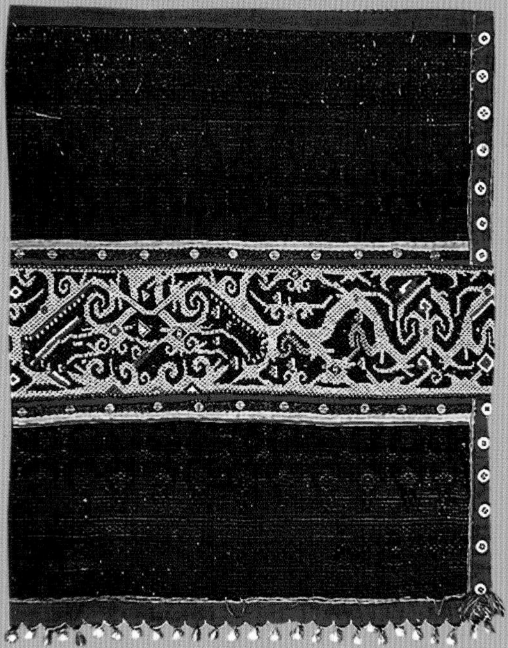

More Maloh beadwork garments. CLOCKWISE FROM TOP LEFT: Skirt with 'slaves' motif fringed with hawk bells; vest with dragon motif; skirt containing button decoration and fringe of hawk bells, and with beaded insertion featuring dragons; and skirt with dragon motif.

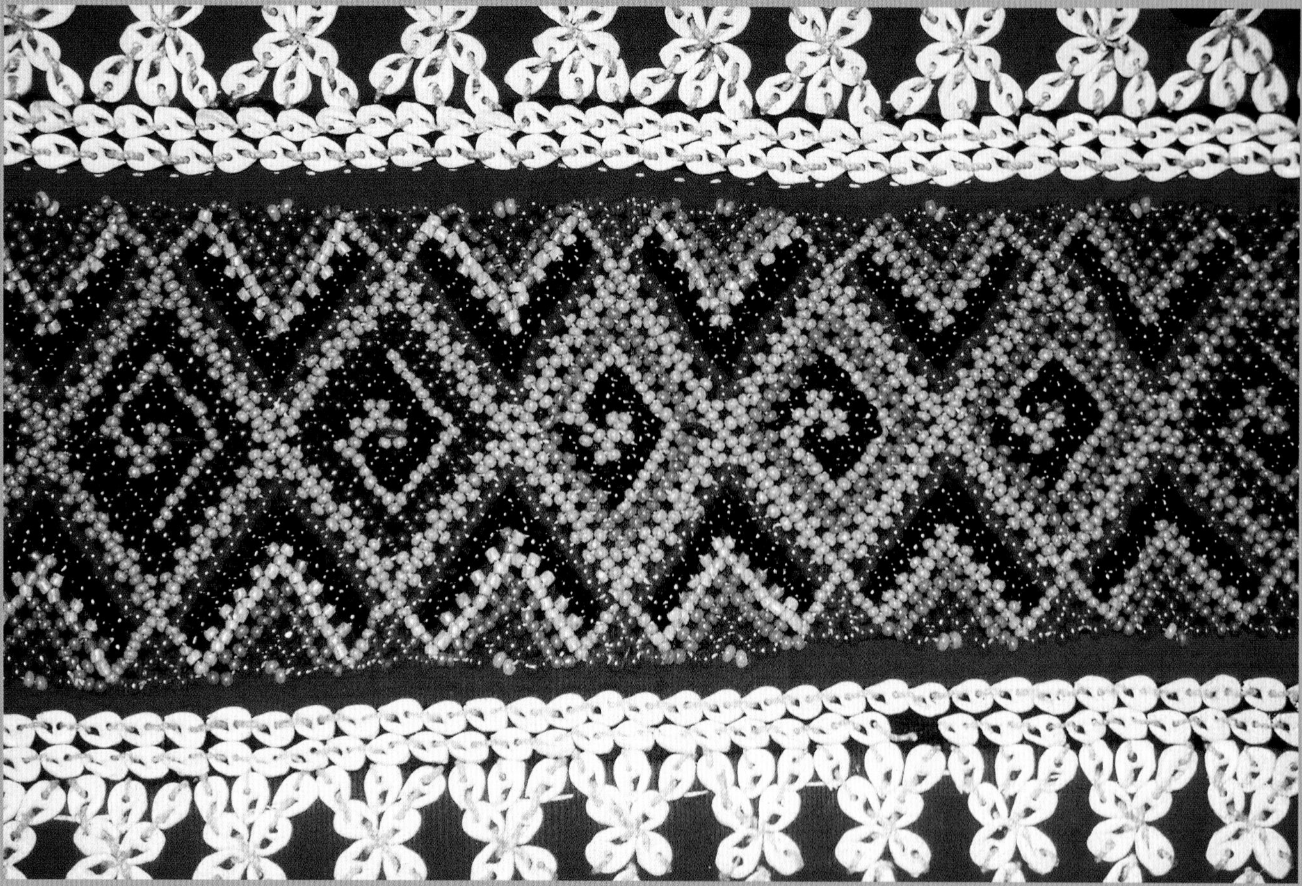

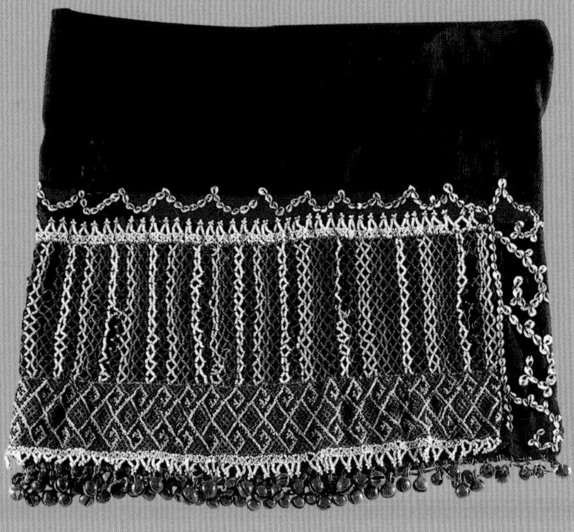

TOP: Beaded Iban skirt panel.

LEFT: Beaded Iban skirt with hawk bells.

OPPOSITE: Maloh woman's skirt with inset beadwork panel featuring 'slave' motif and shell embroidery.

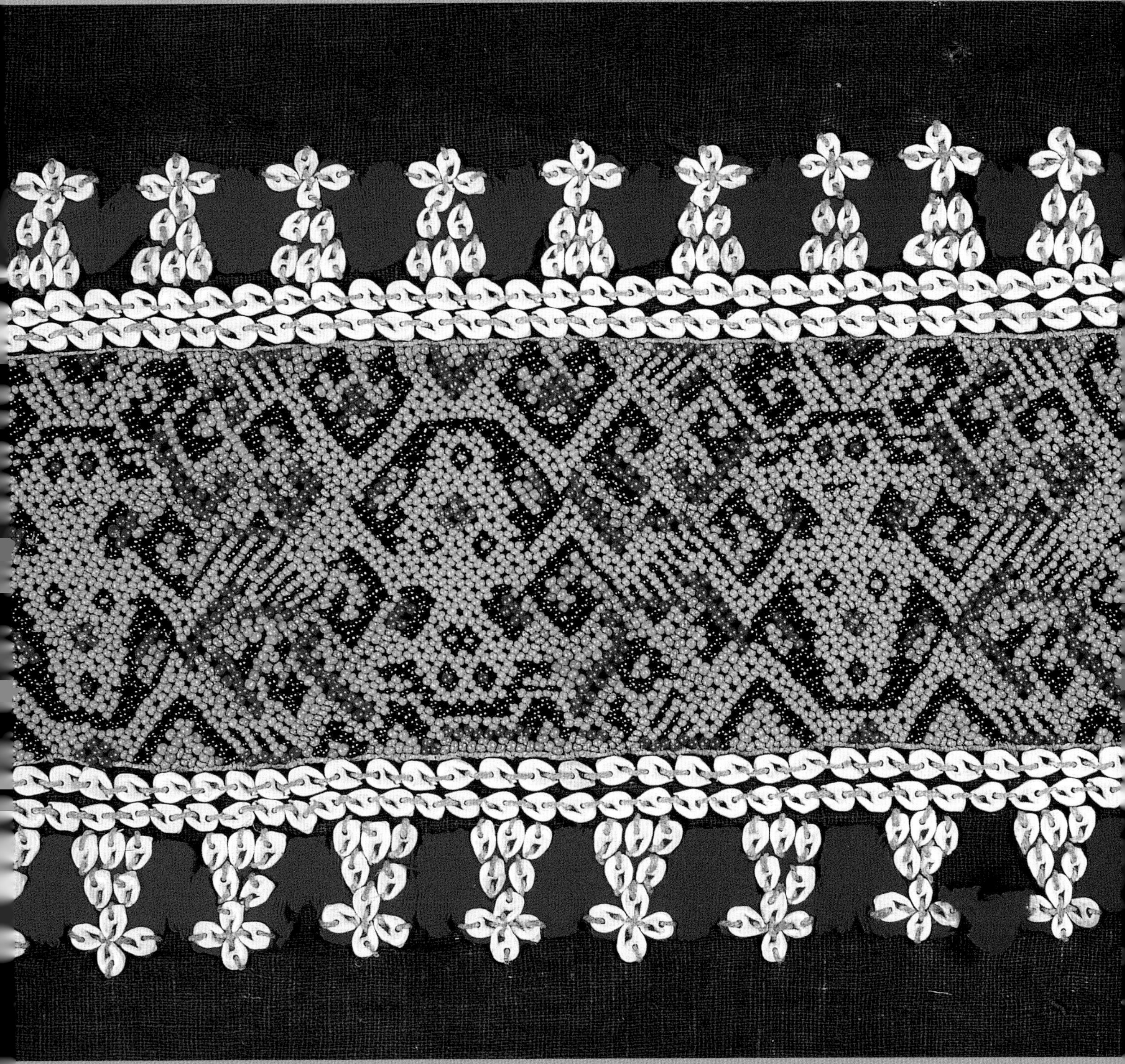

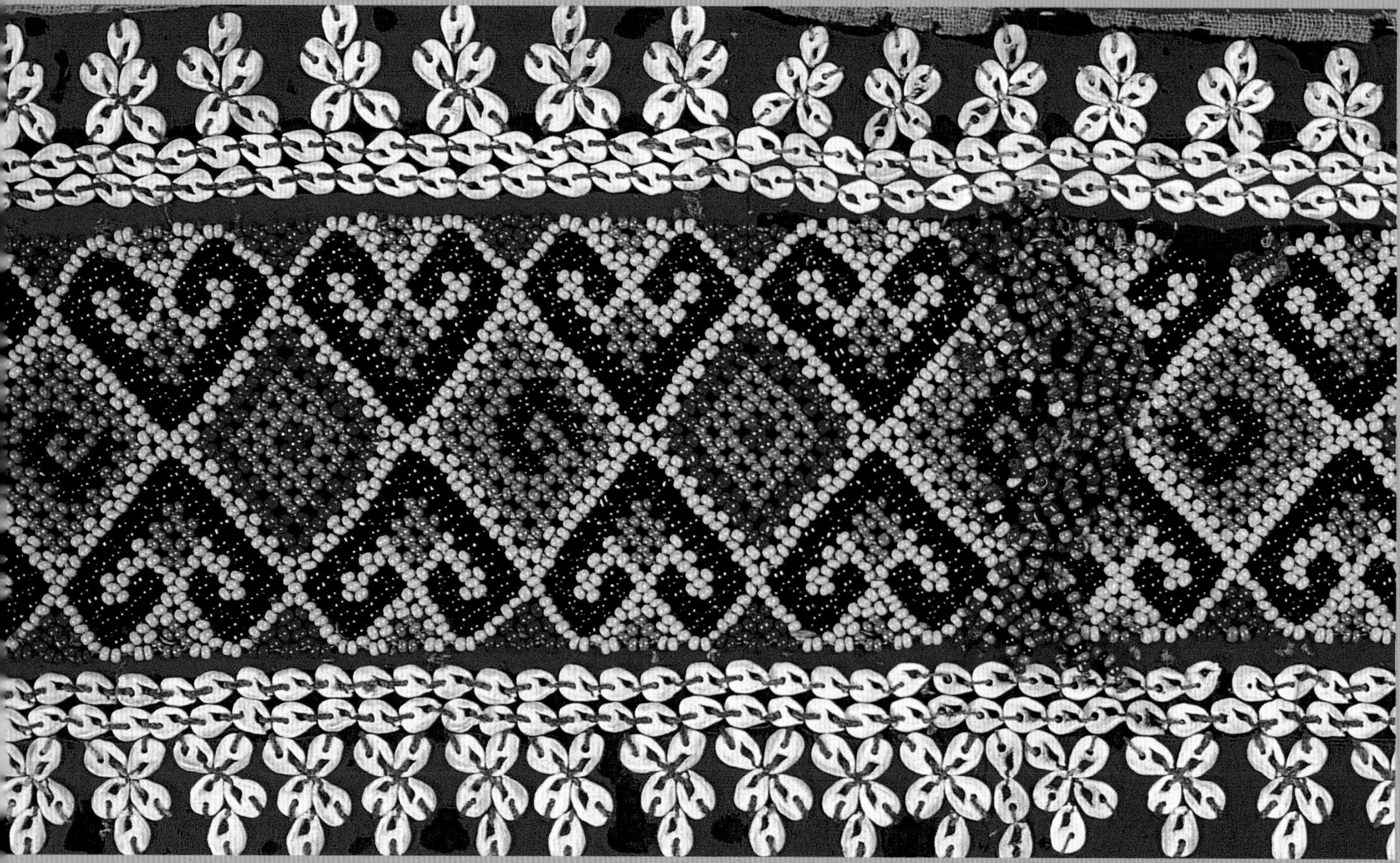

ABOVE AND OPPOSITE:
Women's skirts with inset panel of beadwork and shell embroidery.

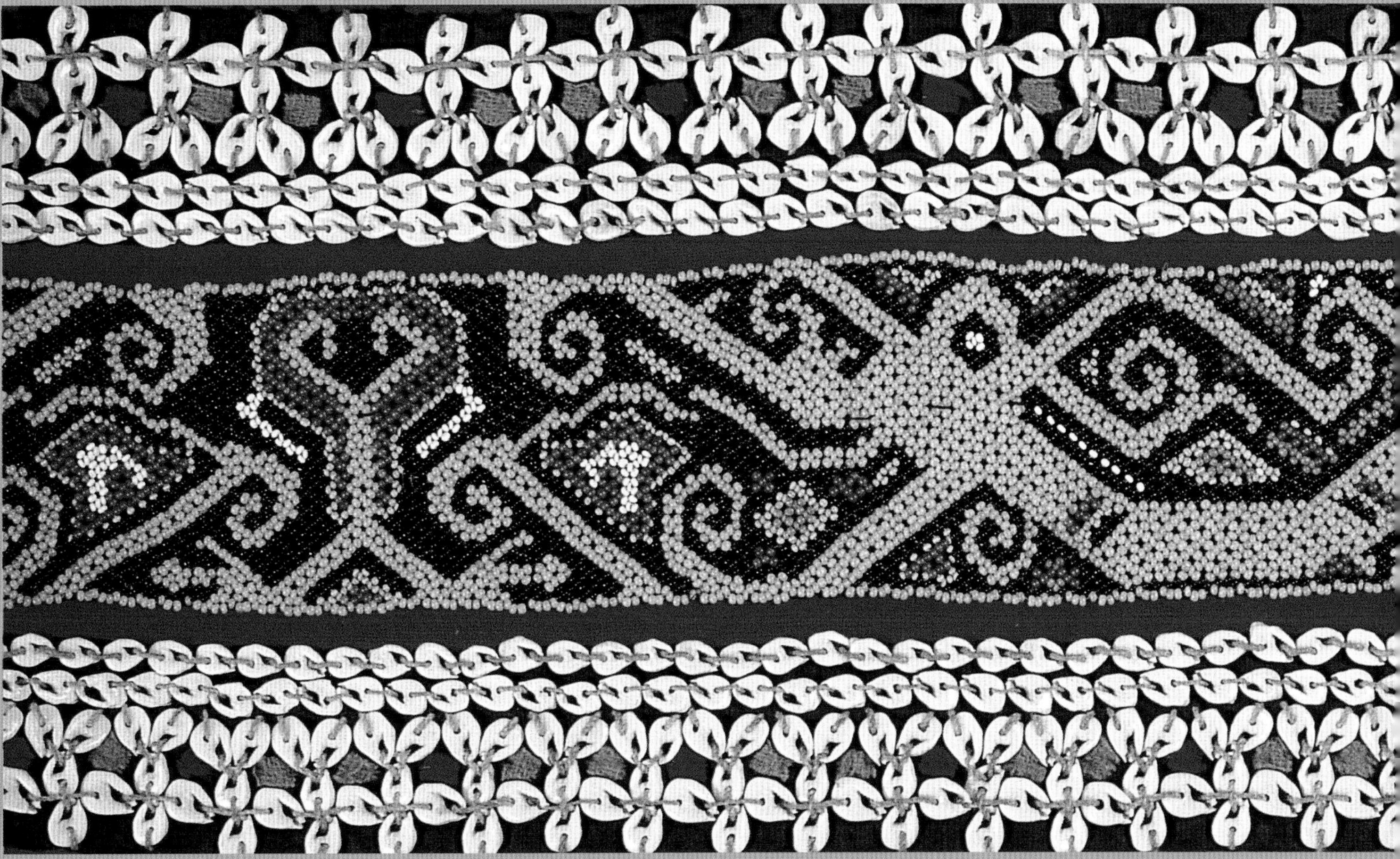

BELOW: Maloh bark cloth jacket, pattern-darned for extra strength and trimmed with red calico.

RIGHT: Detail of middle section of the same jacket in which the beadwork can be clearly seen.

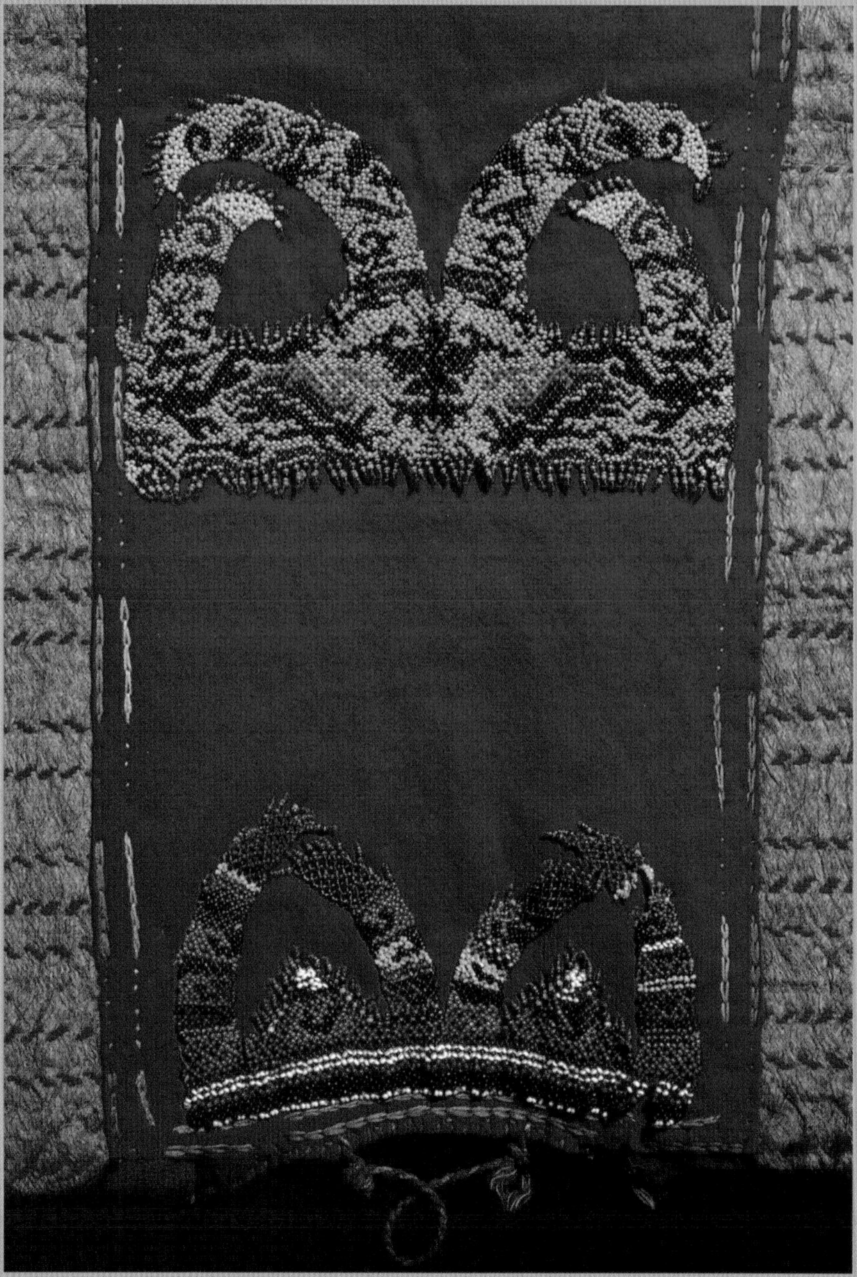

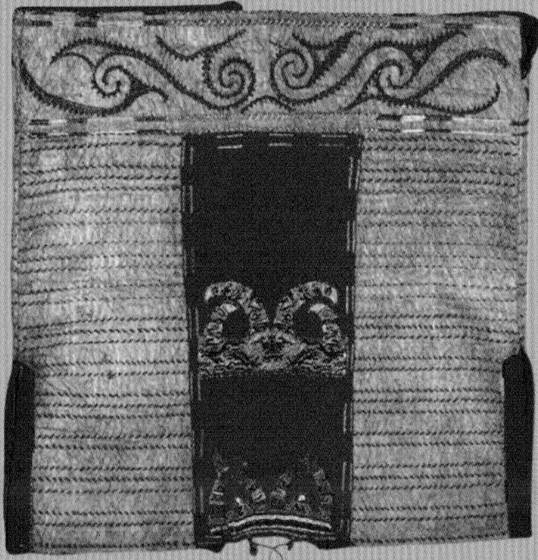

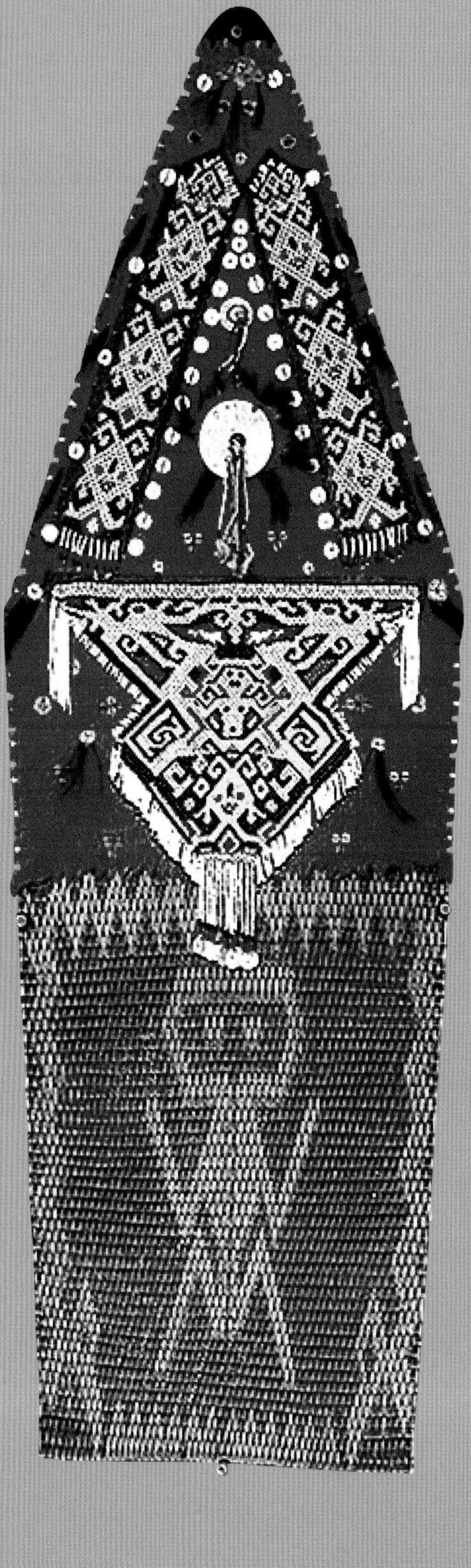

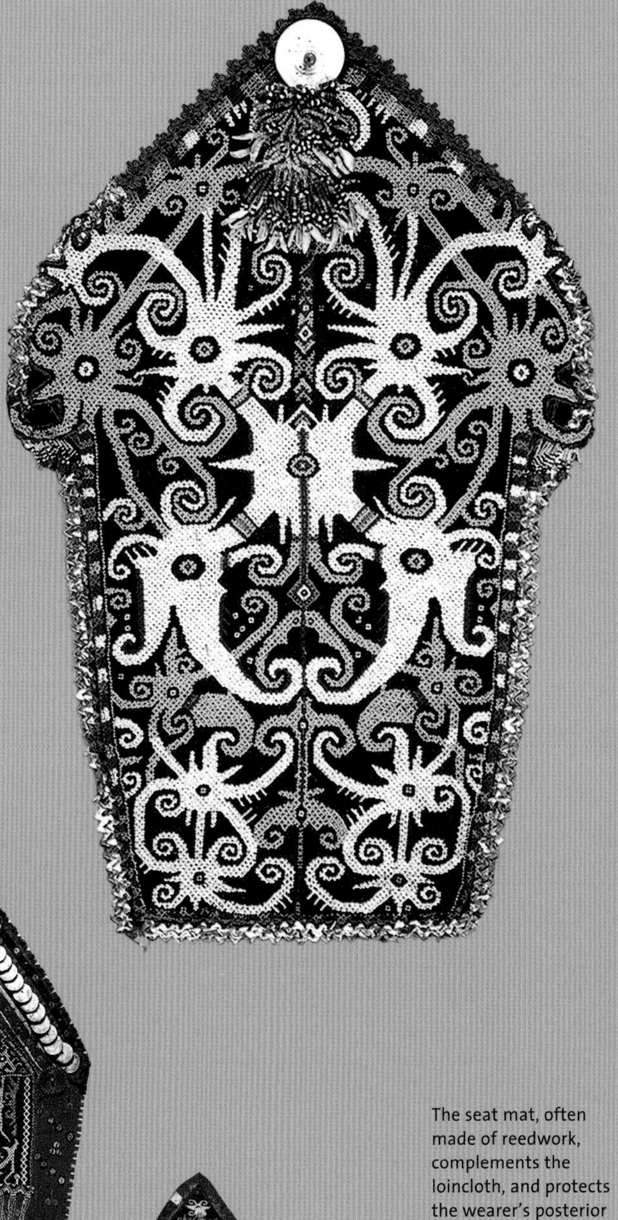

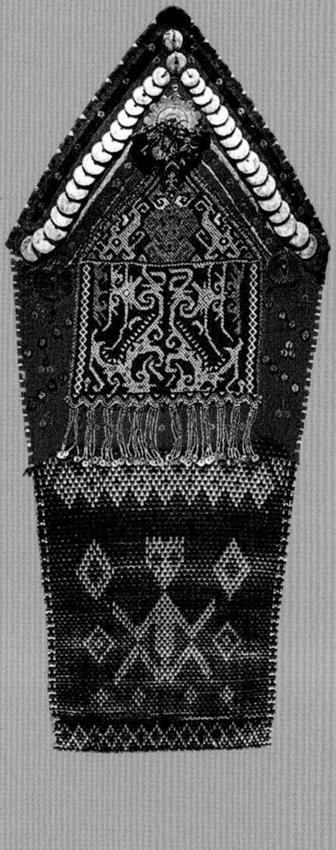

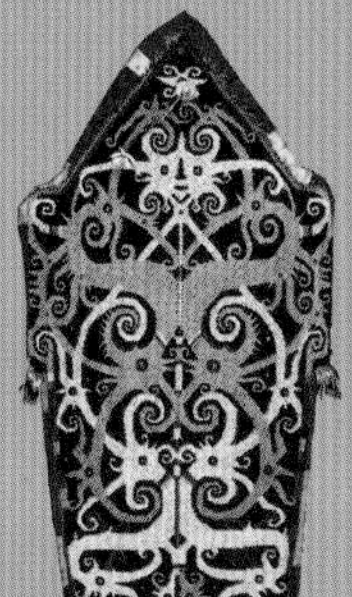

The seat mat, often made of reedwork, complements the loincloth, and protects the wearer's posterior if he has to sit on damp or rough ground. The seat mats here, embellished with fine beadwork, were designed for festival and gala wear only.

ANTI-CLOCKWISE FROM EXTREME LEFT: Maloh (first two), Kayan, and Kenyah with dragon motif.

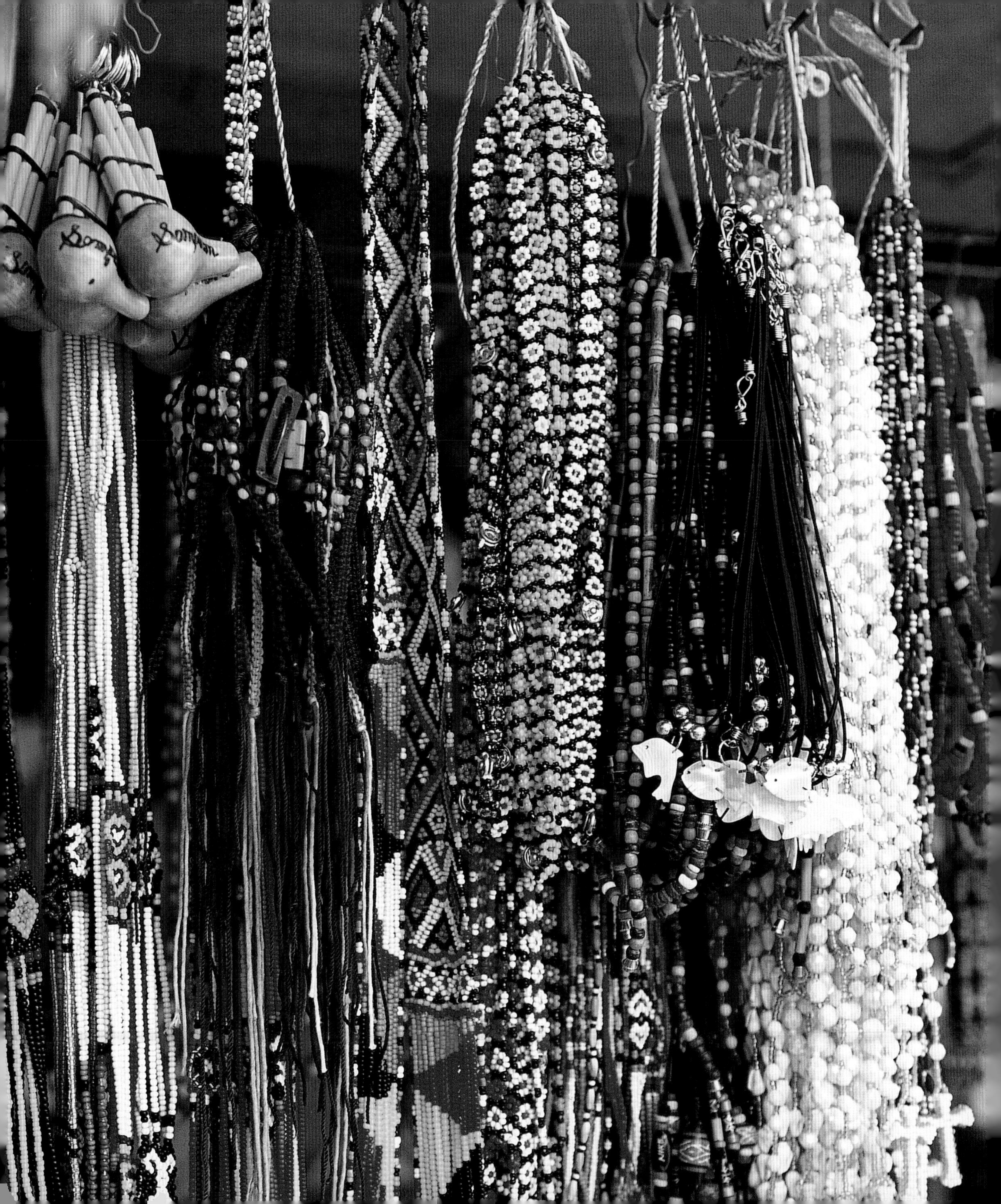

[CHAPTER 6]

THE BEAD TRADE TODAY

A look at how bead usage and manufacture have been reinvented in recent times. Beads are now part of modern fashion wear and are sold as souvenir items.

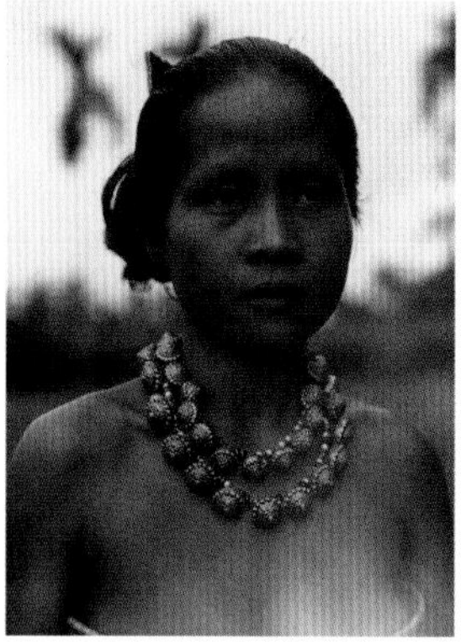

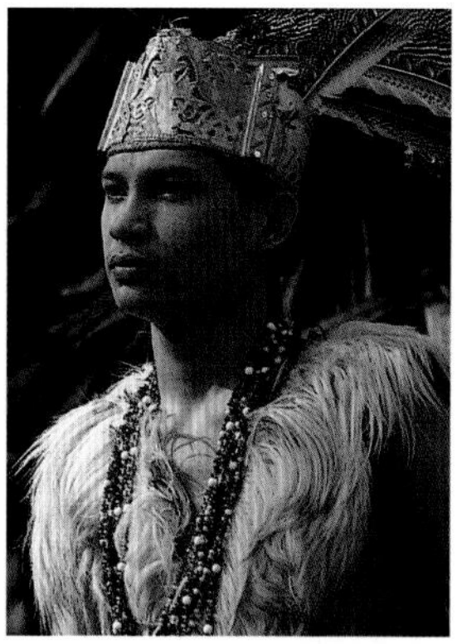

FACING PREVIOUS PAGE: Wide variety of beads on sale at a Sunday market in Borneo. Most beads sold in the Borneo marketplace today, in the form of necklaces, bracelets or beadwork, are new. Government-sponsored handicrafts boards are also helping to determine consumer demand and encourage beadworkers to meet it.

ABOVE, LEFT: Bornean lady wearing silver button beads. Photo taken in the late 19th century.

ABOVE, RIGHT: Iban youth in traditional costume.

CHANGING STYLES

Bead use and bead fashions change all the time. Compared with what is known of 19th and early 20th century costume in Borneo, ornamentation has now become more lavish. In addition to beads, there is a plethora of metal buttons, gold and silver lace and fringe, and sequins. Old beads are now worn together with all this tinsel, and not always to advantage – stringing stone and glass beads with gold is not necessarily an improvement.

The point is: Beads continue to be worn according to the owner's taste and fancy. New beads and styles come in while the old ones are treasured and stored away, and are becoming rare. Old beads have dropped out of circulation in a number of ways – by burial, accidental loss, fire, enemy raids or sale. In the last two cases, the beads were not lost absolutely, only lost to the original owner. The raider or buyer took his spoils to another longhouse but they stayed in Borneo.

This situation has changed since beads became a collector's item on the international arts and antiques scene. Today, some of the most beautiful Borneo beads may be seen in the trendy boutiques of Singapore and further afield. Indonesia, Brunei and Malaysia have laws against the export of antiques but these are very difficult to enforce. Some genuine old beads, bushels and bushels of new beads, fake antiques including "fakes" of beads which never existed (presumably made by the same hand that produced a three-quarter cent coin with the White Rajah's head on the obverse) are sold in gorgeous profusion in all the main townships of Borneo.

The "Kalimantan witchdoctor necklace" so beloved of curio shops is about as authentic as plastic jade, but it finds ready buyers and it keeps a smallish cottage industry gainfully employed. The local bead collectors know very well which piece is genuine and which is not. Most of these are no longer traditional bead owners but members of "downriver" communities who may have more disposable cash than their upcountry compatriots. In addition to the bead collections in museums, there are also some fine bead assemblages in private hands. In the past, beads used to be seen very much as "women's business", but today quite a number of serious amateur collectors are men.

Indigenous bead collectors browse the bazaar – including the goldsmith shop and the pawnshop – and they often buy "in the field" when travelling upcountry on official duty or on business. Being local, they know where good beads may be found and how to get them.

I was with a group of people at one time and was told a story of a high-ranking Orang Ulu lady who travelled upriver to inspect the bead hoards of the lower classes, and identified those she considered "too strong" for their humble owners. She then

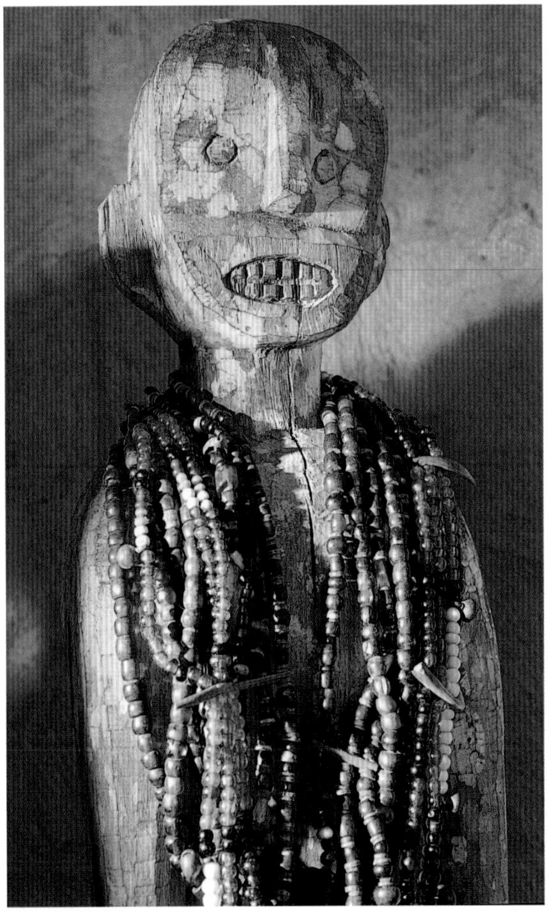

Assorted beads, some of them re-strung, of the kind used by the Bidayuh of west Borneo. For display purposes, they are draped over a *tigundo* wooden figure, which is sometimes found protecting the approach to a longhouse.

proceeded to buy them – at her own valuation. And the longhouse wives did not complain.

When I enquired further on the matter, there were embarrassed shuffles but no straightforward answers. In the matter of beads, so the reluctant sellers seemed to feel, they had to yield to the stronger spirit of an aristocrat even in the late 20th century. A police officer who was in the group and whose relatives lost some of their heirlooms, commented in true official parlance that "this lady exceeded her authority!" But he did not recommend lodging a report.

Local collectors buy beads when they are overseas – the junk shops, flea markets and antique dealers of London and San Francisco are well known to jet-setting Borneans who often find beads "just like granny's" in such unexpected places, and buy them at bargain prices. The newly-bought treasures are added to a collection, or they are re-strung together with grandma's necklaces, either in a traditional pattern, or according to the owner's taste and fancy. Two or three generations from now, who will know the difference?

A small but distinguished number of professional artists is also active in this field. Some re-string a private client's own beads in an aesthetically pleasing fashion while others collect and arrange beads for boutique-type outlets. In Kuching Main Bazaar, the elegant bead creations of Margaret Tan of Gallery M may be inspected at EO Gallery, alongside natural fibre and naturally-dyed textiles. Another denizen of the Main Bazaar, batik Artist Ramsay Ong, collects and occasionally strings beads according to his own imagination or along traditional ethnic lines.

"Stringing beads" includes adding anything that catches the artist's eye which fits harmoniously into the creation. Borneo beads are mixed with others from all parts of the world. These professional artists are not hampered by the taboos of old, which forbade the mixing of "male" and "female" beads. A fishing weight or a spindle whorl may also look interesting enough to be incorporated in a modern necklace. The heart-shaped pubic shields, formerly worn by otherwise naked little girls for modesty, are quaint pieces of silver-work in themselves. One of these may be used as the frontal pendant of a bead necklace.

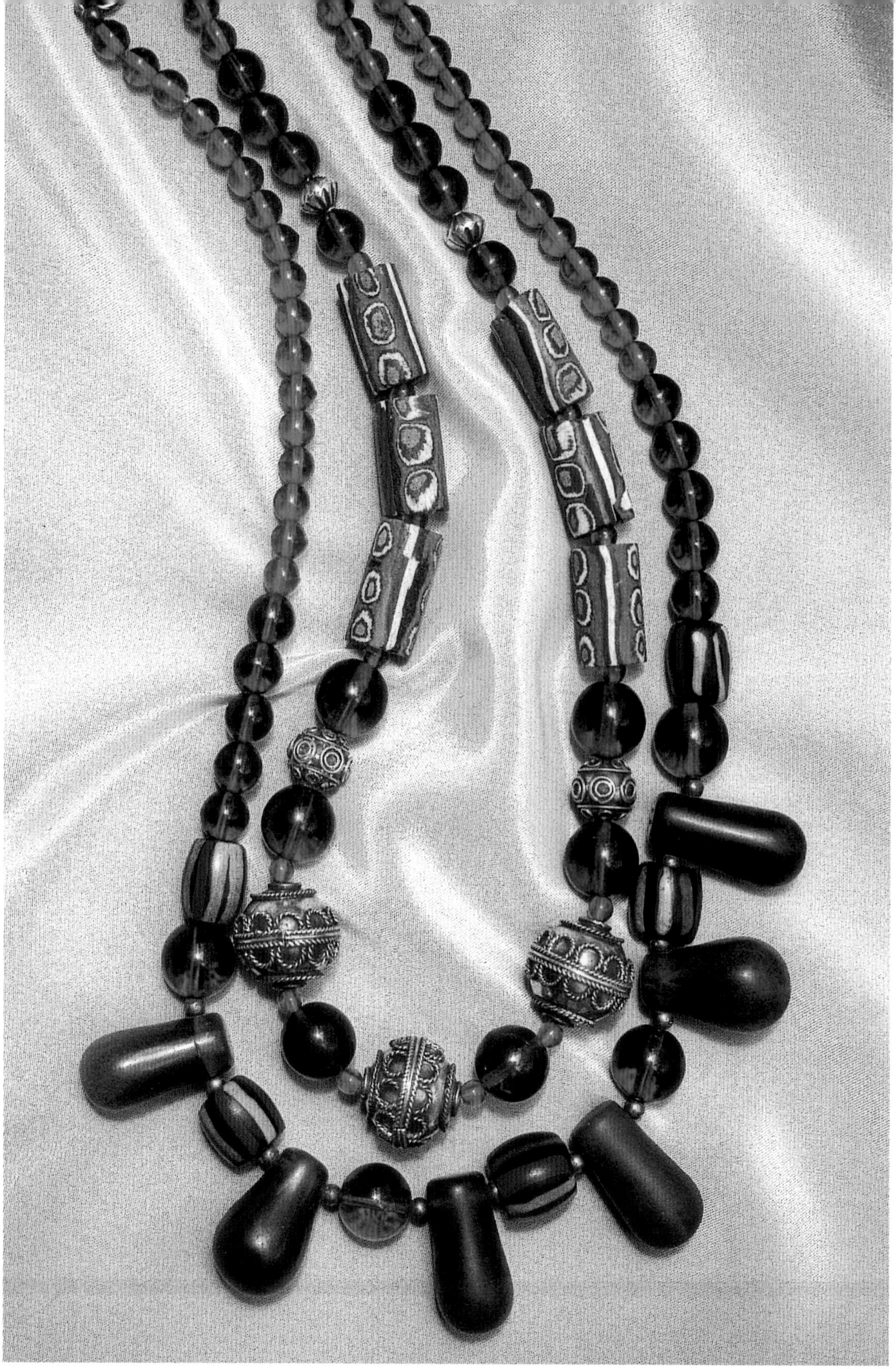

A small number of professional artists in Borneo today re-string clients' beads or collect and arrange beads for boutique-type outlets.

LEFT: Old and new beads re-strung by Margaret Tan of Gallery M, Kuching.

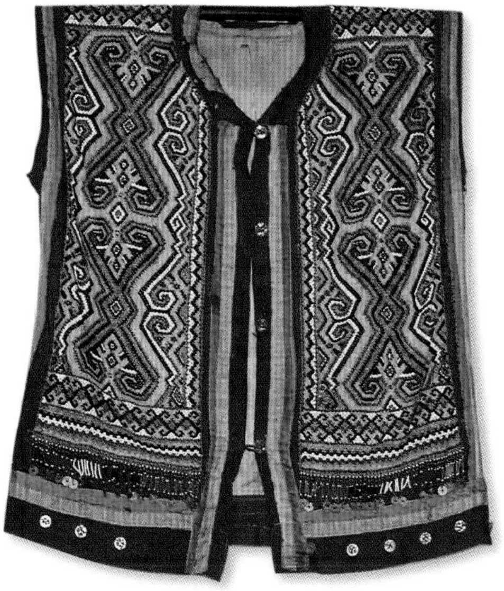

These fashionably-strung beads are worn with modern attire; they go well with severely-tailored office wear or with designer clothing created with an eye for "ethnic chic". The larger old beads in particular are beautifully set off by natural fibres, natural dyes, and hand-spun and hand-woven textiles artistically cut and draped. A number of Malaysian fashion artists, including Sarawakian Edric Ong, are combining old beads with new ideas in their creations.

One young Bidayuh artist, Mikit Nyayig, has turned the same idea upside-down – she faithfully re-creates her people's traditional bead artifacts out of anything but beads, such as nuts and bolts, insulators, coconut scrubbing brushes, fishnet floats and fencing wire. The local hardware shop now yields the ingredients for the tall hat of the *dayung baris* priestess, the ritual specialist's heavy neckpiece or long bandolier.

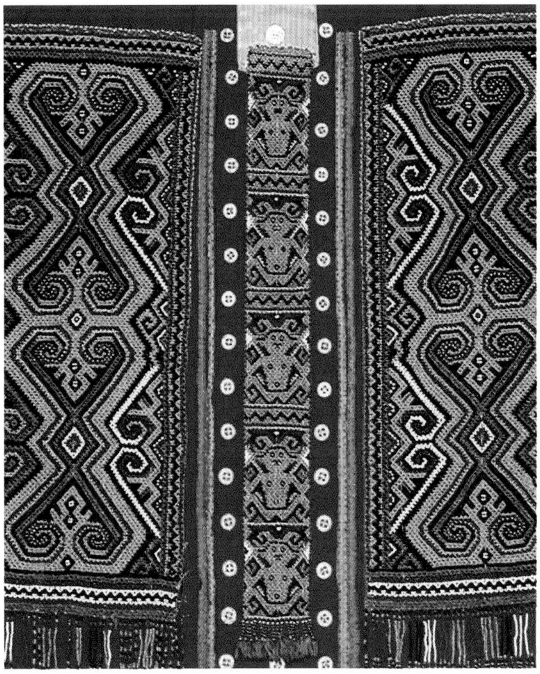

Old beadwork, such as can be seen on these jackets, inspires Bornean fashion designers of today, such as Sarawakian Edric Ong.

LAWAS BEADS

Some Lun Bawang in Long Tumah near Lawas in Sarawak do more than just re-string old beads. In the 1970s, they started to make yellow "peanut" and "cherry" beads out of a fine clay found by the riverbanks. The inspiration is credited to some Indonesian Lun Dayeh, close cousins of the Lun Bawang, who were visiting the village. Reviving interest in the material culture of Borneo drove up

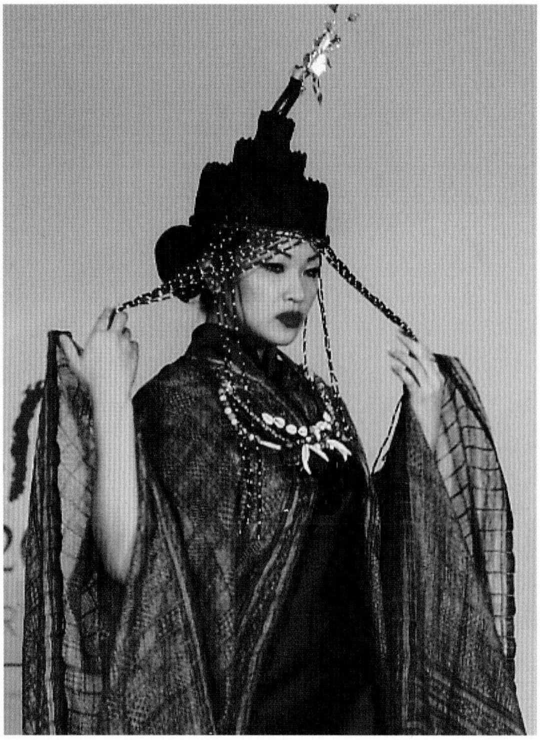

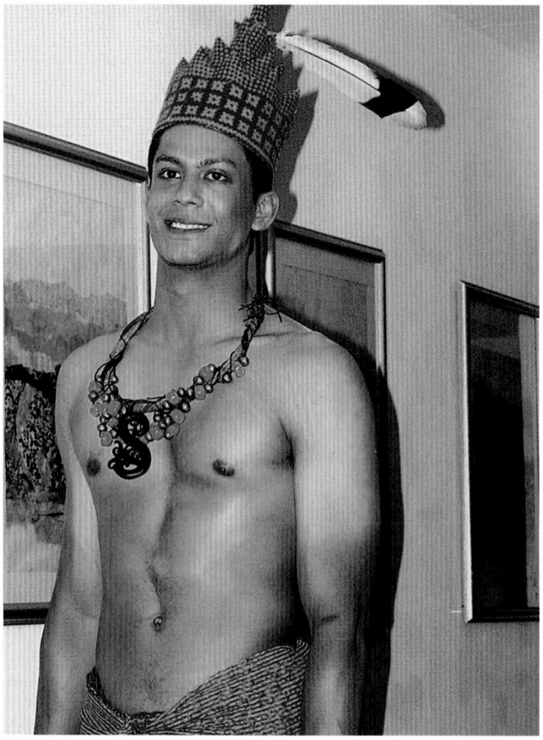

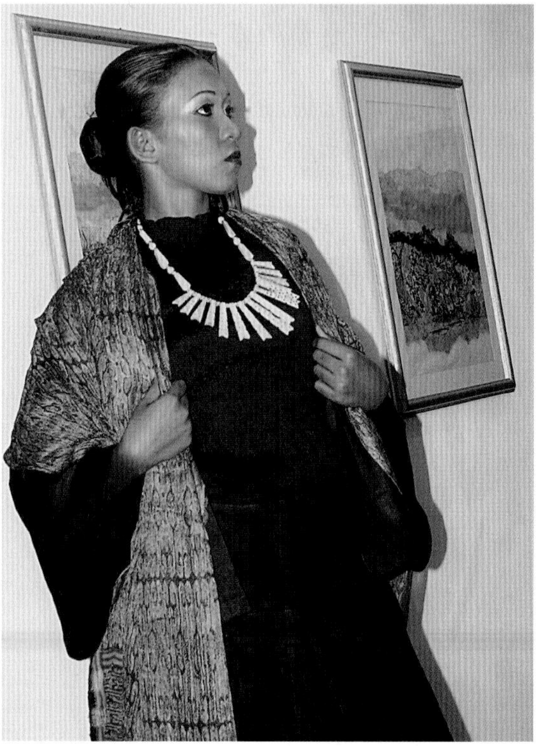

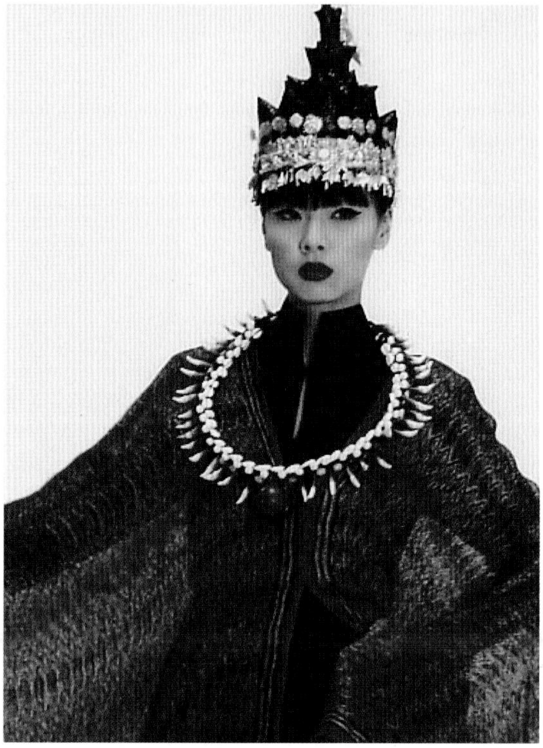

Old beads are combined with designer clothing for an 'ethnic chic' look in these modern presentations by Sarawakian fashion artist Edric Ong.

the value of genuine beads. A parallel folkloristic revival created a demand for traditional costumes and large quantities of Lun Bawang beads, few of which could be substituted with plastic.

Traditional Lun Bawang beads are mainly opaque. The beadmakers of Lawas replicated them quite easily in clay, fired them in a backyard furnace, and painted the finished product with enamel paint – motorbike paint, as one of the original manufacturers and owner of a motorbike told me proudly. This craftsman used the simplest materials, all within easy reach.

Sarawak's Agriculture Department is now supporting this cottage industry by providing electric kilns and proper ceramic paints and glazes. While the main output still consists of "modern traditional Lun Bawang" wares, some of the more adventurous beadmakers also turn out fancy beads and pendants, and even cups and mugs.

The Lawas beadmakers originally started production "to save old beads". Lun Bawang fashion demands the wearing of 10 to 12 necklaces at one time. If a lady accidentally breaks a string or two and loses some or all of her beads, her loss is great for these beads are valued at so many ringgit per piece! Schoolchildren dressed up in traditional costumes and valuable ornaments for all sorts of functions are particularly vulnerable. How can a teacher take responsibility for a dozen little girls wearing RM5,000 worth of beads each? On the other hand, few parents will mourn the loss of a few dozen enamel-painted clay beads.

Once word got around about their product, the beadmakers of Lawas were amazed at how saleable their product proved. Soon they had large orders from dance troupes and villages in Sabah, Kalimantan, Sarawak and Brunei. Some of the craftspeople even gave up padi farming to make beads full-time. One unexpected result of this new bead source is that some Tagal girls in western Sabah have started wearing the yellow bead caps; their own traditional carnelian head-bands are very hard to obtain.

This is how bead fashions and preferences must have been shaped in the past – partly by what people liked or needed, and partly by what was then available. The main purpose of local beadmaking is the replication of antique beads, not the production of fakes. The Lun Bawang beadmakers of Lawas are emphatic on this point: Nobody tells the buyer that these beads are "genuine antiques".

WHEN IS A FAKE NOT A FAKE?

Beads collected in the field are almost impossible to date although it is usually possible to tell a new, shop-bought bead from an older one. This is where the uncertainty starts – how old is "the older"? Family histories may fix a bead at "10 generations", which leads to the next question: How long is "one generation"? Fifteen years or 20? If 10 generations

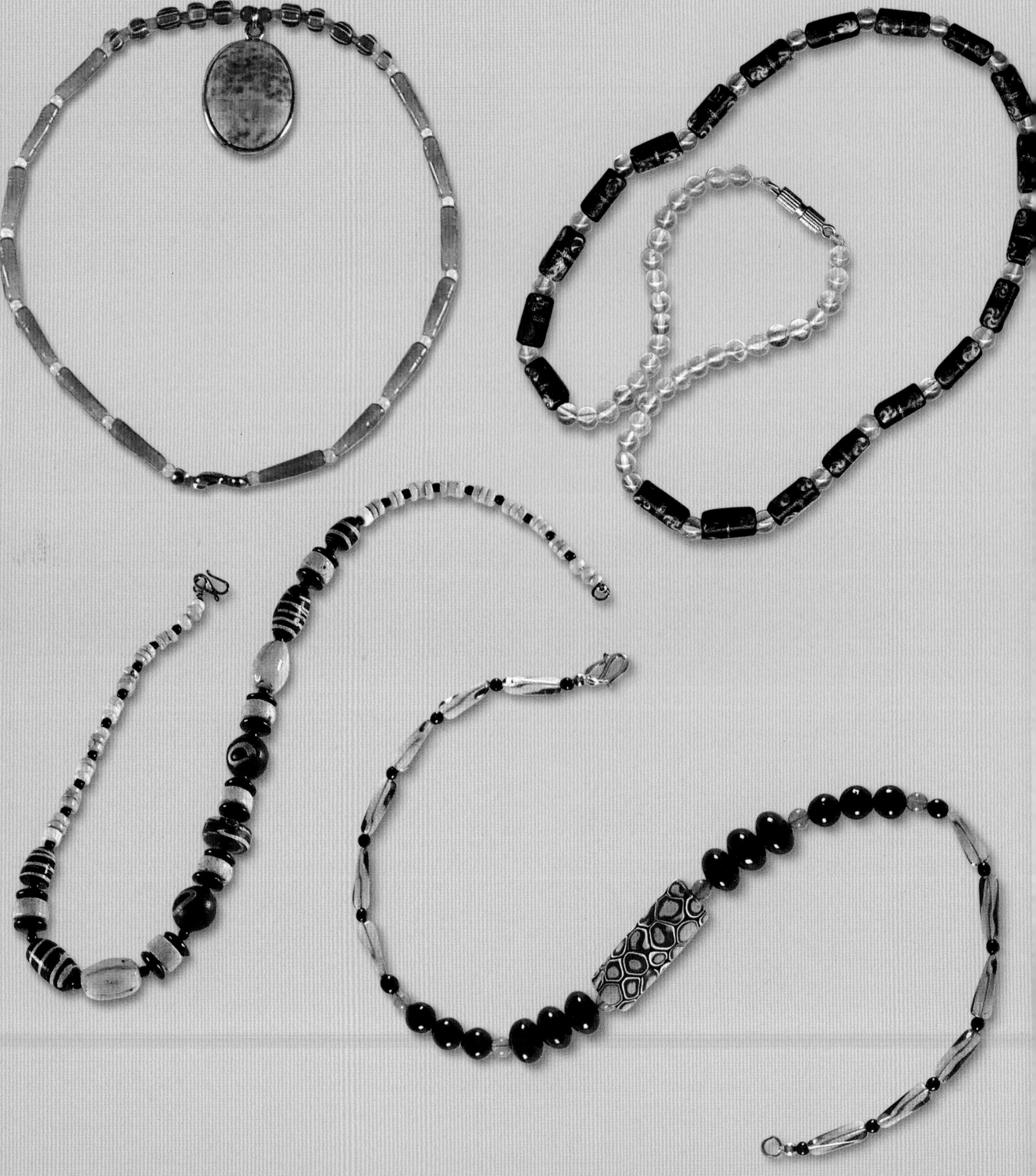

Examples of modern bead stringing which mixes new and old beads.

OPPOSITE PAGE (CLOCKWISE FROM TOP LEFT): String with jade pendant; modern Indonesian string with rock crystal beads; string with millefiori centre; and string with yellow melon, *ketobong* (yellow and black stripes) and *lavang* ('yellow doughnut') beads.

THIS PAGE, LEFT: String featuring old polychrome *mata punai* (pigeon eyes) and jade beads.

BELOW: String containing black and 'spider bottom' beads.

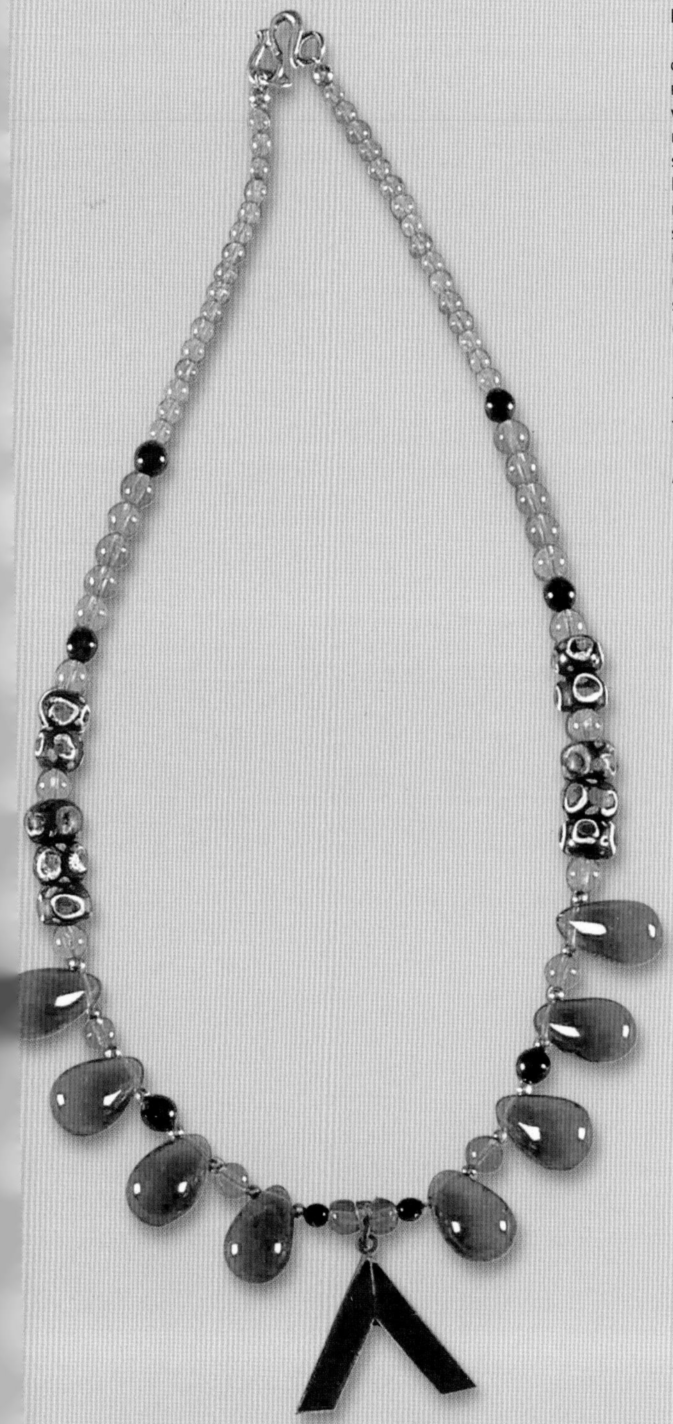

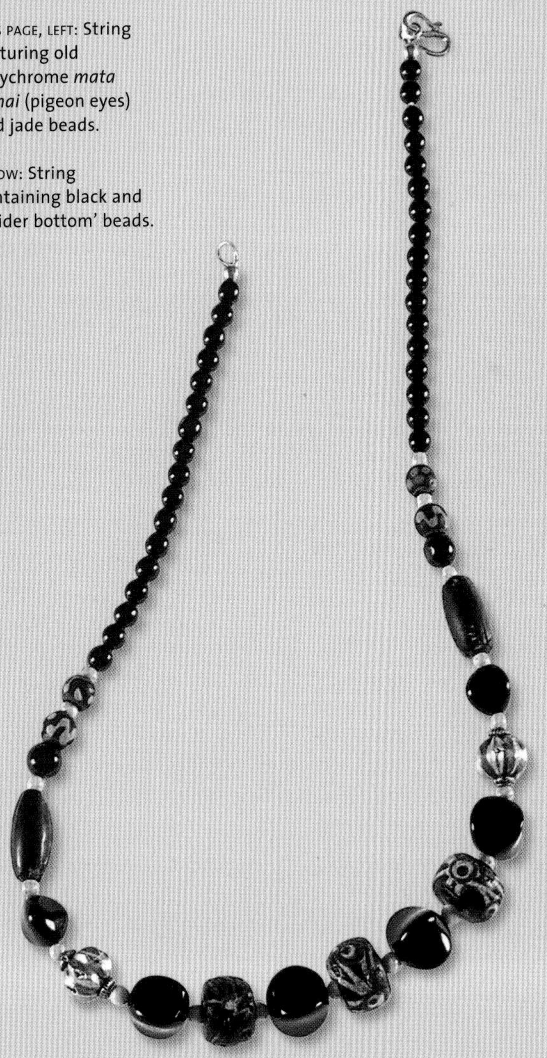

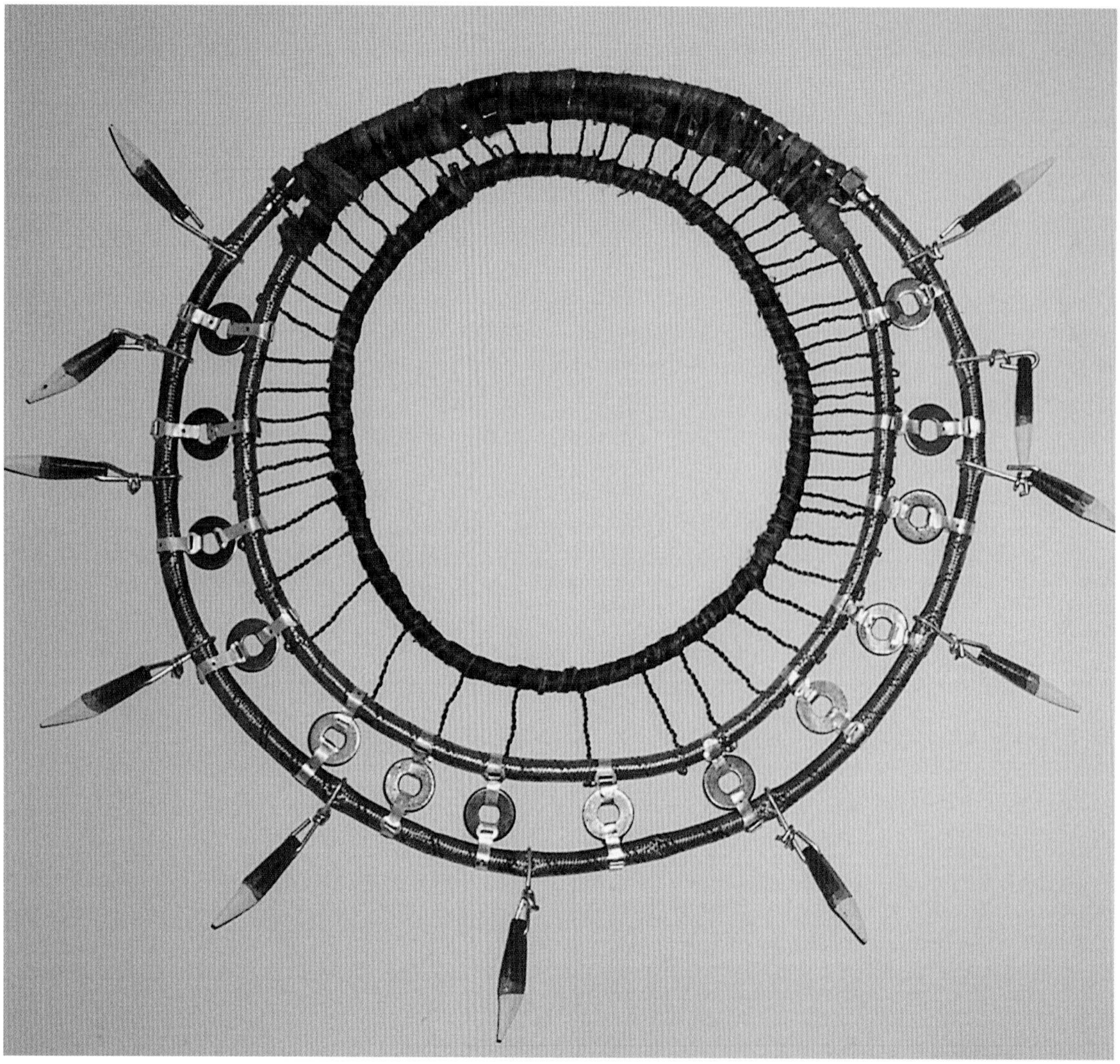

Bidayuh artist Mikit Nyayig re-creates her people's traditional bead artifacts out of nuts and bolts, insulators, coconut scrubbing brushes and other items.

LEFT AND OPPOSITE PAGE, TOP LEFT: A modern interpretation of the traditional Bidayuh warrior's necklace.

BELOW: The Bidayuh female cult leader's beaded headdress is given new form.

OPPOSITE PAGE, BOTTOM LEFT AND EXTREME RIGHT: Re-creation of the Bidayuh female healer's bead necklace.

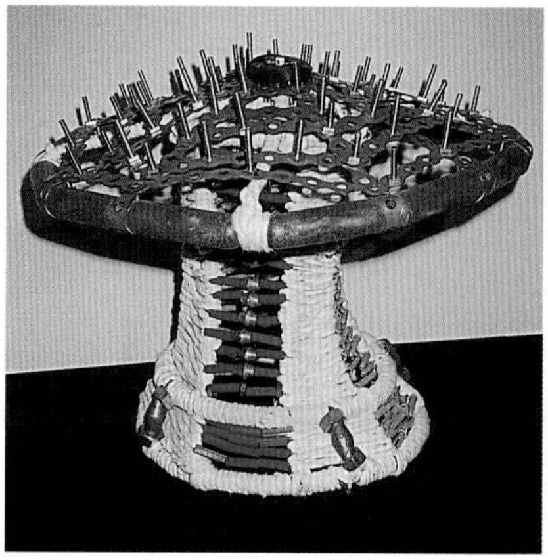

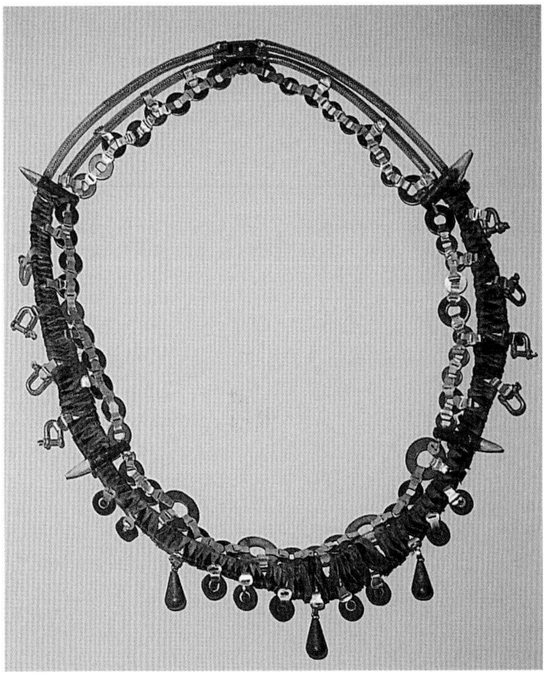

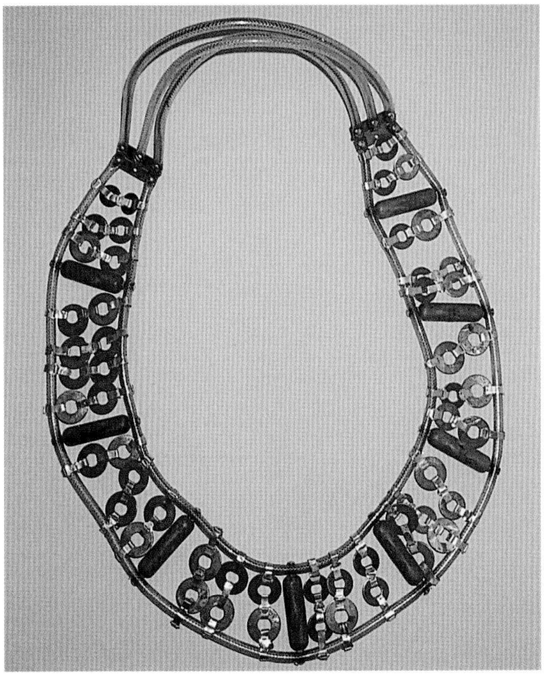

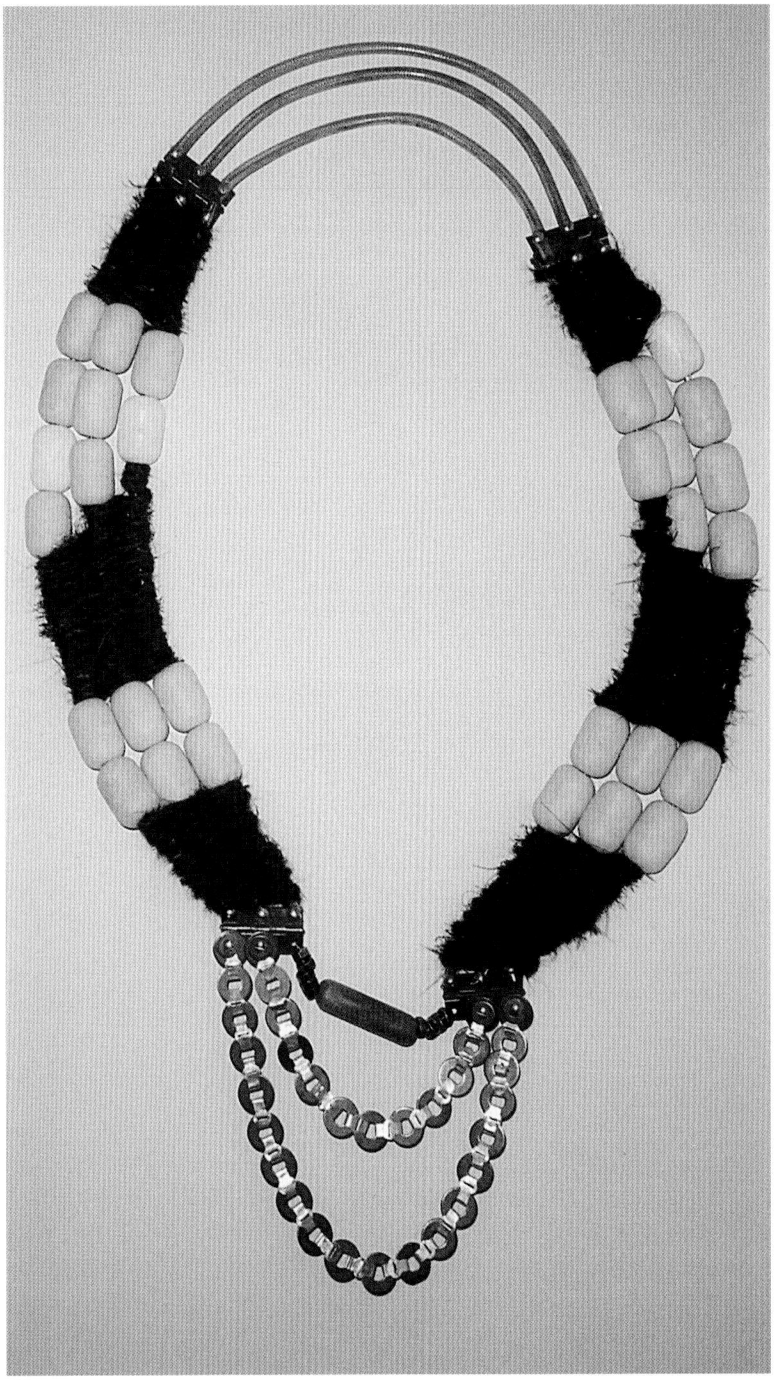

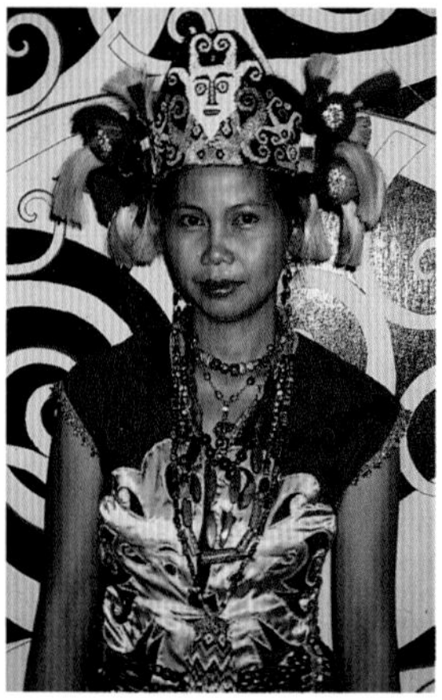

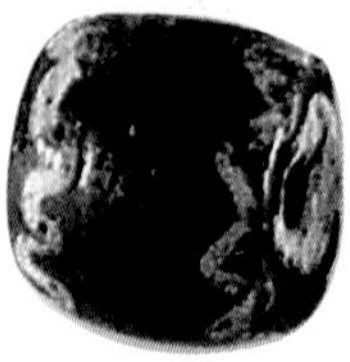

TOP: Orang Ulu woman wearing old and new beads in 'modern traditional' style.

ABOVE: White-core imitation chevron, described as 'more than a thousand years old' by Swedish naturalist and anthropologist Erik Mjöberg in Borneo, was actually being manufactured in Venice in the 17th century.

means 10 owners, it needs to be established whether the item changed hands after each owner's death, or was handed to the first child of the family who got married.

In the first case, this could mean 600 – 650 years if each elder reached the average age of 65 and then passed it to a child of two to five years. In the second, it could be 200, assuming the average age at marriage for males to be 20. If the bead was handed down in the female line it was likely to be 160 to 180.

Considering the shape and colour of the bead is of only limited use in this context. Descriptions like "Roman Beads" and "Egyptian Beads" are casually tossed around, mainly because a bead looks like a product of Alexandria in Roman Egypt, or the somewhat later city of Fustat.

Beads are items of trade; they have been moving from hand to hand and from land to land. As research increasingly documents, the beadmakers themselves were highly mobile people. To this day, beads are manufactured, bought and sold. If a collector from Vancouver buys a 200-year-old bead in Kalimantan, takes it home and re-sells it, it is for all intents and purposes a "new bead" on the Canadian market.

Some beads worn in Borneo today may resemble the ornaments of antiquity. Some visually-identical beads are found at Sungai Mas in West Malaysia and on Orang Ulu necklaces – a time lag of approximately 1,000 years. Bead producers have long been aware of which types were in constant demand.

Translucent blue barrel-shaped glass beads have been found in Babylonian and Egyptian graves. They were also produced in 10th-century Pengkalan Bujang in West Malaysia. They were found again in a 16th-century shipwreck in the South China Sea, off the coast of Malaya, and they were made by Chinese craftsmen in 16th-17th century Java. Best-sellers stayed in production for centuries!

The large white-core glass black bead with surface-applied red and white zig-zags, described as "more than a thousand years old" by Swedish naturalist and anthropologist Erik Mjöberg in 1930 in Borneo, was being manufactured in Venice in the 17th century. A smaller white-core "chevron bead" was also found in 17th-century Amsterdam, featured on a 1926 Venetian sample card which manufacturers sent to wholesalers and traders, and is freely available in Petaling Street in Kuala Lumpur, West Malaysia, today (I bought some there in 1999).

The same principle applies to stone beads. If anything, they are more difficult to pin down because stone, unlike glass, cannot be spectro-graphically analysed to determine at least approximate details about its possible origins. The biconical facetted carnelian bead has been found in graves and old trade sites all over South-east Asia's Sunda region and beyond; it has been produced in

Cambay, north-western India, since 2000 BC and is still in production.

A bead found in an undisturbed site may be dated by association with other articles recovered. This fixes the time when the bead was deposited, not the time when it was made. Did the society which buried one particular set of remains usually give new items as grave gifts, or did they deposit their most ancient goods with their dead?

One man's tomb is also his neighbour's treasure trove. The more lavish the funerary gifts, the greater the temptation to grave robbery. In fact, tombs in Sumatra were used as "quarries" by the local population who mined mutisalah beads for re-sale to Timor as recently as the 1950s.

Collecting such beads which came from tombs beyond memory of people is not regarded as sacrilegious by most Borneans. The finder may simply not be aware of their origin. The Selakau of west Sarawak claim that the barrel-shaped blue bead is sometimes deposited by good spirits into the catch-net of women fishing in a mountain stream. In actual fact, the water may be eroding an old graveyard upstream.

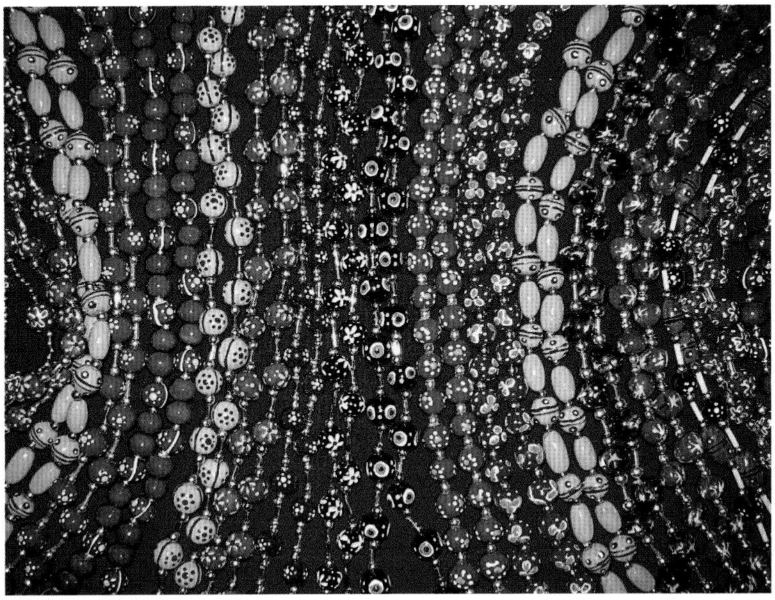

Painted or glazed clay beads made by Lun Bawang cottage workers near Lawas, Sarawak. The beads are replicas of traditional Lun Bawang beads.

THE MARKETPLACE

Most beads sold in the Borneo marketplace today, either in the form of necklaces, bracelets or beadwork, are new. Beadwork items of traditional or

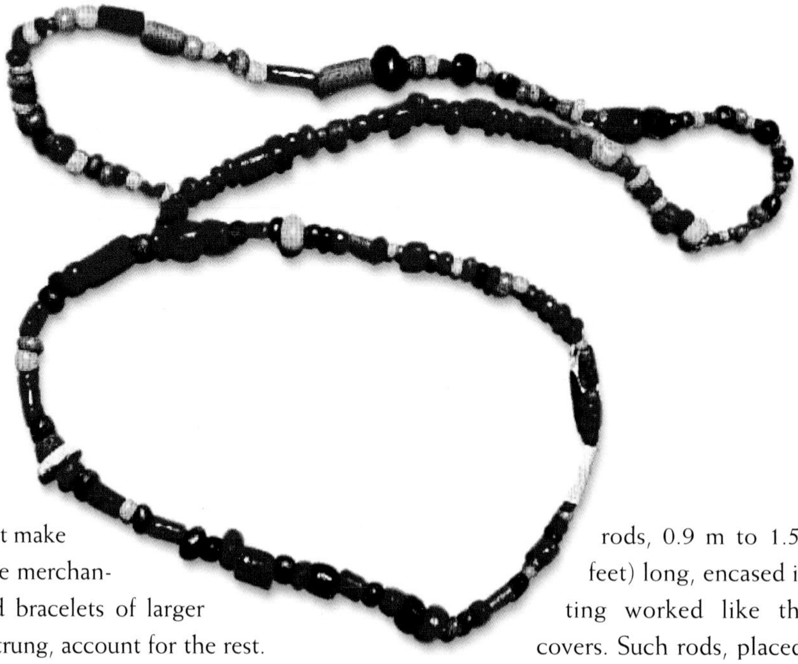

Antique beads from the Sungai Mas historical site in West Malaysia. Many of these discoveries parallel similar finds in Borneo, and a few types are still in use by various indigenous groups.

modern design must make up two-thirds of the merchandise; necklaces and bracelets of larger beads, artistically strung, account for the rest.

Designers have also got into the act. Today, government-sponsored handicrafts boards help to determine consumer demand and encourage the producers to meet it. This situation has resulted in beadworking becoming a popular part-time occupation for many women in the villages and longhouses as well as members of the rural-urban drift living in the larger towns. Some 10 per cent of handicraft produced for sale in Sarawak is beadwork.

The most saleable bead souvenirs have some sort of "traditional Borneo content" – bead hats, headbands, belts and baskets, sashes and pouches. Miniatures of well-known hats, collars and the like are very popular. The typical buyer is a foreign tourist who finds small things easier to pack than big ones like a hat that measures 1 m (3.3 feet) across! The souvenir shops are overflowing with "bead whimsies", from the cute to the useless (a beaded pencil cover is a fine example of the latter). Young women also consider a beaded necklace with dangling mobile phone pouch "cool".

The old beaded lampshades are also making a comeback, if in a somewhat modified form – the entire shade is strung of translucent beads. One interior designer has come up with slender rattan rods, 0.9 m to 1.5 m (3 to 5 feet) long, encased in bead netting worked like those pencil covers. Such rods, placed in tall jars with dry plant arrangements or otherwise deployed, give an attractive touch of colour to a room.

In the longhouses of Sarawak, the innovative spirit of the womenfolk has yielded not just beaded handbags, belts, watch-strap covers and cigarette lighter sheaths, but also beadwork neckties with a built-in knot. I am not aware that any woman has succeeded in making a man wear one of these, but they are frequently displayed at charity sales in aid of the local school or similar occasions.

CONCLUSION

The vast bulk of Borneo beads are not originally from Borneo at all, but were brought in from India, China, west Asia and Europe – exactly the same types of beads found in Africa, the Americas and all parts of Asia. The collector who is looking for spectacular, beautiful beads will find them anywhere, even in the junk shops and flea markets of London.

To qualify as "Borneo beads", the artifacts need to be in their original stringing. Most commercial sellers buy beads in odd lots and sell them either singly or in what they consider an aesthetically-pleasing arrangement, usually mixing many new beads with a few good, old ones.

Beaded touristy souvenirs.

CLOCKWISE FROM LEFT:
Miniature Iban *marik empang* or bead collar, 17 cm in diameter; beaded purse and mobile phone pouches from Miri, Sarawak.

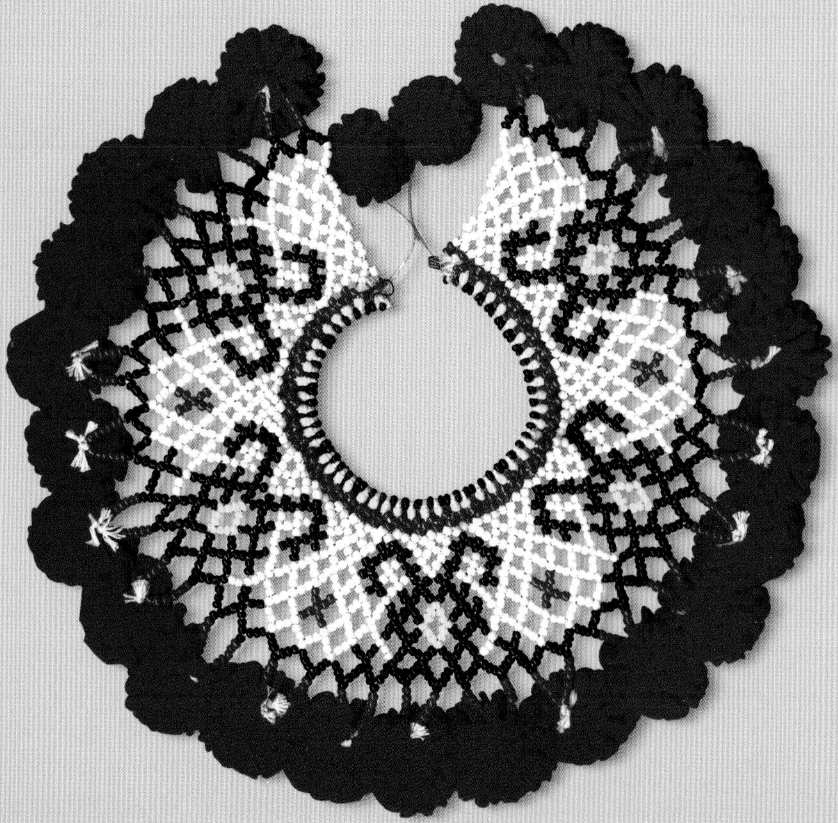

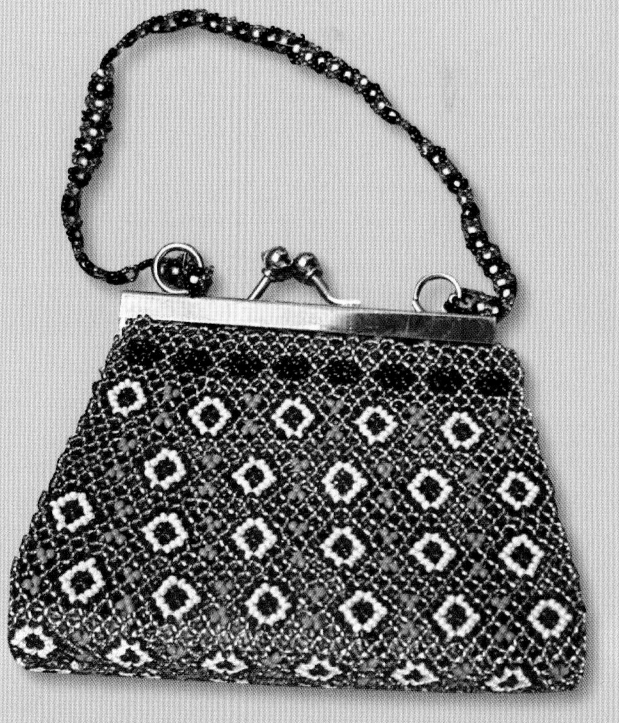

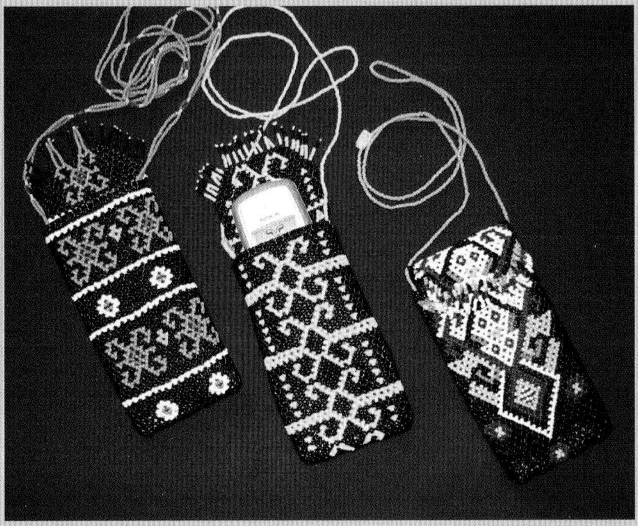

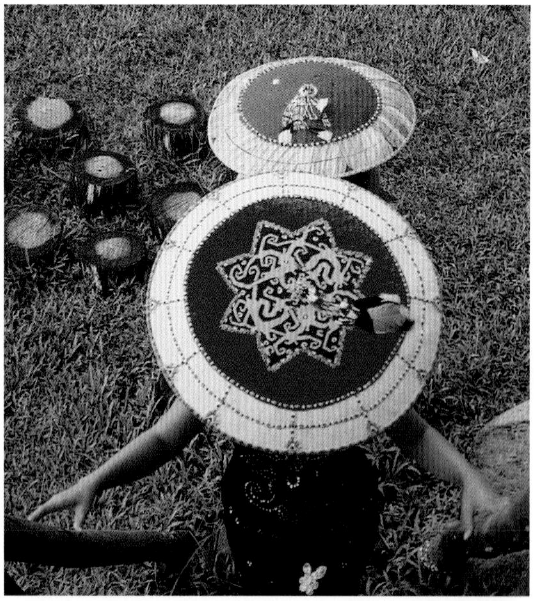

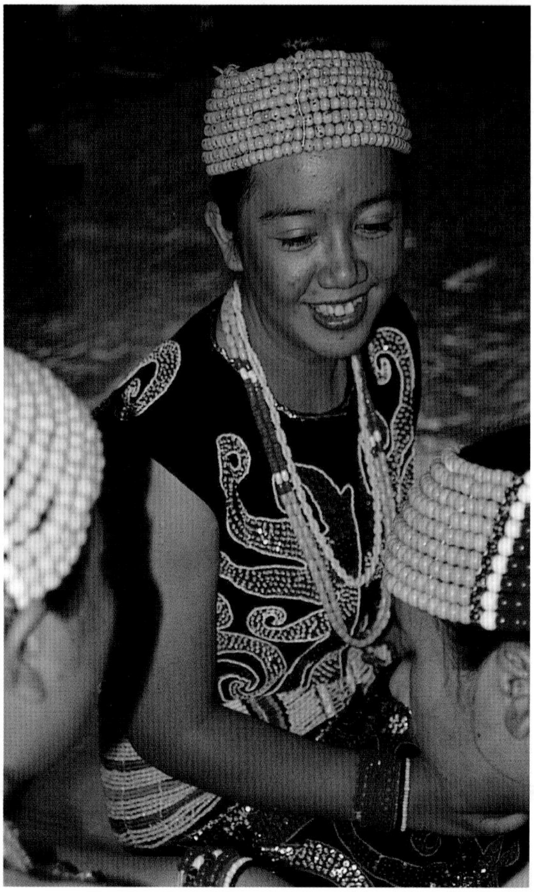

What makes an assortment of beads originating from all over the world 'Borneo beads' is the way they are used by ethnic groups here.

ABOVE: Orang Ulu ladies wearing their beaded sun hats, ascending the stairs to their longhouse.

RIGHT: Lun Dayeh girls wearing their caps of opaque glass beads.

The buyer should not feel cheated or short-changed by this kind of mixing. It is exactly what the people of Borneo themselves have been doing with their beads for centuries. There was a constant trickle of new beads coming in, more easily available to the coastal dwellers who lived within range of the shipping trade, and from there moved and traded up the rivers right into the mountain fastnesses of Central Borneo. It is much better to get a set of new, or new and old mixed, beads which the buyer considers beautiful and enjoys wearing, than to get a string of guaranteed genuine antiques which do not suit her complexion or wardrobe.

That said, what is the difference between "any beautiful beads" and "Borneo beads"?

What makes an assortment of beads originating from all over the world "Borneo beads" is the way they are strung and used by one of the many ethnic groups of this vast island, once fashioned into necklaces, hats, belts, bracelets, charms and garments. This is how they become Rungus beads, Lotud beads, Kayan beads, Maloh beads, Melanau beads, Kenyah beads, Iban beads, Bidayuh beads, Bahau beads, Selakau beads.

These are the real Beads of Borneo.

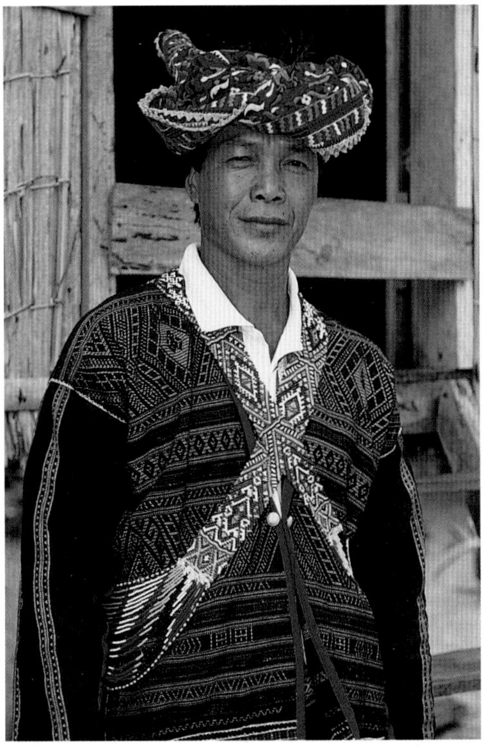

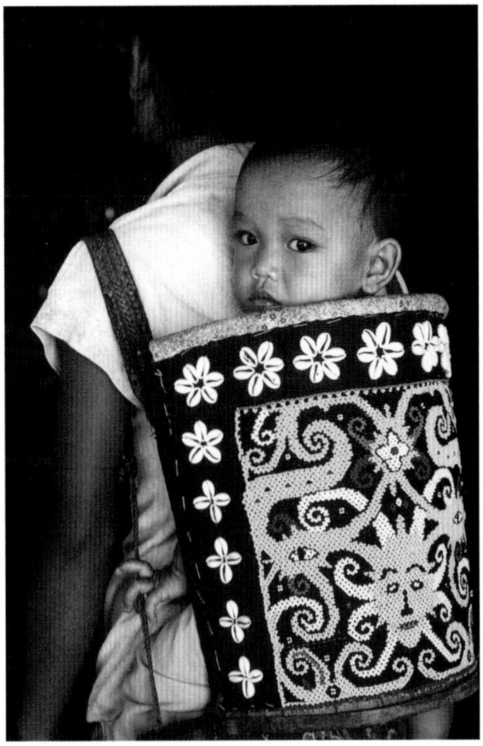

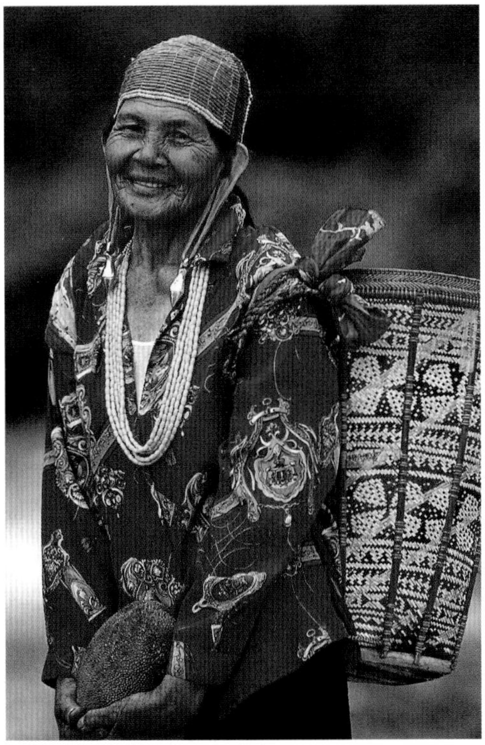

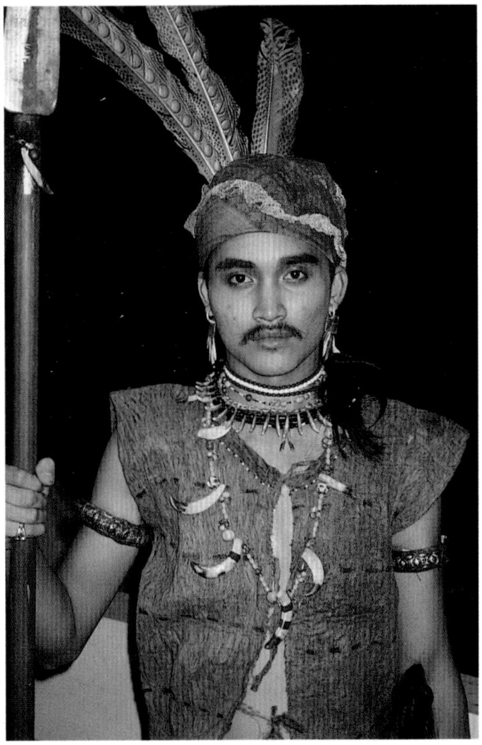

Indigenous people wearing their 'Borneo beads'.

CLOCKWISE FROM TOP LEFT: Rungus man wearing bead bandoliers and handwoven headcloth; mother carrying her child in a traditional beaded baby carrier in Kalimantan; young Bidayuh man dressed up for the annual Gawai festival, wearing newly-made traditional bark cloth and his grandfather's warrior beads; and Kelabit woman from Bario, Sarawak, wearing her set of beads on her way to the local market.

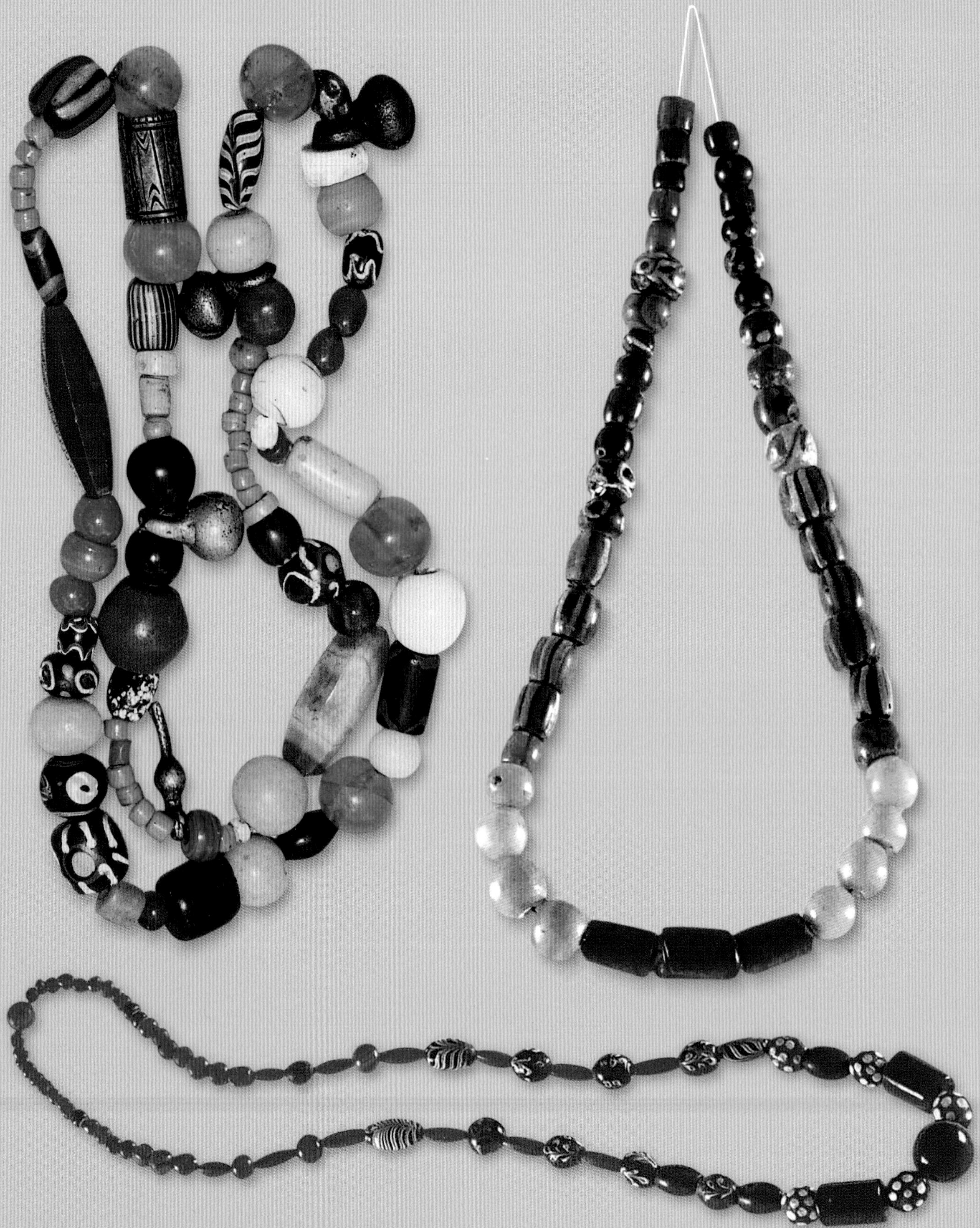

[CHAPTER 7]

BEAD NAMES

A list and description of beads which are either common in most parts of Borneo, or are of unusual historical interest.

BEAD NOMENCLATURE

To those who value them, all beads have names. For polychromes, the names may describe the design – "hornbill eyes", "bird footprints", "hornet", "spider's bum", "length of a longhouse" – or not, as the case may be. Some people use a bead name they heard from neighbours. One opaque pale blue bead described as *inu Kelabit* or "Kelabit Bead" by Charles Hose, a civil officer in the service of the Rajah of Sarawak in the 19th century, is not otherwise known by this name. A Kayan or Kenyah probably told Hose it was a kind of bead the Kelabit like. Other Kayan call it "tube" and the Kelabit would probably call it *let maitam* or any one of the "*let*" classes of beads. Another bead, the *lukut barong*, appears so named because it was sold by traders who came in river-going sailing boats, called the *barong*.

Bead nomenclature is not entirely fixed. Names tend to vary from river to river, even within the same ethnic group. Some names are used for two different beads, each owner vowing that hers is the authentic one. Kayan ladies distinguish between the "length-of-a-longhouse" bead of Sarawak and the identically-named bead of Apo Kayan in Indonesian Borneo, two beads different in size, shape and design. The mosaic *lukut kong ba* in the Southwell collection of the Sarawak Museum does not at all resemble a bead of the same name recorded in Long Laput on the Baram River, only a few longhouses away from where the Rev H. Southwell bought his specimen in the 1950s. Southwell was a missionary active in Sarawak from about 1937 to the 1970s, and a knowledgeable bead scholar.

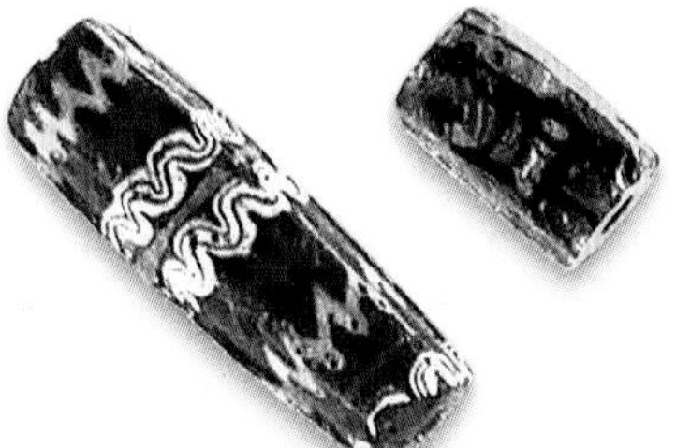

The Kalimantan version of the *buah wang batang uma* is on the left, while the Sarawak version is on the right.

FACING PREVIOUS PAGE, CLOCKWISE FROM TOP LEFT: Typical Borneo beads; bead string which includes pyjama, turquoise and red 'white-heart' beads; and necklace of orange carnelian and decorated red glass beads.

When the commercial production of new-antique beads started in the 1970s and 1980s, the manufacturers realised tha what the Borneo (and also the Sumatra and Celebes) buyers wanted were not simply pretty glass beads but recognizabl replicas of their heirlooms. Many of the new beads are good reproductions, just a bit glossier and brighter than the old. They are called by the same names too.

Borneo's bead owners and collectors know the name of each bead used by the community, and can identify minute shade or shape differences. In a book on beads for bead connoisseurs from different ethnic groups, regions and countries, it is simpler to use descriptive names in English. In the following checklist, each bead is visually described and illustrated. Some of the better-known local names are given, the material and colour are approximately described and typical measurements (length x diameter) are given. This is a very brief list of beads which are either quite common in most parts of Borneo, or which are of unusual historical interest:

BLUE BARREL

Known as *let mitem*, *let itam*, *let silo*, numerous *let* variants (Kelabit) and *manik tolam* or *tumbis tolam* (Bidayuh), these beads are of translucent glass, and colours range from deep bluish-black to almost transparent turquoise. They are barrel-shaped with slightly convex sides, 8–10 mm x 7–9 mm. Each slightly different shade or shape has its own name. The blue barrel is found in most parts of Borneo. As archaeological evidence documents, it was an export from China, and also produced in South-east Asian sites, most likely by immigrant beadmakers, for the local market.

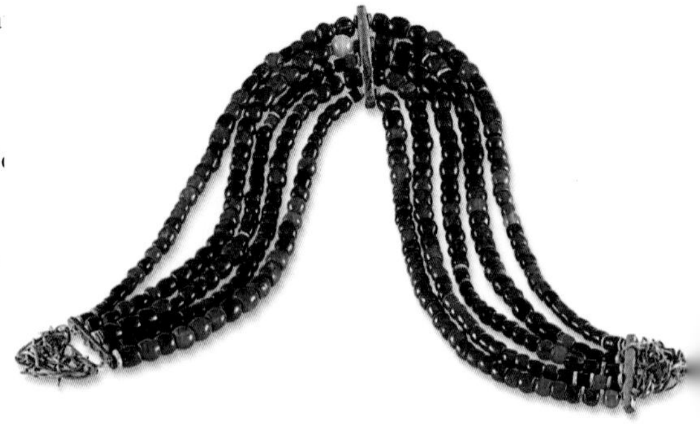

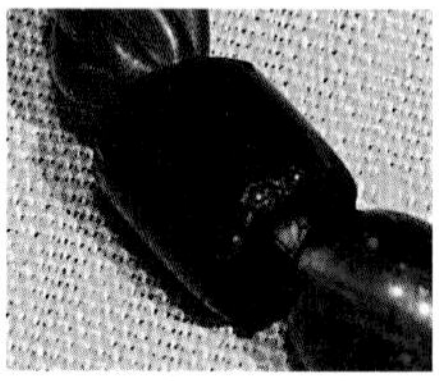

ABOVE: Selakau blue-barrel bead belt.

LEFT: Close-up of a blue barrel bead.

BLUE/GREEN/AMBER SPHERICAL

These beads are known as *manik likis* (Bidayuh) and *marik kelam* (Iban), and are translucent dark blue, green or blue-green, or amber. They are cherry-sized and spherical, 10–12 mm in diameter. They were very common in the past. They were produced, among other places, in China for the "South Sea trade"

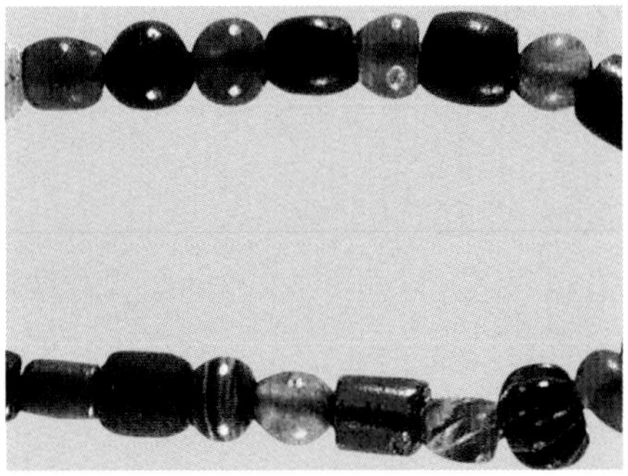

The spherical blue and green beads are the Bidayuh *manik likis*. A blue melon bead lies on the right of the amber one.

until around World War II. Until the 1960s they were still available in the shops in Kuching.

BLUE MELON

Known as *let babak* (Lun Bawang), this gadrooned spherical bead is translucent dark to light blue, green, amber or white, with a diameter of 10–12 mm. It is not a top-value bead, but is regarded as "old" by all communities. The blue variety is acceptable for ritual purposes if "a blue bead" is needed.

BLUE WOUND

The blue wound bead is called *manik binchu buhis* (Bidayuh). It is translucent dark blue, pale blue or blue-green, and is cherry-sized and spherical with a diameter of 12–16 mm. It was made by winding glass in the viscous state around a mandrel, and then holding the finished artifact in the flames again to consolidate it. The striation marks can be seen quite well and the bead resembles a tightly wound ball of knitting wool.

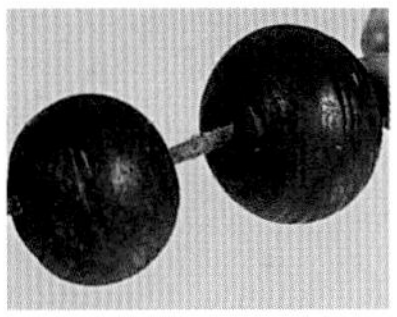

This bead is seen in various Borneo contexts. The Bidayuh Jagoi priestesses value it for the back portion of their ceremonial necklaces. Deep blue beads and ancient coins worn across the nape of the neck "protect the head", a not unnatural consideration in a place where headhunting was rife until the early years of the 20th century.

BLUE VASELINE

Called *manik tilek* (Melanau), this bead is of semi-translucent blue glass and is often rough and pitted; the collectors' term "vaseline glass" indicates the texture. It may be roughly spherical or biconical and measures up to 20 mm x 18 mm. Visually, it resembles some of the large blue beads from the Bian Chiang excavations in Vietnam.

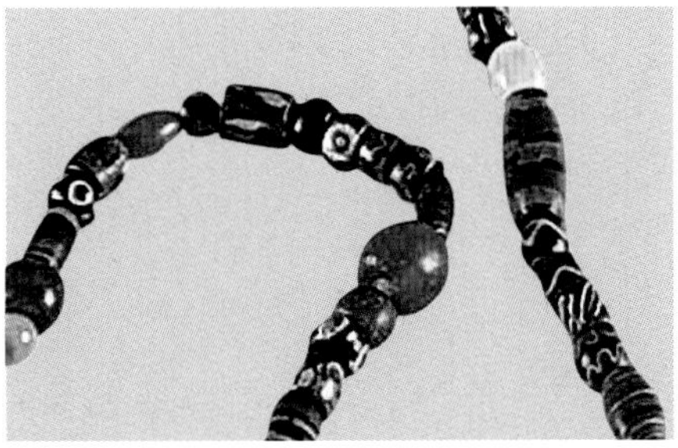

The blue vaseline bead can be seen in this Melanau string.

BRICK-RED SPHERE

The brick-red sphere bead is known as *ino bunan* (Kayan), *bau tina sia*, *alet sia* (Lun Bawang) and *let ma'on* (Kelabit). It is of opaque reddish-brown glass and is roughly spherical, of 10–15 mm diameter. The Selakau or Kendayan of west Borneo keep but do not wear this bead, which is believed to be able to dispel the

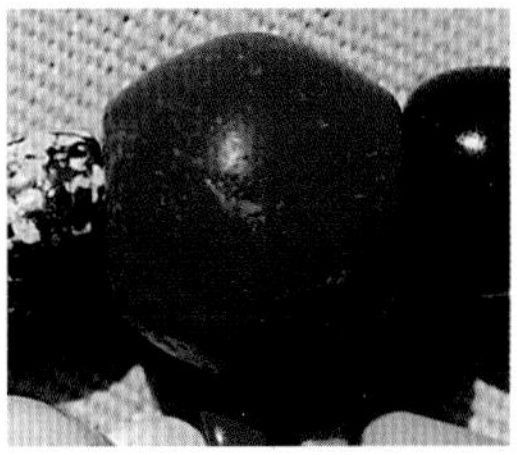

effects of a bad dream. Lun Bawang ladies incorporate it in the sides and back of their bead caps, or in belts. It is visually of the same glass metal as the much smaller mutisalah (see below, Peppercorn). This class of beads has been described as "terracotta" or "paste" by earlier writers who failed to recognize it as opaque glass. The colouring matter is cuprous oxide. Viewed in transmitted light this glass appears grey-blue.

CARNELIAN SPHERE

Known as *lem pudun kora* (Kelabit), this is a reddish-brown rough sphere, ranging from pea size to as large as 25 mm in diameter. This bead is used by the Tagal and related peoples of Sabah to make headbands or incorporate in belts. Elsewhere it is used in necklaces and wristlets. It is considered very old and spiritually powerful, and is believed to have the ability to protect the wearer. The bead is becoming rare. It has not been imitated in glass like other, more commonly popular types of carnelians.

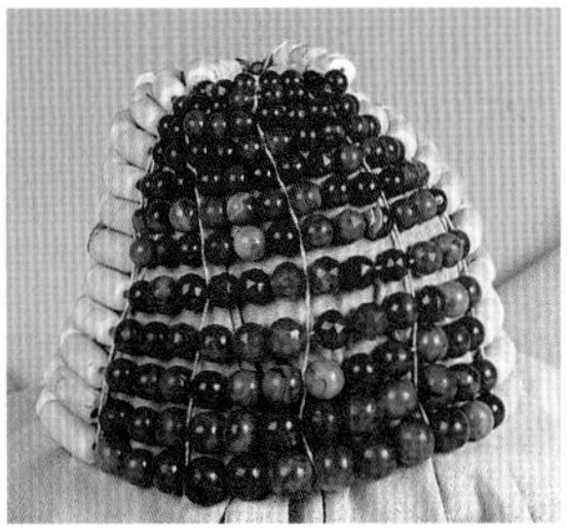

CARNELIAN SPINDLE

Called *tong ba'o buror ma'un* (Kelabit), *marik pelaga* (Iban) and *aki* (Lun Bawang), this stone bead of reddish-brown carnelian is a long-facetted bicone of 30–40 mm x 8–10 mm. It is found in many Malaysian and other South-east Asian archipelago archaeological sites and is still in common use. It is used in the older style of the Kelabit bead cap, in necklaces, in Tagal and Lun Bawang headbands, and in Rungus bandoliers. The Iban bridal dress from the Kapit area is composed partly of carnelians, both round and long.

Semi-precious stone beads were originally a product of the Indian lapidary industry. In the 19th century, however, the German bead industry imported stone from Brazil to produce the "carnelian spindle" for the lucrative colonial market. Bohemian glass imitations of this bead are also common, and by the late 19th century appear not only in red and green (imitating carnelian and jade) but in all colours, up to10 cm in length. The long glass versions of this bead are more commonly found in Sabah and East Kalimantan, possibly due to the North Borneo Company's German trade contacts. In the 19th century, Sarawak supplies were more likely to come via Singapore, the "English connection".

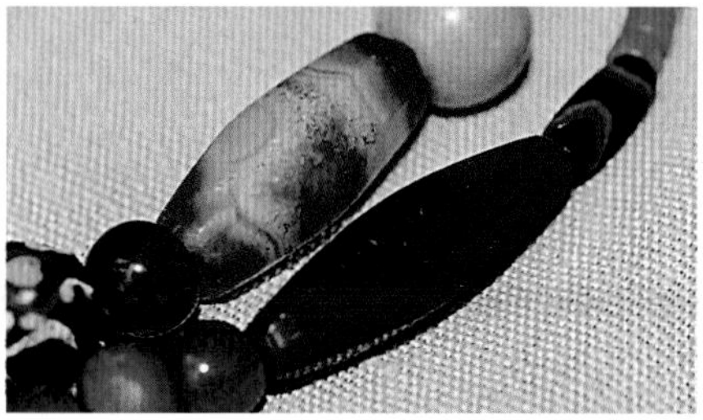

A stone carnelian spindle (left) lies next to a glass one.

CHEQUERBOARD BEAD

Known as *lukut kong ba* (Kayan), this is a large barrel-shaped bead measuring 18 mm x 18 mm, with a plain core of grey or yellow, and a mantle of glass mosaic. This elaborately-decorated bead is possibly Viking or early Islamic, though mosaic glass was known in Roman Egypt mainly as a material for making decorative small dishes and vessels.

The chequerboard bead is rare and highly prized in Borneo. In the 19th century, the Sultan of Kutei, Kalimantan, owned one, and was reported to have told a traveller it was worth 40,000 florins. None of the ruler's subjects could have commanded even a fraction of this sum. In other words, the bead was "not for sale".

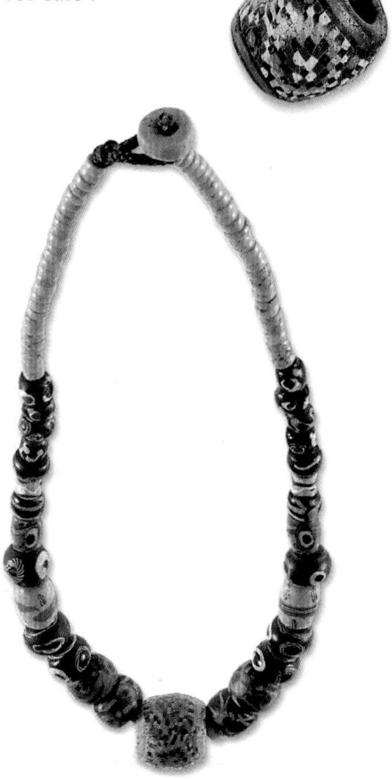

The *lukut kong ba* can be seen at the end of this bead string and in the picture above it.

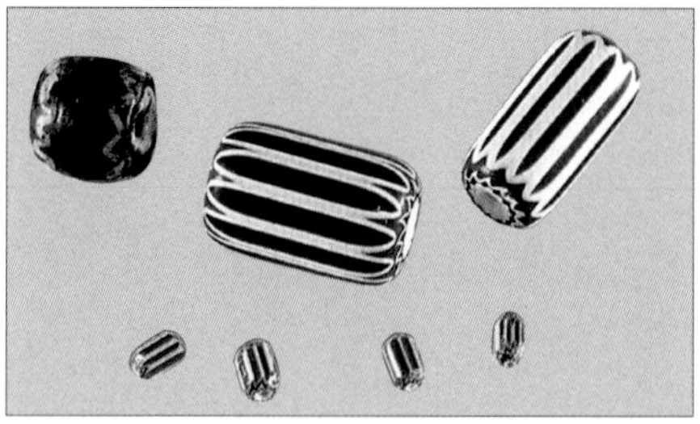

Chevron beads come with zig-zag decorations and in various sizes. The black one on the extreme left is a 'fake'.

CHEVRON BEAD

This bead is called *purung manuk kiking*, *purung matu* (Kayan), *bao mon* (Lun Bawang), *manik burong tiong* (Melanau) and *manik chunto* (Bidayuh). It has a zig-zag decoration and comes in various sizes (9–35 mm x 5.5–22 mm). True chevron beads are sliced off a glass tube incorporating zig-zag layers of contrasting colours. When the ends are ground off, the pretty pattern appears.

"False" chevrons (up to 21 mm x 19 mm in size) are decorated with a surface-applied zig-zag pattern. Both types are popular in Borneo. The chevron was never a top-value bead, but it was popular with all ethnic groups. Known as a "steady seller", it has been produced in many places over the centuries, and currently in India and Indonesia.

DRINKING STRAW BEAD

Known as *bao tulang buror* (Lun Bawang) and *ba'o rawir* (Kelabit), this bead is orange, and opaque, and is made of thin-walled smooth glass and long thin tube segments. It measures about 12–15 mm x 3–4 mm. The bead is used to make the front section of Kelabit bead caps, and is worn as necklaces and belts by the Kelabit and Lun Bawang. The "drinking

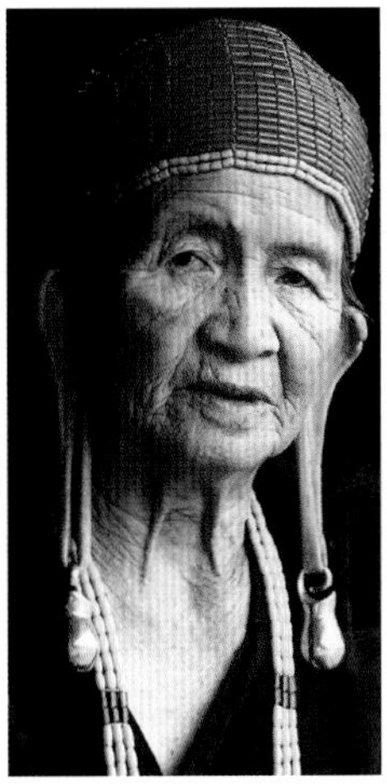

straw bead" is a very old bead type. A few were recovered in an Early Metal Age site in the Madai Caves in east Sabah. New, Indonesian-produced "drinking straw beads" find a good market among the Kelabit and Lun Bawang bead fanciers.

EYE BEADS

Eye beads are called *let sukor* (Lun Bawang), *bua wang nejak* or *bua wang nedak*, *lukut awe* and other names (Kayan).

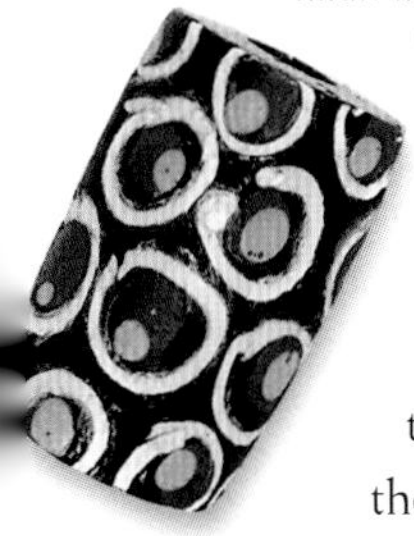

They come in many types, sizes and colours. Most of these pretty polychromes appear to be from Europe, imported over the last 100 to 400 years, judging from the early Portuguese and Dutch presence in the South China Sea from the 15th century right up to the early 20th century. Eye beads are generally considered ornamental, but few have any special ritual significance.

JATIM

Generally known to collectors as Jatim (named after Java Timor or East Java, its best-known provenance) or the "Majapahit" bead, it is roughly

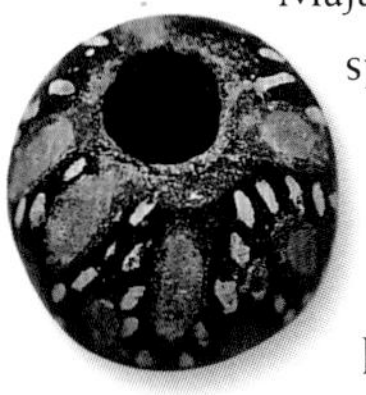

spherical or oblong and can range from 22–40 mm in diameter. The Jatim bead used to be very rare in Borneo, which is strange in view of the comparative proximity of the two islands. Since the 1980s, Jatim beads have begun to turn up in increasing numbers, with most appearing to be newly-made replicas. A few appear original, highlighting the possibility of new illegal excavations.

MARBLE BEAD

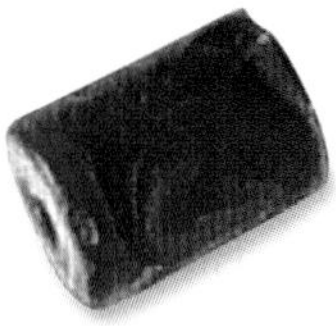

The marble bead and a related combed bead are of opaque glass, with two colours imperfectly mixed to produce a marble effect. It measures 10–15 mm x 9–13 mm.

One marble bead, oxblood-red marbled with white (above), is found mostly in the Kapuas/West Borneo area. The polychrome combed bead is rare in Sarawak, but more common in Sabah and East Kalimantan as well as the southern Philippines. It is generally believed to be of Chinese origin.

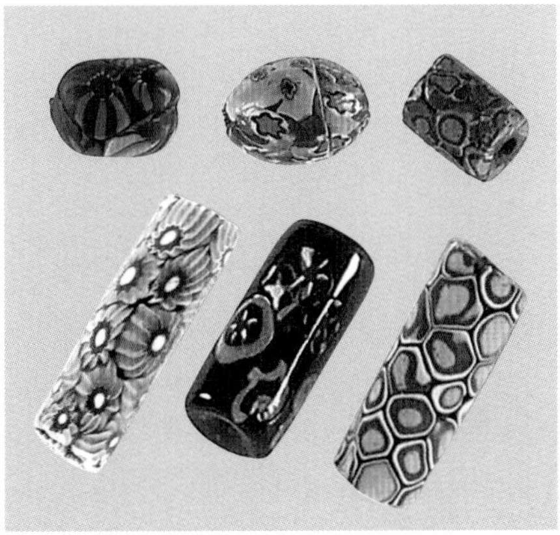

MILLEFIORI BEAD

The colourful millefiori beads (above), mainly from Venice, are popular among all Borneo groups. The Orang Ulu treasure some of them as top-value beads.

PEPPERCORN , BRICK-RED AND OTHER COLOURS

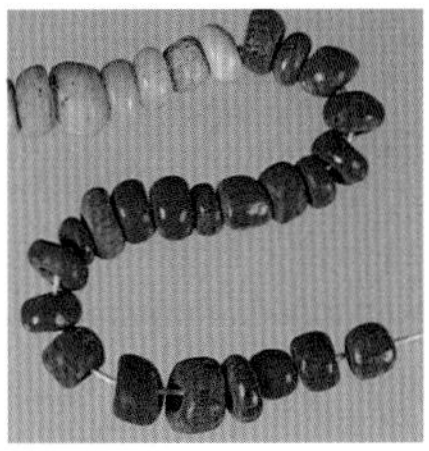

These imported glass beads came first from India and then China. They are 2–4 mm in diameter. The earliest type is a small opaque bead about the size of a peppercorn, in a range of muted colours – brick-red, black, white, yellow and turquoise. Visually, all "peppercorn" beads look alike, namely irregularly-shaped spheres. Technically, they are different – the Indian bead was cut from a tube of drawn glass, while the Chinese product was wound on a mandrel. This bead is known as the "mutisalah" in parts of Indonesia, and still highly valued in Flores. Excavations in Fort Canning Hill in Singapore have brought to light the fact that yellow "peppercorns" had been manufactured there about the 14th century, presumably for the regional market of Sumatra, Borneo and Celebes.

PLAIN BUBBLY GLASS

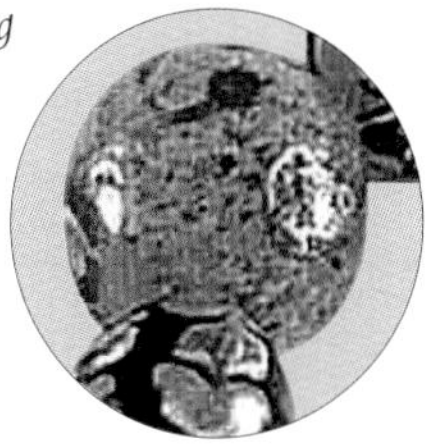

Known as *buah wang lutong* (Kayan), this near-transparent green bubbly glass bead is roughly spherical, about 14–18 mm in diameter, and has surface-applied red decorations. It is found mainly within trading distance of the Kapuas River and does not seem to be known anywhere else. It appears to be of poorly-produced or perhaps even recycled glass, and local manufacture should not be ruled out. People interviewed about the bead generally have rather vague childhood memories of it. The "green bubbly" may well remain one of Borneo's many mysteries.

PYJAMA BEAD

Called *kelem bela, kelem angah* (Kayan) and *marik gamang* (Iban), this bead is of blue-black or black glass, is barrel-shaped and has surface-applied stripes of light yellow, turquoise, pink and white. Some have white stripes only. The bead measures about 10–12 mm x 8–10 mm and is used to make belts and necklaces. Judging by the numbers still in circulation, it must have been very common once. Striped beads of this type were manufactured in 18th-century Venice. The pyjama bead was one of the first to be produced by the emerging Indonesian bead industry in the late 20th century.

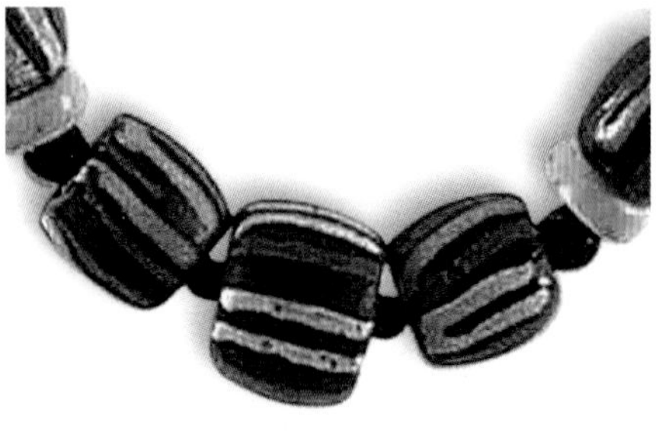

ROSETTE BEADS

Known as *lukut* (Kayan, Kenyah), this bead is a black flattened sphere with an average size of 8–9 mm x 9–11 mm, decorated with twisted rosettes of pink, yellow, turquoise, blue and white. The most "aristocratic" of these beads is the *lukut sekala*. Experts are able to distinguish between a "male" and a "female" bead,

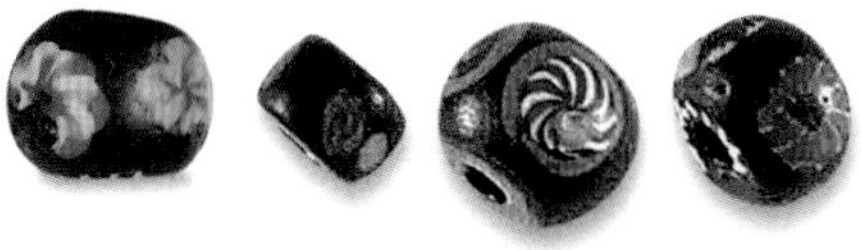

and concede there are a few acceptable but lower-ranking variants. The bead tends to be less than 10 mm in both diameter and length.

The *lukut bela daba* is a smallish bead of the same family and is black with bright red or yellow rosettes. It is used for ritual purposes although it may be worn as part of a necklace. The *lukut sekala telang usan*, according to the Orang Ulu, is a near-perfect variety of the *lukut sekala*, while the *lukut sekala barong* and the *lukut selibau* are larger, coarser variants of the rosette bead. The term *lukut* is used to define a number of high-value beads with decorations other than the rosette typical of the *lukut sekala*.

SHELL BEAD, LARGE

This cylindrical bead is called *ba'o ulum* or *ba'o ulub* (Kelabit) and *tebalu* (Lun Bawang). It is about 20 mm x 14–16 mm and is cut from giant clam shells. Large shell beads are used to make the side portion of bead caps. Some are incorporated in belts or necklaces, mainly by the Lun Bawang and Kelabit, who say this type of bead comes from Brunei. The largest shell beads in the Sarawak Museum collection, over 12 cm in length, make up a very heavy neckpiece, but this is a rarity.

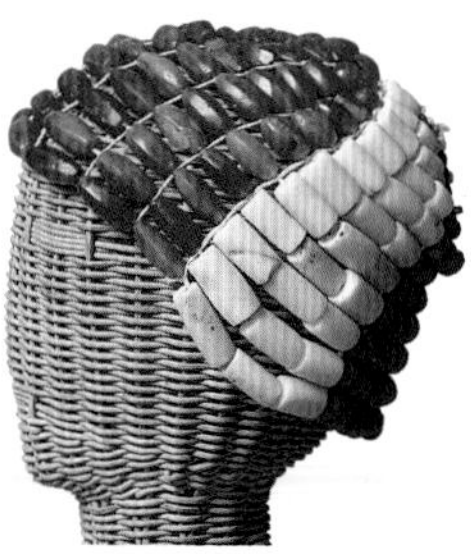

Kelabit woman's cap of reddish-brown carnelian and white shell beads.

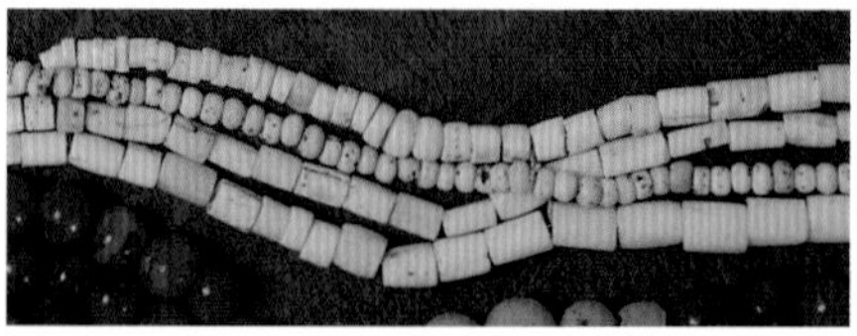

SHELL DISC

Known as *palus* (Bidayuh), this is a flat disc worked from shell, about 2 mm x 4–7 mm. Telok Kimanis in west Sabah was a well-known centre of shell bead-making, as was nearby Brunei Bay. In the early 20th century, a North Borneo Company officer in Tempasuk, on the west coast of Sabah, noted somewhat disapprovingly that Dayak from Sarawak came to buy shell disc beads for trade. Some female Kadazandusun clothing, such as skirts, jackets and hoods, are richly embellished with shell discs. Shell is generally considered to be "cool" and able to ward off fevers. Bidayuh healers use shell or opaque white beads to cure babies of convulsions. Belts made of five to seven strands of shell discs are highly prized by the priestesses.

STONE EAR WEIGHT

This is one of the few bead-related artifacts produced in Borneo but is now obsolete. Dutch traveller Nieuwenhuis observed Bahau people polishing a dark, green-flecked stone, possibly serpentine, to make large beads and ear hangings around 1900.

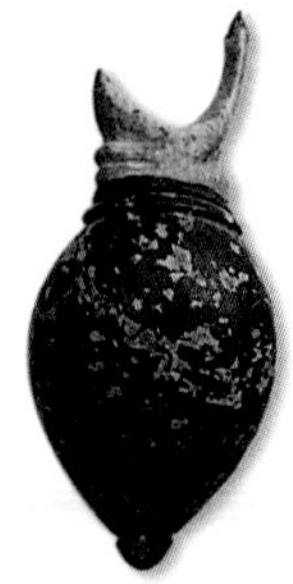

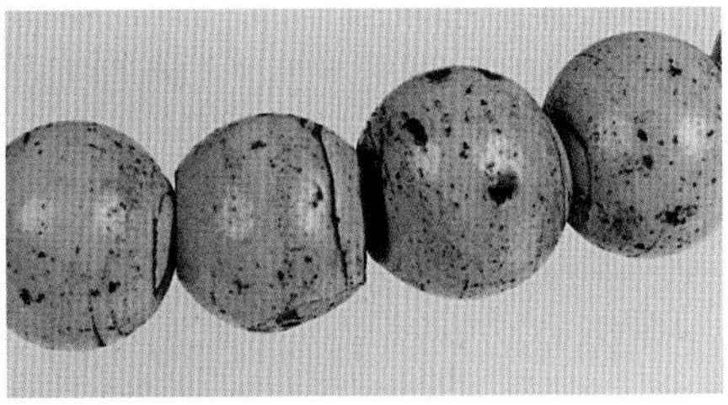

YELLOW CHERRY

Known as *bao alet birar mon* and *alet mon meching* (Lun Bawang), this spherical opaque glass bead comes in various shades of yellow and measures about 9–11 mm in diameter. Older specimens tend to be pitted and time-worn.

This bead forms the main portion of the Lun Bawang bead cap. Yellow beads have also been recovered in various parts of Peninsular Malaysia. Those in use today are most likely of Chinese origin.

YELLOW DOUGHNUT

This bead is called *lavang* (Kayan), and is a yellow opaque glass bead with a texture ranging from very shiny to rough and sandy. It is about 3–5 mm x 7–10 mm in size and is very popular among the Orang Ulu, who use it for the side portion of necklaces.

It is of considerable ritual value, which

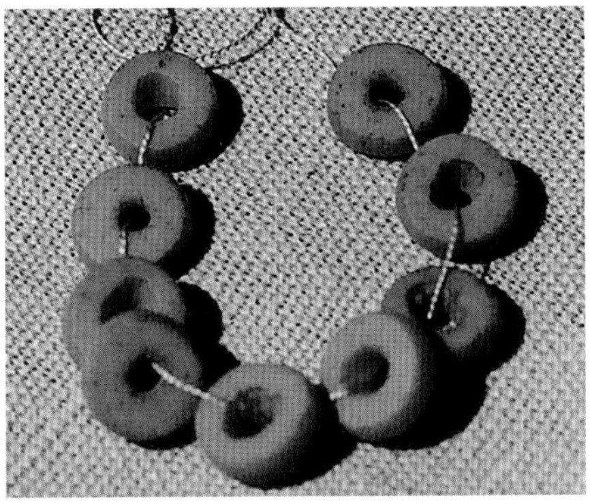

indicates that it must be an old bead. Even very wealthy families give some yellow doughnut beads as engagement tokens, together with the more expensive and colourful *lukut*.

This is the one bead known to have been manufactured in Borneo, in Tanjung Selor on the north-east coast, in the early 20th century. Imported yellow beads were pounded in an iron mortar and the resulting grit carefully filled into clay moulds and fired in a backyard furnace. After the glass had fused, the still-viscous beads were perforated with an iron awl.

The whole manufactory took place under an open-sided, leaf-thatched shed, the workmen squatting on the ground as they went about their work. The 17th-century bead factory in Java probably looked more or less the same.

YELLOW PEANUT

Known as *let alai* (Lun Bawang) and *manik pasin* (Melanau), this opaque oval bead (8–11 mm x 4–7 mm) with a smooth surface is known all over Borneo. It is particularly valued by the Kelabit and Lun Bawang for necklaces. The Melanau also esteem it and use it to embellish the hem of their "bead tunics".

This bead could possibly be of Chinese origin, although Robert Liu, an authority in the field of collectible beads, points out that this type of bead is not found on the mainland and was probably produced purely for export.

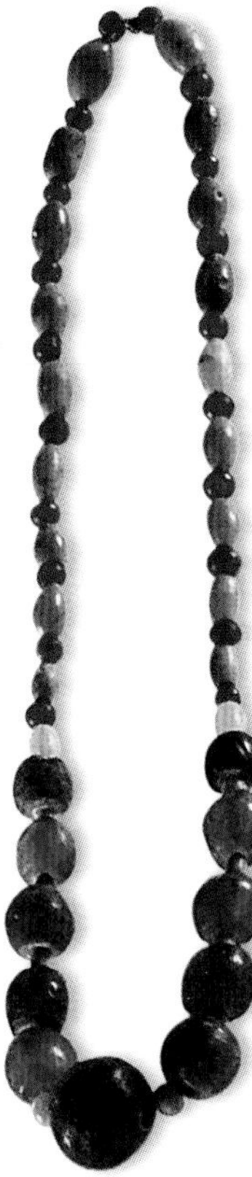

'Yellow peanut' beads can be seen at the side portions of the bead string on the left, between the red beads, and at the side portions of the bead string below.

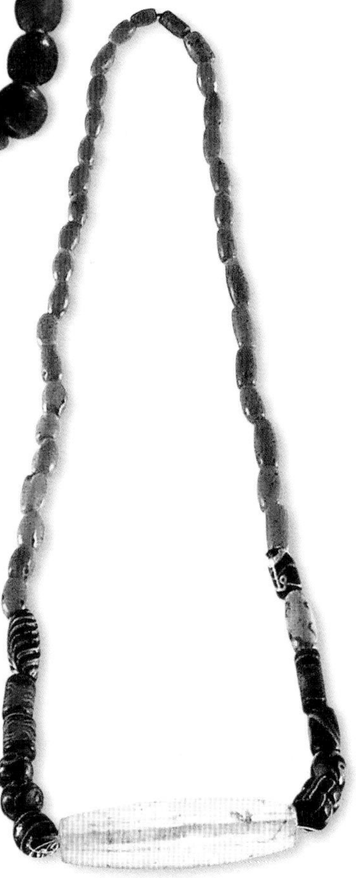

PICTURE CREDITS

The author and publisher would like to thank the individuals and organisations whose photographs are reproduced in this book.

A. Lamb. 13 (top right)
A.W. Nieuwenhuis. *Quer Durch Borneo*. Vol. 2. Leiden: E. J. Brill, 1904–1907. 51 (centre and bottom), 97 (bottom right)
Albert Teo. 12, 13 (top left), 14 (top left), 16 (right), 44 (top left), 91 (top left and bottom), top right, 98 (top right)
Ariel Tunguia. 90 (top)
B. Hermann. 76 (right)
Bank Negara Malaysia. 80
Bernard Sellato. 19 (top), 98 (top left, bottom right)
C. Knight. (Courtesy of The Malaysian Today) 50
C. L. Chan. 89 (top right), 93 (top left), 112, 129 (top left)
Charles Hose. (Courtesy of the British Museum, UK) 35, 37 (bottom), 85 (top right), 86 (centre), 114 (left)
Carl Bock. *The Head-hunters of Borneo*. Singapore: Graham Brash, 1988. Rpt. of London: Sampson Low, Marston, Searle and Rivington, 1881. 85 (top left and bottom right), 92
Carol Colfer. 42 (top left), 89 (bottom right)
Deddy Muliastra. 15 (bottom right), 58
Dennis Lau. 13 (bottom), 16 (extreme left), 18 (bottom), 41 (top left), 94 (top left), 114 (right)
Dicky W. P. (Courtesy of Bernard Sellato) 88 (right), 89 (top left, bottom right)
Edric Ong. 117, 118
Gérard Houlbrèque. (Courtesy of Bernard Sellato) 4, 104 (left)
Gilles Perret. (Courtesy of Bernard Sellato) 40 (bottom), 43 (top), 66, 110
H. F. Tillema. *Apo-Kajan, Een filmreis naar en door Centraal-Borneo*. Amsterdam: Van Munster, 1938. 27
Heidi Munan. Cover (extreme left), 13 (centre), 17, 19 (right), 23 (top left and bottom), 29 (top right), 31 (top left), 33, 41 (top right), 43 (bottom), 44 (bottom), 46, 47 (left), 48, 55, 56, 60, 65 (top right), 75 (top), 76 (left), 78, 79 (top), 80 (bottom), 82, 86 (top left and top right), 87 (top right), 96 (second and third in second row), 97 (second row), 102, 116, 120 (top right), 122, 123, 124 (top), 125, 126 (courtesy of Museum Negara, Malaysia), 127, 128 (top), 129 (bottom right), back cover (extreme right bead)
Hermann Scholz. 20 (right), 45 (top), 98 (bottom left)
Jo Rose. 31 (top right), 34 (left), 61 (right), 63, 67, 130 (top left), 132 (bottom left), 133 (top right), 134 (bottom left), 135 (bottom left), 137 (bottom left)
Kent Watters. 51 (top), 52 (bottom four), 53 (all except top left), 96 (second and third in bottom row), 105, 111
Lawrence Lim. 54, 96
Luca Tettoni. 2, 38, 48, 52, 53, 57, 68, 95, 100, 103, 107, 108, 109, 115 (top right), 136 (centre column, bottom; top right)
Michael Cadman. 14 (top right), 20 (bottom), 21 (right), 32 (top), 88 (top left), 91 (top right), 93 (top right), 128 (bottom)
Mike Yamashita. 15 (top right), 18 (top), 34 (top right), 86 (top left), 99
Museum Negara, Malaysia. 30 (top left)
Patricia Regis. 20 (left), 21 (left)
Rio Helmi. Cover (top centre), 9, 11, 15 (left), 129 (top right)
Sabah Museum. 22, 101
Sarawak Museum. 27 (top left), 30 (top right), 32 (left), 42 (top right), 47 (right), 59 (second picture), 79 (bottom), 85 (bottom left), 94 (right), 96 (centre row, extreme left), (bottom row, extreme left), 106 (top), 133 (bottom left and bottom right), 134 (top centre), 135 (first column, centre; top right), 136 (centre column, top extreme left; third column, bottom), 137 (top left)
Sarawak Tourism Board. 75 (bottom), 89 (top)
Simon Tchee. Cover (main), 3, 24, 28, 29 (top left), 40 (top), 44 (top right), 73 (fifth to eighth beads from bottom), 124 (bottom), 130 (top right), 133 (top left), 134 (top right), 135 (centre column, top and bottom – all beads except bottom left and bottom right), back cover (all except extreme right bead). Courtesy of Gallery M, Kuching: 26, 120 (all except top right), 121, 135 (middle column, bottom right). Courtesy of Nelson Tan, Kuching: 61 (left), 62, 72 (top, bottom centre and bottom right), 73 (bottom four beads), 96 (bottom row, extreme left), 97 (top), 132 (bottom left), 135 (middle column, second row, extreme left), 136 (first column, and top of second column), 137 (third column). Courtesy of Phillip Yong, Kuching: 59 (top), 71 (bottom), 72 (bottom left), 134 (bottom centre). Courtesy of Sarawak Museum: 65 (top left), 70, 71 (top), 73 (seven beads top of page), 74, 104 (right), 106 (bottom), 130 (bottom), 132 (top right), 133 (centre), 135 (bottom right)
Sten Sjostrand. 31
Sylvester Wee. Cover (top right), 77, 129 (bottom left), 135 (top left)

REFERENCES

Abbreviations:

JGS Journal of Glass Studies
JFMSM Journal of Federated Malay States Museums
JMBRAS Journal of the Malayan Branch Royal Asiatic Society
JRASSB Journal of the Royal Asiatic Society, Straits Branch
SMJ Sarawak Museum Journal

BANKS, E. "Megalithic Remains from Kelabit Country." *SMJ* 4.15 (1937): 413–438.

BOCK, Carl. *The Head-hunters of Borneo.* Singapore: OUP, 1985. Rpt. of London: Sampson Low, Marston, Searle and Rivington, 1881.

BOYLE, Frederick. *Adventures among the Dyaks of Borneo.* London: Hurst & Blackett, 1865.

BRADDELL, R. "An Introduction to the Study of Ancient Times in the Malay Peninsula and the Straits of Malacca." *JMBRAS* 13.2 (1936): 70–109.

—. "An Introduction to the Study of Ancient Times in the Malay Peninsula and the Straits of Malacca." *JMBRAS* 14.3 (1937): 10–71.

—. "Notes on Ancient Times in Malaya — The Ancient Bead Trade." *JMBRAS* 20 (1947): 1–10.

BUCK, W. S. "Notes on Oya Milanos." *SMJ* 4.13 (1933): 157–173.

CHAU Ju Kua. *Chu Fan Chi (A Record of Barbarian Nations).* c.1235. Trans. Friedrich Hirth and W. W. Rockhill. St Petersburg: Printing Office of the Imperial Academy of Sciences, 1911. New York: Paragon Book Reprint Corp., 1966.

CHONG Chin Seng. *Traditional Melanau Woodcarving (Bilum) in Dalat, Sarawak.* Kuching: Persatuan Kesusasteraan Sarawak, 1987.

CRAIN, J. B. "The Lun Dayeh." *Essays on Borneo Societies.* Ed. Victor King. Oxford: OUP for the University of Hull, 1978. 122–142.

DATAN, Ipoi. "A Brief Ethnography of the Lun Bawang of Sarawak." *SMJ* 61 Part iii (1989): 143–156.

—. "Archaeological Excavations at Guah Sireh/Lubang Angin." *SMJ Special Monograph 6* 45.66 (1993).

DEEGAN, James. "Some Lun Bawang Spirit Chants." *SMJ* 18.36-37 (1970): 264–280.

DRIS, Aloysius. "Melanau Healing Images." *Sarawak Cultural Legacy.* Ed. Lucas Chin and Valerie Mashman. Kuching: Society Atelier Sarawak and Shell Companies of Malaysia, 1991. 53–60.

EVANS, Ivor H. N. *Among Primitive Peoples in Borneo.* London: Seeley Service & Co., 1922.

EVERETT, H. H. and J. Hewitt. "A History of Santubong." *JRASSB* 52 (1909): 1–30.

FORBES, Henry O. *A Naturalist's Wanderings in the Eastern Archipelago.* London: Sampson Low, Marston, Searle and Rivington, 1885.

FRANCIS Jr, Peter. *Asia's Maritime Bead Trade: 300 B.C. to the Present.* Honolulu: University of Hawaii Press, 2002.

—. "Chinese Beadmakers in Java ca.1600?" *The Margaretologist* 1.1 (1985): 4–6.

—. "Chinese Coil Beads." *Ornament* 14.1 (1990): 66–70.

—. "Manatai, Bead Crossroads of the Medieval World." *Ornament* 12.3 (1989): 82–91.

—. "The Asian Maritime Bead Trade." *The Margaretologist* 2.2 (1988): 3–12.

—. *The Czech Bead Story.* New York: Lapis Route Books, 1979.

—. "Two Distinctive Chinese Glass Beads." *Ornament* 14.4 (1991): 82–83.

GEDDES, W. R. *Nine Dayak Nights.* Melbourne: OUP, 1957.

HAMDAN bin Buyun B. *The Melanau Community.* Kuching: Majlis Adat Istiadat Sarawak, 1998.

HARRISSON, Tom. "Kelabit, Land Dayak and Related Beads in Sarawak." *SMJ* 5 (1950): 201–220.

—. "Monochrome Beads from Malaysia and Elsewhere." *Man* 64 March–April (1964): 37–41.

—. "New Analyses of Excavated Prehistoric Glass from Borneo." *Asian Perspectives* 11 (1968): 125–133.

—. *The Malays of South-West Sarawak before Malaysia.* London: Macmillan, 1970.

HOSE, Charles. *Natural Man: A Record from Borneo*. London: Macmillan, 1926.

HOSE, Charles and William McDougall. *The Pagan Tribes of Borneo*. London: Macmillan, 1912.

HOWELL, W. *Sarawak Historical Notes*. Guildford: St.Thomas's Trust, 1993.

LAMB, A. "A Note on Glass Beads from the Malay Peninsula." *JGS* 8 (1966): 80–94.

—. "Notes on beads from Johor Lama and Kota Tinggi." *JMBRAS* 37.1 (1964): 88–98.

—. "Some Glass Beads from Kakao Island, South Thailand." *FMJ* 6 (1961): 48–55.

LIU, Robert K. *Collectible Beads*. San Marcos: Ornament Inc., 1995.

MJÖBERG, E. *L'Ile des Chasseurs de Têtes*. Paris: Libraire Plon, 1934.

MORRIS, H. S. *Report on a Melanau Sago Producing Community in Sarawak*. London: HMSO, 1953.

MORRIS, Stephen. *The Oya Melanau*. Kuching: Malaysian Historical Society (Sarawak Branch), 1991.

—. "The Oya Melanau: Traditional Ritual and Belief." Ed. B. Clayre. *SMJ Special Monograph 9* 52.73 (1997).

MORRISON, A. "Murut Pottery." *SMJ* 6.5 (1955): 295–296.

MUNAN, Heidi. "A Kayan Bead Song." *SMJ* 56.77 (2001): 19–28.

—. "Bead Cap 64/88 in the Sarawak Museum Collection." *SMJ* 32.53 (1983): 89–96.

—. "Beads." Chin and Mashman. 177–190.

—. "Lun Bawang Beads." *SMJ* 48.69 (1995): 49–64.

—. *Sarawak Crafts: Methods, Materials and Motifs*. Singapore: OUP, 1989.

—. "The Southwell Collection of Kayan Beads." *SMJ* 39. 60 (1988): 105–110.

MUNAN-OETTLI, A. "Bead Necklace 1598." *SMJ* 29.50 (1981): 18–26.

NIEUWENHUIS, A.W. *Quer Durch Borneo*. Vol. 1 and 2. Leiden: E. J. Brill, 1904–1907.

—. "Kunstperlen und ihre kulturelle Bedeutung." *Internationales Archiv fuer Ethnographie*. (1904): 136–153.

POLLARD, F. H. "The Muruts of Sarawak." *SMJ* 4.13 (1933): 139–155.

—. "Some Comparative Notes on Muruts and Kelabits." *SMJ* 4.14 (1933): 223–227.

RICHARDS, A. J. N. *An Iban-English Dictionary*. Kuala Lumpur: OUP, 1981.

ROTH, Henry Ling. *The Natives of Sarawak and British North Borneo*. London: Truslove and Hanson, 1896.

RUBENSTEIN, Carol. "Poems of Indigenous Peoples of Sarawak." *SMJ Special Monograph 2* 21.42 (1973).

SANDIN, B. "The Bisayah and Indigenous Peoples of Limbang." *SMJ* 20.40–41 (1972): 41– 52.

—. *The Living Legends: Borneans Telling their Tales*. Kuala Lumpur: DBP, 1980.

TILLEMA, H. F. *Apo-Kajan, Een filmreis naar en door Centraal-Borneo*. Amsterdam: Van Munster, 1938.

TUAI RUMAH LAH WAN, narr. *Kayan Bead Origin Myth*. Recorded and edited by Heidi Munan. Trans. Lah Jau Uyoh, 1998.

VAN DER SLEEN, W. G. N. "A Bead Factory in Amsterdam in the Seventeenth Century." *Man* 219 (1963): 172–174.

—. *A Handbook of Beads*. Liège: Musée de Verre, 1967.

—. *A Handbook on Beads*. Liège: Librairie Halbart, 1973.

VROKLAGE, B. A. G. *Ethnographie der Belu in Zentral-Timor*. Leiden: E. J. Brill, 1952.

WALLACE, A. R. *The Malay Archipelago*. London: MacMillan, 1869.

WHEATLEY, Paul. *The Golden Khersonese*. Kuala Lumpur: University of Malaya Press, 1980.

WHITTIER, H. L. *Social Organization and Symbols of Social Differentiation: an Ethnographic Study of the Kenyah Dayak of East Kalimantan*. PhD Thesis. Michigan State University, 1973.

INDEX

Note: Numbers in *italics* refer to illustrations.